Charles Towne on the Cape Fear

The Rise and Fall of the First Barbadian Settlement in Carolina

by
Jack E. Fryar, Jr.

Copyright 2019 by Jack E. Fryar, Jr.

All rights reserved. No part of this book may be reproduced in any form or by any electronic or mechanical means, including information storage and retrieval systems, without written permission from the publisher, except by a reviewer who may quote brief passages in a review.

Published in the United States of America by
Dram Tree Books

Publisher's Cataloging-in-Publication Data

Names: Fryar, Jack E., Jr., author.
Title: Charles Towne on the Cape Fear : the rise and fall of the first Barbadian settlement in Carolina / by Jack E. Fryar, Jr.
Description: Includes bibliographical references and index. | Wilmington, NC: Dram Tree Books, 2019.
Identifiers: ISBN 9780984490035
Subjects: LCSH North Carolina--History--Colonial period, ca. 1600-1775. | Cape Fear River (N.C.)--History. | Fear, Cape, NC--History. | North Carolina--History. | United States--Colonization--History. | Frontier and pioneer life--United States. | BISAC HISTORY / United States / State & Local / South (AL, AR, FL, GA, KY, LA, MS, NC, SC, TN, VA, WV) | HISTORY / Modern / 17th Century | HISTORY / Americas (North, Central, South, West Indies) | HISTORY / Caribbean & West Indies / General | Classification: LCC F262.C2 F79 2019 | DDC 975.62--dc23

Dram Tree Books
P.O. Box 7183
Wilmington, N.C. 28406
dramtreebooks@gmail.com
(910) 538-4076

For Dr. Alan W. Watson and Dr. Chris E. Fonvielle, Jr. ...

Friends and mentors who took an enthusiastic amateur and taught him how to be a real historian;

and as always, to Cherie with love

Table of Contents

- Introduction..1

- Of Empires, Explorers, and Mariners Bold..................9

- Of Cavaliers and Roundheads....................................27

- Barbados, the Sugar Island...37

- Eight Loyal Men..63

- Carolana/Carolina...81

- The Barbadian Adventurers......................................103

- On the Cape Fear..115

- Victims of the Times...137

- Uncovering Charles Towne......................................155

- **Appendix I:** Declarations and Proposals of the Lords Proprietors of Carolina (1663)....165

- **Appendix II:** Concessions and Agreement between the Lords Proprietors of Carolina and Wm. Yeamans et al. ...169

- **Appendix III:** Persons Known to have Explored Cape Fear with William Hilton, Jr. or who settled at Charles Towne with John Vassall of Sir John Yeamans...189

- **Appendix IV:** William Hilton, Jr.'s Description of Cape Fear (1663)...193

- **Appendix V:** Signatures of the Lords Proprietors of Carolina and a facsimile of the Lone Surviving Record Book of the Lords Proprietors of Carolina...201

- **Bibliography**...215

Index...236

Introduction

There are ghosts on the Cape Fear, spirits of those who lived along its banks and left their mark on the place where the river meets the sea. They are Indians and Englishmen, redcoats and rebels, African slaves, and soldiers clad in butternut and blue. They include men and women who bent great forests of longleaf pine, cypress, and the very tides to their will, pioneers who sowed rice and indigo and built great estates from their industry. They made their lives on the periphery of the British Empire, and eventually outgrew their dependence on British kings to become a nation in their own right. Their stories are fascinating, and among the most fascinating is that of the Barbadians and Puritans of the Charles Towne settlement.

South Carolina can claim the most famous Charles Town in the Carolinas, but the first settlement to honor the name of England's King Charles II was on the Cape Fear River between 1664 and 1667. There, just north of the place where Town Creek empties into the river below modern Wilmington, a group of Barbadians and Massachusetts Puritans planted the English flag below the Albemarle for the first time. The colony, which numbered in the hundreds if promotional literature that appeared in London at the time is to be believed, was to provide raw materials and food for trade with England and Barbados, where sugar cultivation left little room for the production of anything else.

As promising as the Charles Towne settlement seemed to its members and backers, it only lasted three years. Its failure lay in a combination of factors – poor planning, neglect by its supporters, and both natural and man-made disasters. While John Vassall and the hardy souls who followed him to the proprietary settlement south of Virginia were ultimately unsuccessful, their attempt to carve a home from the Carolina wilderness provided a testing ground for later, more successful attempts. The eight Lords Proprietors who held the King's grant for a vast area between the Chesapeake Bay and Spanish Florida used the experiences of the Cape Fear colony to fine-tune their subsequent settlement at Port Royal. In that respect, at least, the Vassall colony did a service for those that came afterward.

To consider Charles Towne through a narrow lens that views only the settlement itself is a short story. The colony had its share of drama, and its history is fascinating for those who are captivated by the grit of that first wave of Englishmen who braved winds and waves to establish a home in the daunting rough country of the North American mainland. While there are doubtlessly many tales that could be told of Charles Towne and its inhabitants, documentary evidence of those years is scant. The letters of John Vassall and other principles in the effort to settle on the banks of the Cape Fear River offer tantalizing clues as to what happened between the first New England attempt at settlement in 1663 and when the colony collapsed in 1667, but no diaries or journals have yet been found that recount the day to day lives of the people there.

The problem with assembling a historiography of the Charles Towne settlement on the Cape Fear River is that there are no historical treatments, in either book or article form, that focus specifically on the Puritans and Barbadians who lived there. The settlement is mentioned in many monographs and journals, usually in connection with the more widely known story of the Yeamans colony established at Port Royal three years after John Vassall's Cape Fear settlement failed. The researcher is left to comb through primary sources and the collected bits and pieces of other secondary sources that refer to Charles Towne in order to assemble enough of a patchwork to tell the story of the first Englishmen to call the Cape Fear home. Yet when considered in the broader context of Atlantic history, Charles Towne's tale becomes a richer account. The England of the Stuarts, the English Civil War, the discovery and development of Barbados, the evolution of southern English colonization into a system dependent on slavery, and the geopolitical machinations of European nations vying for a slice of New World riches, all contribute to the story of the little colony at Cape Fear.

For any researcher delving into North Carolina's seventeenth and eighteenth century past, the *North Carolina Colonial and State Records*, either in print or digitized online at the University of North Carolina's Documenting the South website, are an indispensible resource. The correspondence and reports contained therein represent virtually every known document in the founding of both the colony and state. William Noel Sainsbury's *Calendar of State Papers, Colonial Series, America and West Indies, 1661-1668,* is also a key primary source for the period. Several key communications of Anthony Ashley Cooper, 1st Earl of Shaftesbury and one of Carolina's original eight Lords Proprietors, are preserved in *The Shaftesbury Papers*, published by the South Carolina Historical Society. The sole surviving accounts book of the Lords Proprietors provides telling insight into the extent that each proprietor invested in their Carolina patent.

Perhaps the most useful secondary sources consulted for this work are by scholars of Carolina's proprietary period. Daniel W. Fagg's 1970 doctoral dissertation, "Carolina 1663-1683: The Founding of a Proprietary," is a wealth of information on how the English came to settle Carolina, and their experiences there. It is perhaps most valuable for its extensive bibliography, although Dr. Fagg also provided a masterful examination of Carolina in the late seventeenth century. Herbert R. Paschal, Jr.'s dissertation, "Proprietary North Carolina: A Study in Colonial Government" is another work that details how proprietary government operated, and the several efforts to plant colonies on the Lords Proprietors' Carolina patent. Charles Suttlemeyre's Ph.D dissertation at Oxford University in 1991, "Proprietary Policy and the Development of North Carolina, 1663-1729," expands on Fagg and Paschal's earlier studies to explain the workings of the Carolina proprietary. These dissertations, among others, were most helpful in deciphering the mysteries of Charles Towne and its relation to the larger plans of the Lords Proprietors.

Among the many monographs consulted for this study, Louis H. Roper's *Conceiving Carolina: Proprietors, Planters, and Plots, 1662-1729* was among the best about the evolution of the Carolina proprietary and Charles Towne's place in it. Russell R. Menard's *Sweet Negotiations: Sugar, Slavery, and Plantation Agriculture in Early Barbados,* and Richard S. Dunn's *Sugar and Slaves: The Rise of the Planter Class in the English*

West Indies, 1624-1713, both provided handbooks describing the development of tiny Barbados into the jewel of England's overseas colonies thanks to Europe's sweet tooth. The growing demand for sugar was a crucial element of the Charles Towne story. Without it John Vassall may never have convinced his island neighbors to sail for the mainland in the first place. April Lee Hatfield's *Atlantic Virginia: Intercolonial Relations in the Seventeenth Century* illustrates just how dependent England's colonies were on each other as both markets and providers of raw goods. She also shows how other nations, including the Dutch, facilitated that network.

No study of colonial North Carolina is complete without a perusal of E. Lawrence Lee's *The Lower Cape Fear in Colonial Days* and *The History of Brunswick County*. Both works remain indispensible sources for the history of the region in which Charles Towne was located.

Among the many journal articles referenced in this book, Richard S. Dunn's "The English Sugar Islands and the Founding of South Carolina" stands out as among the most useful. Daniel Fagg offers another perspective with "Sleeping Not with the King's Grant: A Rereading of Some Proprietary Documents, 1663-1667," a particularly enlightening piece that illuminates the thinking of the Lords Proprietors concerning their Carolina schemes. Max S. Edelson's "Clearing Swamps, Harvesting Forests: Trees and the Making of a Plantation Landscape in the Colonial South Carolina Lowcountry" provided examples of the hard work put in by the early Carolina settlers planting crops and turning the abundant forest into a source of much needed income.

Timothy P. Grady's "Vomit His Fury and Malice: English Fears and Spanish Influences on the Exploration and Establishment of Carolina through 1670," explained the mainland rivalries between Spain and England that affected Charles Towne and the Port Royal settlements. Louise Hall did yeoman's work sifting through New England Puritan records to write "New England at Sea: Cape Fear Before the Royal Charter of 24 March 1662/3." This single article provides the names of a host of the Puritans who departed from Massachusetts to either accompany William Hilton on his 1662 voyage of discovery at Cape Fear, or later to establish a colony there (though the settlement never took place). Richard Waterhouse details the conditions on Barbados that led to adventurers seeking new lands on the North American mainland in "England, the Caribbean, and the Settlement of Carolina."

In addition to the source material I utilized in preparing this manuscript, I was fortunate to call on the talents and expertise of several people who made valuable additions to the final product, either in terms of what went on the page, or by stimulating lines of inquiry and offering avenues of leads to answers sought. Others offered encouragement and inspiration to see me through to the completion of this story. Dr. Chris E. Fonvielle, Jr. is not just a fine teacher, editor, author, and historian, but he is also my friend. His input was indispensible to producing a manuscript worthy of consideration as a serious piece of scholarship. Dr. Alan Watson is, to my mind, the finest colonial historian in North Carolina. He is also a friend and mentor whose guidance and expertise not only helped me make this book better, but also set an example of what a historian should be that I will strive to reach for the rest of my career. This book grew out of my Master's thesis in History at the University of North Carolina Wilmington. I am privileged to have the signatures of both of these fine historians, along with that of a third excellent historian, author, and friend, Dr. David La Vere, on that document.

Finally, none of this would have been possible without the love and support of my wife, Cherie Willetts Fryar. Convincing her to marry me is undoubtedly the greatest achievement I have ever earned, and I am infinitely better off for her kindness, patience, support, and love.

Charles Towne did not exist in a vacuum. John Vassall's hapless settlers at the Cape Fear were part of a wider English world, and ripples in one part of that world inevitably had an impact on the rest of it. That being the case, perhaps the best way to study Charles Towne is to place it within the framework of the English and Atlantic worlds of the seventeenth century. This book attempts to cast a wider net than existing literature, that encompasses more of the events and personalities that influenced the establishment of the Charles Town settlement. I have tried to place the Vassall colonists within the context of the times that the settlement existed. By using existing literature and records that bear on the English colonial expansion to Carolina, and by showing how events before and during Charles Towne's existence impacted the destinies of the people who settled there, it is hoped a fuller picture of the first English outpost in Carolina below the Albemarle will emerge. Though the research to do so is a piecemeal product, calling on works about a myriad number of topics, the end result is hopefully enough to provide an understanding of Charles Towne's story and legacy.

John Vassall and the other members of his group of Barbadian

Adventurers were what Christian J. Koot has termed Englishmen "on the periphery." Barbados was the center of the English world in the Western Hemisphere in the mid-seventeenth century, and the evolution of that small Leeward Island impacted English colonization elsewhere in the Caribbean and in North America. The idea of Atlantic history is that events in places touched by the ocean's tides influenced the history of every other place. Nowhere is that truer than in the case of Charles Towne. What happened at the Cape Fear was directly attributable to events in other parts of the world.

This book pieces together the story of the roughly 800 souls who came to the Cape Fear during the early years of the reign of King Charles II, when sugar and slaves were turning Barbados into England's wealthiest overseas possession, when other European nations jockeyed for position at home and in the Americas, when commerce and enterprise drove people to become adventurers, and when a mix of cultures, religions, and motives shaped the fate of that first attempt at settlement in Carolina below the Albemarle. If the story is incomplete, it is not from lack of effort.

Jack E. Fryar, Jr.
Wilmington, N.C.
April 2019

A
RELATION
OF
A Discovery lately made on the Coast of
FLORIDA,
(From Lat. 31. to 33 Deg. 45 Min. North-Lat.)

By *William Hilton* Commander, and Commissioner with Capt. *Anthony Long*, and *Peter Fabian*, in the Ship *Adventure*, which set Sayl from *Spikes* Bay, *Aug.* 10. 1663. and was set forth by several Gentlemen and Merchants of the Island of *BARBADOES*.

Giving an account of the nature and temperature of the Soyl, the manners and disposition of the Natives, and whatsoever else is remarkable therein.

Together with Proposals made by the Commissioners of the Lords Proprietors, to all such persons as shall become the first Setlers on the Rivers, Harbors, and Creeks there.

LONDON,
Printed by *J. C.* for *Simon Miller* at the Star neer the West-end of St. *Pauls*, 1664.

The title page of William Hilton's 1664 report on what he found along the Cape Fear. Hilton was just one of several explorers who found the region a likely place for settlement.

I
Of Empires, Explorers, and Mariners Bold

"Twelve feet and sandy!" came the cry from the bow, where a seaman was casting a lead line to gauge the depth of the water under *Adventure*'s keel. The plug in the end of the lead was coming up with silty sand from the river bottom, an indication that the riverbed would be a shifting one, and the channel inconsistent. William Hilton looked above, where the mainsail was reefed and an offshore breeze filled the ship's topsails to provide headway, then shifted his gaze to take in the lush vegetation growing along the west bank. Hilton's commission was to find a place for Puritans from Massachusetts to establish a colony below Virginia. Looking at the rich land abeam of the *Adventure*, he believed he might have found it. William Hilton was just another in a long line of explorers to become acquainted with the Carolina coast.

Carolina was not unknown to Europeans, at least in the abstract. Some explorers knew of the land that would come to be called Carolina as early as the third decade of the sixteenth century. Florence's Giovanni de Verrazzano sailed the length of the North American east coast on behalf of Francis I of France in the second decade of the sixteenth century. Verrazano's expedition made landfall at Cape Fear in March 1524. He subsequently sailed 150 miles southward to a point somewhere along the modern South Carolina coast, then north as far as present-day Maine, before returning to France. Spain's Lucas Vazquez de Ayllon may have plied the waters of the Cape Fear River in 1526, although if he did he did not stay for any great length of time. Between 1566 and 1567, another Spaniard, Juan Pardo, led an expedition into the Carolina backcountry, establishing a small outpost called Fort San Juan near modern Morganton, North Carolina, and visited Indian villages along the Catawba River. Two decades later, Sir Walter Raleigh, a favorite of Queen Elizabeth I of England, sponsored three efforts to plant a colony on Roanoke Island. Raleigh's experiment ended badly, becoming the enduring mystery that is the famed Lost Colony. For decades, the lure of the American coast drew European explorers to the Western Hemisphere's lush shores.

Verrazanos Grand Tour

The discoveries of Ferdinand Magellan were still fresh in the minds of Europeans, including a group of Tuscan merchants living in Lyon and Rouen, who petitioned the King to authorize an expedition to seek out new trade routes. Verrazano's voyage to the New World was the result of their encouragement and King Francis I's own curiosity.

Giovanni de Verrazano

Giovanni de Verrazano was the perfect man to conduct an exploration of the uncharted lands that Europeans called America, after Amerigo Vespucci, Christopher Columbus' navigator on his expedition of discovery that put the continents of the Western Hemisphere on the map. A Florentine by birth, Verrazano was a mariner who had lived for many years in France. Residing in the seaport town of Dieppe, Verrazano's experience on previous successful voyages of exploration spoke well of his ability to lead a flotilla of four vessels into the Western Sea.

With the blessing of King Francis I of France, Verrazano led four ships into the Atlantic Ocean and towards the new continents in 1523, though only *La Dauphine* and *La Normande* survived poor weather to sail on the final Atlantic crossing. His mandate from the King was to explore the lands between Spanish Florida and Newfoundland, seeking gold and a possible Northwest Passage. Rough seas sank two of Verrazano's ships and forced the remaining two to return to port. Verrazano effected repairs and set out from Brittany with the surviving vessels of his command in the closing weeks of 1523.

Crossing the Atlantic to reach North America was never easy. Verrazano sailed southward until he reached a position off the coast of Spain, then put his helm over, assuming a tack that took the expedition farther into the Atlantic. Again, complications forced *La Normande*, the companion ship to Verrazano's flagship, *La Dauphine*, to return to France. Sailing alone, Verrazano and his crew crossed the ocean and made landfall along the Cape Fear coast on March 21, 1524. After exploring to the south, Verrazano foraged on shore to refill his depleted stores, dangerously low after the trans-Atlantic voyage. On returning to the Cape Fear, he ordered landing parties to go ashore to find fresh water and food. Verrazano made carefully detailed notes about the flora and fauna his men encountered.

Verrazano wrote that the land he saw was, "…completely covered with fine sand XV feet deep, which arises in the form of small hills about fifty paces wide. After climbing farther, we found other streams and inlets from the sea which come in by several mouths, and follow the ins and outs of the shoreline. Nearby we could see a stretch of country much higher than the sandy shore, with many beautiful fields and plains full of great forests, some sparse and some dense; and the trees have so many colors, and are so beautiful and delightful that they defy description."

Verrazano did not remain ashore long before returning to *La Dauphine*. The Frenchmen not only found plants and foliage that suggested a land of plentiful resources, but also made contact with Native Americans inhabiting the Carolina coast. Despite a tentative first meeting, Verrazano's record of the encounter suggested that the Indians were quite friendly. When the expedition returned to France a year later, Verrazano's narrative encouraged subsequent explorations of the Americas, including modern North Carolina.[1]

Lucas Vasquez de Ayllon and the Cape Fear

Two years after Giovanni de Verrazano delivered a glowing report about the potential of the lands along the east coast of North America, Spanish explorer Lucas Vasquez de Ayllon established an outpost at present day Tybee Island, Georgia. De Ayllon's expeditions in the 1520s stemmed more from his own curiosity than any directive from the Spanish King. In 1526, he sent two parties out to explore the lands known as

Lucas Vasquez de Ayllon

Chicora to its Indian inhabitants. One group traveled westward into the interior, while a second one took to the sea and sailed up the coast, perhaps as far as the Cape Fear.[2]

As they crossed the inlet bar, the Spanish discovered why later mapmakers would give the land jutting into the Atlantic its enduring name - Cape Fear. One of the ships was lost with all its supplies, perhaps on Frying Pan Shoals, though the crew was rescued. Local legend contended for years that the Spanish mariners immediately began construction on a replacement vessel. If true, that would have made the Cape Fear the site of the first western-style vessel built in North America. New scholarship, however, discredits the Cape Fear theory and instead suggests that the shipbuilding episode occurred closer to the Tybee Island outpost. Other members of de Ayllon's expedition established a short-lived fort near the same site the Jamestown settlement would occupy some eighty years later. Before the end of 1524, the settlements had succumbed to disease and epidemics that claimed a host of lives, including de Ayllon. While de Ayllon's attempts to plant a Spanish colony along the Atlantic seaboard were unsuccessful, another Spaniard had better luck exploring the Carolina interior from 1566-1568.[3]

Juan Pardo's Western Sojourn

From the earliest discovery of the Americas, Spain, more than any other European country, invested time, men, and material into exploring and exploiting the Americas. The main thrust of Spain's efforts focused on Central and South America because of the mineral wealth they discovered and the slaves they exploited. As early as 1528, however, Panfilio de Narvaez's men endured a difficult trek across the lands of the Florida panhandle and Gulf Coast before finally winding up in Mexico, by way of lands that make up part of modern California. The Spanish fort at St. Augustine, established in 1565, was just one of several outposts established on behalf of King Philip II, as far north as the Chesapeake Bay.[4]

In 1566, Juan Pardo, under the command of General Pedro Menendez de Aviles, struck out into the Carolina interior from Santa Elena

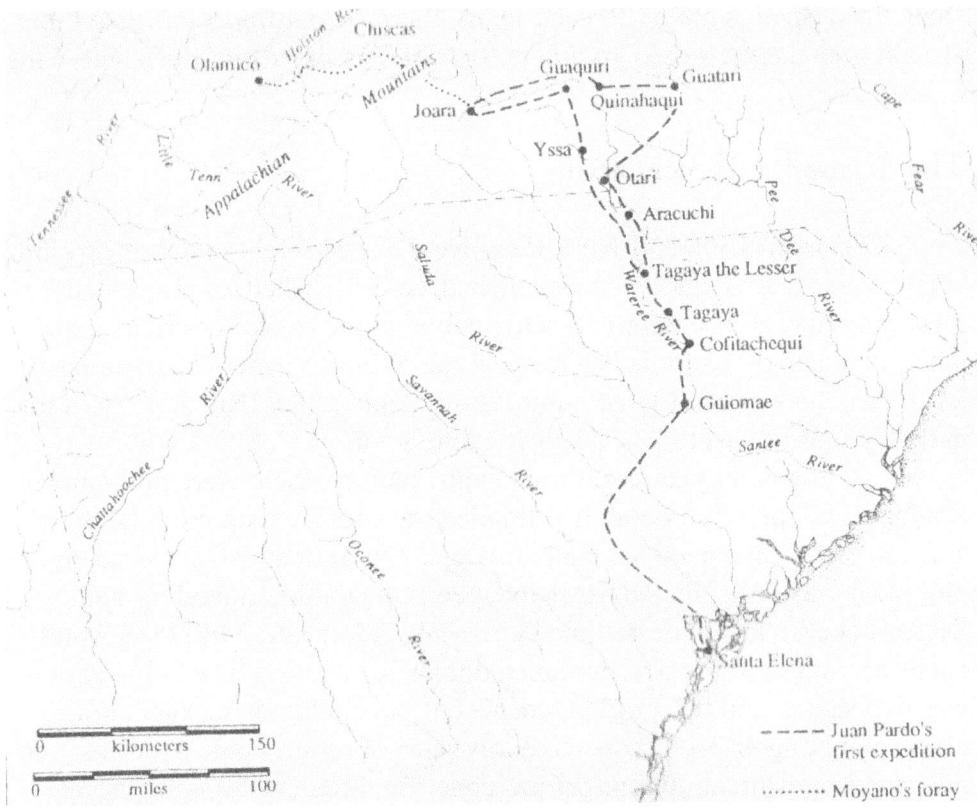

Juan Pardo's expedition into what would become North Carolina, 1566.

on the first of two explorations of unknown lands.[5] Pardo's men encountered swampy lowlands along the Carolina coast before turning westward to reach a point near modern Linville, North Carolina. A little farther on, the Spanish established a military outpost near modern Morganton, North Carolina, which Pardo left in the command of his sergeant, Hernando Moyano de Morales, with a small garrison of thirty soldiers. General de Aviles recalled the remainder of Pardo's men when fears of a French raid against Santa Elena compelled him to gather his forces at the coast. When the threat passed, a second expedition led by Pardo with as many as 120 men explored as far north as the site of modern Asheville, North Carolina, before turning westward into Tennessee.

Spain claimed the entirety of North America by right of discovery, but found that claiming it and possessing it were two different matters. Beginning with Raleigh's toehold on North Carolina's Outer Banks, then at

Jamestown and elsewhere (including the Cape Fear in 1663), the English challenged Spain's ability to back up its claim by putting colonists on the ground to make their own argument for who possessed the lands below the Chesapeake.

The Roanoke Experiment

Between 1606 and 1681, there were twenty-eight major territorial charters and grants made that established, re-established, or confirmed English (and in one case Scottish) settlements on the North American mainland. Increasingly charters began speaking of North American colonies in terms of places to plant large numbers of people rather than as sources for natural commodities to fuel English manufacturing.[6]

By the latter years of the sixteenth century, there were problems in England. A population boom had flooded the country with more laborers and craftsmen than need demanded. Wages fell dramatically, and unemployment was rampant. Advisors to Queen Elizabeth I, including both Richard Hakluyts, advocated the large-scale colonization of North America as a solution to the overburdened domestic situation. But colonization was expensive, and the Virgin Queen's coffers could not sustain a long term colonizing effort. Prospective low rates of return made overseas colonies poor investment options for merchants and traders who might otherwise have mitigated the high costs of colonization. Consequently, a policy was established that saw the English Crown offering Western Hemisphere territory to investors willing to underwrite the expense of colonization.[7]

Sir Walter Raleigh (left), a favorite of Queen Elizabeth I (right), used his influence with the monarch to mount an expedition to plant an English colony in the New World.

While Spain pillaged the earth of its treasures at sites like Potosi, she constantly had to look over her shoulder to keep an eye on the other European powers that were nipping at her heels for their own piece of the Americas. Portugal and France were especially keen to acquire a slice of the bounty coming from the new lands of the Western Hemisphere.[8] For the most part, England, wrapped up in its own domestic troubles, seemed content to leave the other powers to their own devices. Instead, the English allowed sea rovers like Francis Drake to poach the Spanish treasure fleets sailing out of Havana to get their share of American riches for the Crown's treasury. While Sir Humphrey Gilbert envisioned settlements in what would become Canada between 1578 and 1584, England had no serious colonial ambitions. That all changed when Queen Elizabeth I granted Sir Walter Raleigh a charter to send colonists to Virginia.[9]

Raleigh funded three expeditions to the Western Hemisphere, the first coming in 1584, when Philip Amadas and Arthur Barlowe made a three-month voyage across the Atlantic to plant the English flag in America for the first time, on North Carolina's Outer Banks. The Amadas/Barlowe expedition was not intended to establish a colony, so the explorers returned to England. The report they filed with Raleigh, including a favorable initial encounter with local Indians, was promising enough that Raleigh immediately began outfitting a second expedition to stake a claim among the sand dunes, forests, and sounds of the barrier islands off the Carolina coast – specifically on Roanoke Island.[10]

That second expedition, disembarking at Roanoke in 1585, carried Ralph Lane, the newly appointed governor of the proposed colony, and Sir Richard Grenville, Raleigh's cousin, along with a male-only military contingent, whose mission was to establish a site for settlement and secure the surrounding area. Grenville was eager to return to England for supplies (and also to write-up his discoveries of New World flora and fauna), and left Lane and his men almost immediately. While Grenville was gone, the Englishmen poisoned their relationship with local Indians by accusing one of stealing a silver cup. The accusation made the prospect of finding sustenance among the Native Americans poor at best. By the late spring of 1586, Lane and his surviving men were more than eager to accept a ride home to England from Sir Francis Drake.[11]

The third and final expedition, which led to a second John White colony at Roanoke Island, departed in July 1587. White's contingent included approximately 120 men, women and children, including his own pregnant daughter, Eleanor. The plan was to establish an independent enclave of settlers based on an agricultural economy that could survive on its own, a place that could serve as an entry point for other Englishmen and women who would soon follow. White's daughter, married to fellow settler Ananias Dare, presented her father with a grandchild, Virginia, during the hot, dog days of August 1587.[12]

The Algonquian Indians at Roanoke were initially friendly to the 1584 English settlement with whom they shared the surrounding sounds and streams. One "weroance"[13] in particular, named Manteo, became fast friends with the colonists and worked to help White's settlers establish their new home. That period of good will did not endure. Animosity festered when white settlers began abusing their neighbors, raiding their villages for food and slaves, ruining relations with the very people upon whom the Englishmen had come to depend. Another weroance, Wingina, at first also friendly to the newcomers in 1584, became an implacable enemy of the whites and encouraged all Indians in the region to make war upon them.

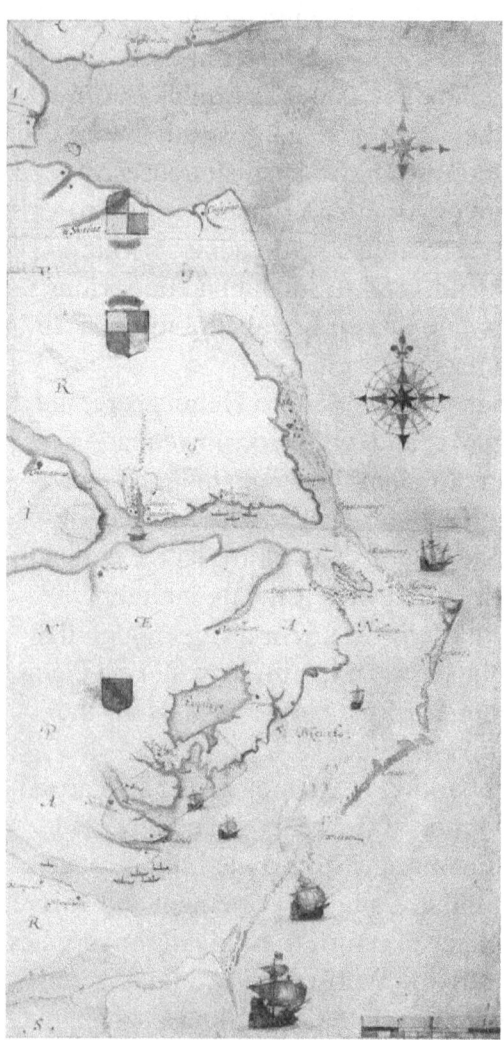

John White's map of the Roanoke colony.

Shortly after Virginia Dare's birth, Governor John White was compelled to make a return trip to England to report to Raleigh on the progress of the colonial enterprise, and to secure additional supplies for the settlers. Before he could return, the undeclared Anglo-Spanish War (1585-1604) heated up and forced him to postpone his departure. When Spain's Great Armada sallied forth against Queen Elizabeth's woefully outnumbered and outgunned Royal Navy in the summer of 1588, all available ships were dragooned into the effort to fend of the warships of His Catholic Majesty, King Philip II.[14]

Desperate to return to Roanoke, White engaged the services of two small vessels unsuitable for military service, the *Brave* and the *Roe,* and attempted to re-cross the Atlantic to his family. Bad luck continued to dog the Roanoke governor when the two ships were captured by French pirates who absconded with everything White had purchased for the succor of his far away colonists. For the second time, White's efforts to return to Virginia were thwarted.

Sir Walter Raleigh was able to outfit two more ships, the *Hopewell* and *Moonlight*, after the Spanish Armada was destroyed and the threat to England abated somewhat, and John White was finally able to begin his journey anew. The ships departed England in March 1590, but still it seemed the cosmos was conspiring to prevent White from reaching Virginia (as all of the region claimed by the English in America was called at the time). Poor weather, fending off attacks by hostile French and Spanish privateers, and a proclivity for commerce raiding on the part of the ships' masters kept them from reaching Roanoke until August 1590 – a full three years after White had sailed away from Eleanor, Virginia, and his other colonists. By that time the settlement on Roanoke was abandoned, strewn with discarded pieces of White's armor and personal effects. The only clue as to the fate of the English was the word "CROATAN" carved into the wood of the palisade gate.[15]

Gov. White returned to Roanoke to find his colony gone.

To this day theories abound as to what happened to the hapless colonists of the infamous "Lost Colony" of Roanoke. Many assert that unfriendly Indians, such as Wingina, massacred the English. Others say one of the Outer Banks' frequent encounters with a hurricane either swept them away, or prompted them to seek shelter in the forests on the mainland, a theory that has gained some traction due to archaeological finds in the vicinity of Edenton, N.C. Still others posit that Spanish raiders out of Havana or St. Augustine learned of the English encroachment and dealt with them. Yet another theory proposes that the English, starving and desperate, threw themselves on the mercy of the Indians, eventually assimilating with them to become part of the Indian societies. In any case, the truth of the disappearance remains one of history's most persistent mysteries.[16]

Virginians in the Albemarle

Before the restoration of the English monarchy in 1660, Carolina was simply perceived as a vaguely defined land mass on the other side of the vast Atlantic Ocean, a place of savage indigenous peoples, but rich in potential resources for those with the moxie to discover and exploit them. On maps of the sixteenth and early seventeenth centuries, the land that would become Carolina was simply referred to as New France or Virginia. It was not until the Lords Proprietors began crafting the Carolina Charter that more accurate maps were needed to enhance the recruiting pitch made to prospective settlers. Even before mapmakers gave it a name of its own, however, Englishmen were already building lives in the northern part of what would become Carolina.[17]

Incursions into the Albemarle region of Virginia were nothing new by the time Nathaniel Batts began trading with Indians in the lands surrounding the Albemarle Sound in 1655, and by 1663 the proprietary province of Carolina had been inhabited by Virginians for at least five years. As early as 1602, Sir Walter Raleigh had dispatched an expedition, led by Samuel Mace, to try to locate the lost Roanoke colonists. Another exploration of the lands to the south of Jamestown occurred in 1622 when John Pory, secretary of the Virginia colony, made an extensive search of the territory that Virginians suspected might have become the refuge of Virginia Dare and her fellow colonists. In 1643, a military expedition under Major General Richard Bennett and Colonel Thomas Dew converged on the Chowan River to put down an Indian uprising. Among the men mustered under

This Mercator map from 1606 is a typical example of maps of the era that have Carolina as part of Virginia.

arms for the campaign were Henry Plumpton of Nansemond County, and Thomas Took (Tuke) of Isle of Wight County. Both men liked what they saw in the fertile lands surrounding the Albemarle. Plumpton and Took combined their resources to buy a parcel of land along the Chowan in 1648, although they never settled on it.[18]

But while land in Virginia was not an issue in the early years of the seventeenth century, by the middle decades rich bottom lands suitable for agriculture were becoming scarce. A burgeoning population led enterprising newcomers and second-generation colonists to cast their eyes southward for new lands on which to stake a claim and make their fortunes. Men such as Francis Yeardley were happy to oblige.

Francis Yeardley, the son of Virginia's governor, like most people in the Tidewater settlements, was eager to find ways to enhance the size of his personal fortune. Yeardley had done a bit of exploring below the Chesapeake himself, with ideas to expand English settlement beyond the bounds of the Chesapeake. Yeardley, like most Virginians, always kept a wary eye on the moves of the Spanish to the south, who claimed all of the

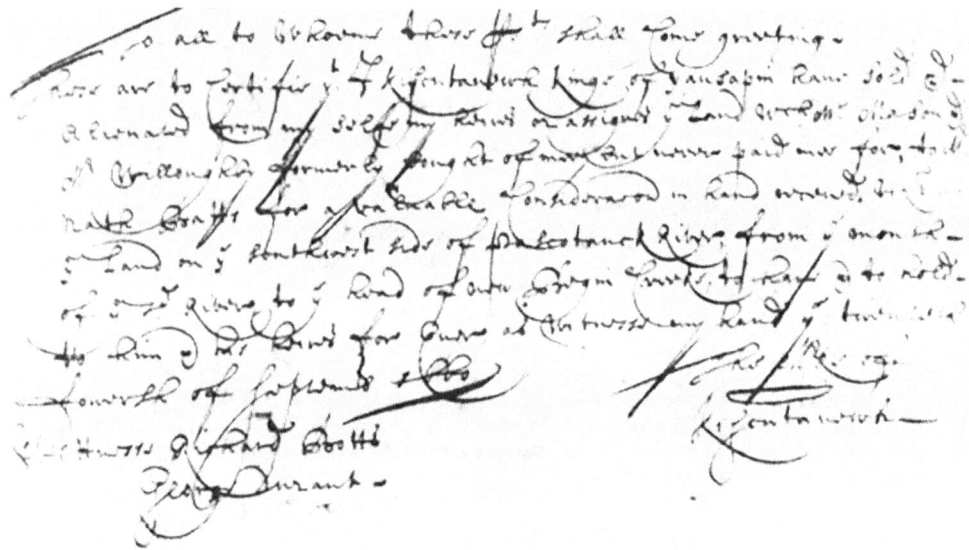

Nathaniel Batts became an early settler in North Carolina's Albemarle by virtue of this deed, granting him land along the Chowan River (above). Batts' claim is recorded on the Comberford map from 1657.

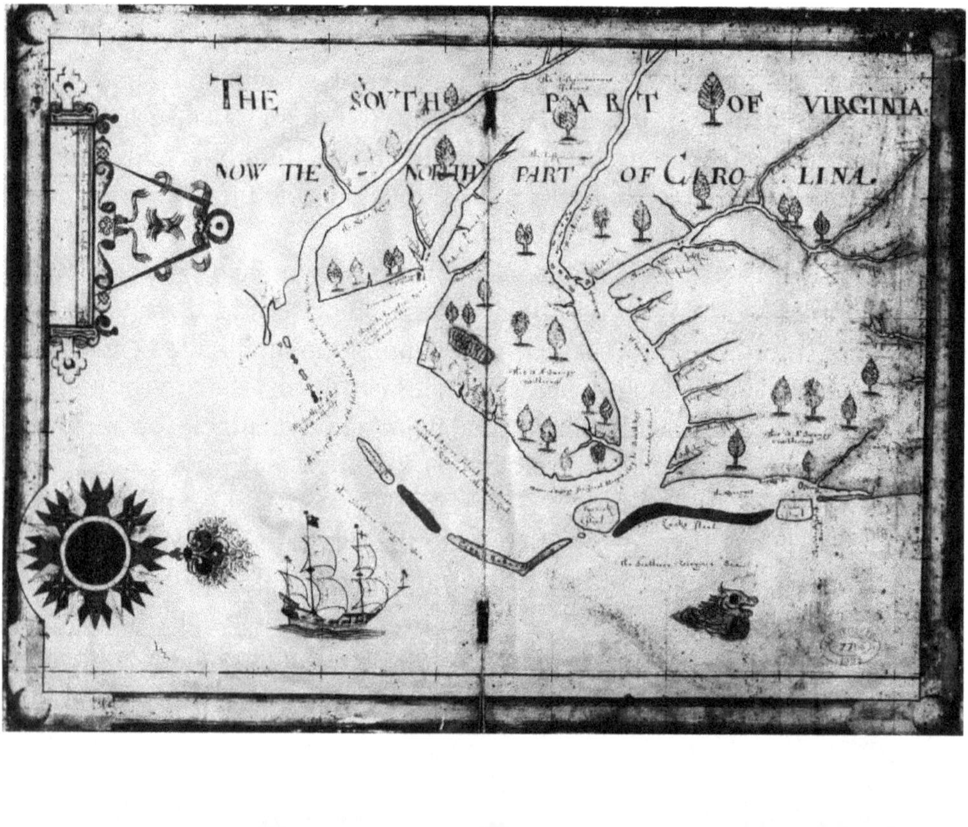

territory from Florida to the Chesapeake. Settling in what would be Carolina could be dangerous.[19]

Nevertheless, the opportunities in the Albemarle were too tempting to ignore. To that end, Yeardley contracted with fur trader Nathaniel Batts to explore the lands below the Virginia colonies, seeking new sources of revenues and suitable lands for new English enclaves. Batts spent a year surveying the new area, as more than fifty years after its founding, Jamestown had become crowded. Newcomers were eager to strike out from the Chesapeake to establish their own estates. His work can be seen in part in the Nicholas Comberford map of 1657.[20]

After purchasing land of his own, Batts built a home along Salmon Creek (identified as Fletts Creek on the Nicholas Comberford map) on a tract of land that became Perquimans and Bertie Counties. According to surviving records, his home measured twenty feet by twenty feet and had a large chimney. Batts abandoned the house after troubles with the Tuscaroras made it untenable, but it remained in use as a trading post for years afterward.[21]

When Batts ventured into the uncharted wilds south of the Chesapeake in 1658, seven men were hired to accompany him. Records list them as John Battle, Thomas Relfe, Roger Williams, Thomas Jarvis, John Harvey, John Jenkins, and George Durant. Batts' deed lists Durant as a witness to the transaction between the fur trader and King Kiscutanaweh of the Yeopim, and his name is found in a similar capacity in several other deeds over the next several years. When Durant filed his own claim for a tract of land in what is now Perquimans County in 1661, he became the second man to claim land in Carolina (and the first to file that claim in the southern colony instead of Virginia), and joined the first settlers of the Carolina mainland. It would be some years more before Englishmen attempted to settle the southern portion of the territory. Before that could happen, events had to run their course in other parts of the world.[22]

Endnotes

1. Giovanni de Verrazano, "Letter to King Francis I of France, 8 July 1524: reporting on his voyage to the New World," National Humanities Center, http://nationalhumanitiescenter.org/pds/amerbegin/contact/text4/verrazzano.pdf (accessed 1/17/12); Samuel Eliot Morison, *The European Discovery of America: The Northern Voyages*, (New York: Oxford University Press, 1971), 260-261 (hereafter cited as Morison, *European Discovery of America*).
2. Morison, *European Discovery of America*, 30-31; Paul Quattlebaum, *Land Called Chicora: The Carolinas Under Spanish Rule With French Intrusion, 1520-1670* (Spartanburg, S.C.: The Reprint Company, 1973), 19. Lucas Vasquez de Ayllon was a wealthy lawyer and official of the Spanish administration on Hispanola. De Aylon would fund three expeditions to explore North America between 1520 and 1524. According to Quattlebaum, Chicora encompassed roughly all the land between the Cape Fear and Santee Rivers (see endpapers for map).
3. James Sprunt, *Chronicles of the Cape Fear River: 1660-1916*, 2nd ed. (Wilmington, N.C.: Dram Tree Books, 2005), 1 (hereafter cited as Sprunt, *Chronicles of the Cape Fear River*). Cape Fear, the scourge of mariners for centuries due to its nearly twenty miles of shoals stretching into the Atlantic, was sometimes labeled "Cape Faire" on early maps and charts. This is likely due to inconsistencies in spellings rather than any benign aspect of the land mass.
4. Alvar Nunez Cabeza de Vaca; Rolena Adorno and Patrick Charles Pautz, eds., *The Narrative of Cabeza de Vaca* (Lincoln, NE: University of Nebraska Press, 2003), passim; Charles Hudson, *The Juan Pardo Expeditions: Exploration of the Carolinas and Tennessee, 1566-1568* (Washington, D.C.: Smithsonian Institution Press, 1990), 7, (hereafter cited as Hudson, *The Juan Pardo Expeditions*). Narvaez and his companions, including Cabeza de Vaca, were shipwrecked near modern Tampa Bay. In their attempts to find rescue at a Spanish outpost, they endured a horrifying journey that featured a chase by hostile Indians, but also succor by friendly Native Americans. His account of that journey is a fascinating look at native culture and environment at a time when white men had never touched those lands. Other Spanish outposts along the American east coast include the de Ayllon outpost at Winyah Bay, South Carolina (1526), Fort Caroline/San Mateo, Florida (1564/1565), San Miguel de Gualdape (location unknown), Santa Elena, South Carolina (1565), and Bahia de Santa Maria in the Chesapeake Bay.
5. Hudson, *The Juan Pardo Expeditions*, 23-50. The first expedition was from December 1566 - March 1567. The second took place from September 1, 1567 – March 2, 1568.
6. Christopher Tomlins, "The Legal Cartography of Colonization, the Legal Polyphony of Settlement: English Intrusions on the American Mainland in the

Seventeenth Century." *Law & Social Inquiry*, Vol. 26, No. 2 (April 2000): 315-372. The twenty-eight land grants were the first, second, and third charters of VA (1606, 1609, 1611); the London and Bristol Company charter for Newfoundland (1610); the New England Council charter (1620); the three Alexander charters for Nova Scotia (1621, 1625, 1628); the Maine grants (1622, 1639, 1664, 1674); The Avalon charter of Newfoundland (1623); the Heath patent for Carolina (1629); the Plymouth charter (1629); the Massachusetts Bay Company charter (1629); the New Hampshire grants (1629, 1635); the Maryland charter (1632); the Kirke charter for Newfoundland (1637); the Connecticut charter (1662); the Rhode Island charter (1663); the Carolina charters (1663, 1665); the New Jersey charter (1664, 1674, 1682); the Pennsylvania charter (1681). Most chartering activity after Charles II returned to the throne in 1660 abrogated earlier patents while leaving intact established jurisdictional ideologies.
7. Carville V. Earle, "The First English Towns in North America," *Geographical Review*, Vol. 67, No. 1 (January 1977): 42.
8. French, Portuguese, English, and Basque fishing fleets had already been plundering the abundant cod fisheries of the New World for years.
9. N.C. History Project, http://northcarolinahistory.org/encyclopedia/25/entry (accessed 9/12/12). Raleigh received his grant in 1584, and the queen's blessings to his venture, commanding him to "discover, search, find out, and view such remote heathen and barbarous Lands, Countries, and territories . . . to have, hold, occupy, and enjoy."
10. David B. Quinn, *North America from the Earliest Discovery to First Settlements: The Norse Voyages to 1612* (New York: Harper & Row, 1977), 322-346 (hereafter cited as D.B. Quinn, *North America*).
11. David B. and Alison Quinn, eds., *The First Colonists: Documents on the Planting of The First English Settlements in North America, 1584-1590* (Raleigh: N.C. Department of Cultural Resources, Division of Archives & History, 1982), 1-12.
12. David La Vere, *The Lost Rocks: The Dare Stones and the Unsolved Mystery of Sir Walter Raleigh's Lost Colony*, (Wilmington, N.C.: Dram Tree Books, 2010), 63 (hereafter cited as La Vere, *Lost Rocks*). Virginia Dare's birth is noteworthy in that she was the first English child born in the New World. She was also added motivation for her grandfather to return to Roanoke as quickly as possible when forced to return to England for supplies and to report to his sponsors the autumn of 1587.
13. LaVere, *Lost Rocks*, 31. Weroance (or sometimes wiroance) is a Native American word for wise man, or man of power, that was ascribed to chieftains of the various coastal Indian groups.
14. Colin Martin and Geoffrey Parker, *The Spanish Armada* (New York: Penguin Books, 1999), 40, 185. King Philip II claimed a share of the English Crown by

his marriage to Mary, Queen Elizabeth's sister. When Mary died, Philip considered Elizabeth a pretender to the throne. That Elizabeth enacted measures against the Catholic Church in England only exacerbated Spain's eagerness to see her deposed. The Armada was simply the culmination of the Spanish venom toward England's "virgin queen." That it was all but destroyed by a storm before it could ever come to blows with the English fleet must have seemed like the ultimate Divine betrayal to Philip.

15. La Vere, *Lost Rocks*, 1-5. CROATAN might have indicated the colonists had moved inland to shelter with friendly Indians, as agreed upon before White left the colony.

16. Thomas C. Parramore, "The Lost Colony Found: A Documentary Perspective," *North Carolina Historical Review*, Vol. 78, No. 1 (January 2001): 67-83. Dr. Parramore contends that the colonists did as they had said they would in the event that Roanoke Island became untenable, and moved fifty miles into the mainland to live with friendly Weapemeoc Indians. To go anywhere else would have been to deliver themselves into the hands of unfriendly natives. Recent evidence discovered on a map offers tantalizing clues that the settlers may have settled near modern Edenton, N.C.

17. S. Max Edelson, "Defining Carolina: Cartography and Colonization in the North American Southeast, 1657-1733," in Michelle LeMaster and Bradford J. Wood, *Creating and Contesting Carolina: Proprietary Era Histories* (Columbia: University of South Carolina Press, 2013): 27-48; William P. Cumming, "Naming Carolina," http://www.ah.dcr.state.nc.us/sections/hp/colonial/Nchr/Subjects/cumming.htm (accessed 11/17/10). Joseph Moxon's was the first map (1664) to note the "Carolina" toptonym. Robert Horne's 1666 map was the first to place Carolina as a distinctive region below Virginia and above Florida. In the charter printed in the *Colonial Records of North Carolina*, the province was identified as both "Carolana" and "Carolina." Cumming's research finds that before the Restoration, the different spellings were almost always due to transcription errors. When Charles II presented the proprietors with a patent for "Carolina," the name was finally changed permanently.

18. Lindley S. Butler, "The Early Settlement of Carolina: Virginia's Southern Frontier," *The Virginia Magazine of History and Biography*, Vol. 79, No. 1, Part One (Jan. 1971): 20-28 (hereafter cited as Butler, "The Early Settlement of Carolina," *Virginia Magazine*). The Albemarle region became widely known to Virginians after Governor William Berkeley, a future Lord Proprietor, sent a military expedition south of the Chesapeake to quell an Indian uprising that was interfering with trade. The land purchase by Plumpton and Took in 1648 is the first recorded purchase of land in North Carolina history. Their case is distinctive in that, unlike Nathaniel Batts and George Durant, they never settled on the land. Their property was situated along the Chowan River and extended as far south as

the Morratuck (Roanoke) River.

19. Timothy P. Grady, "'Vomit His Fury and Malice': English Fears and Spanish Influences on the Exploration and Establishment of Carolina through 1670," *The Proceedings of the South Carolina Historical Association* (2010): 31-42, http://www.palmettohistory.org/scha/proceedings_2010.pdf, (hereafter cited as Grady, "Vomit," *SCHA*). Yeardley wrote to John Farrar in 1654 encouraging exploration of the Albemarle region, but cautioning Farrar to be on the lookout for the Spanish. According to Yeardley, on one of his trips south "the Tuskarorawes emperor, with 250 of his men, met our company, and received them courteously; and after some days spent, desired them to go to his chief town." The Tuscarora chief informed the English that at his main village "was one Spaniard resideing, who had been seven years with them, a man very rich, having about thirty in his family, seven whereof are negroes; and he had one more negro, leiger [resident] with a great nation called the Nexwes. He is sometimes, they say, gone from thence a pretty while." Though the business of the Spaniard is unclear (he was likely an itinerant trader), Spain's influence in the area was clear to Yeardley, but he also noted that not all of the natives in the Albemarle were happy with the Spanish presence.

20. Hugh T. Lefler and William S. Powell, *Colonial North Carolina* (New York: Charles Scribner's Sons, 1973), 29-32; N.C. Museum of History Timeline, http://ncmuseumofhistory.org/nchh/seventeenth.html; William P. Cumming. "Naming Carolina," http://www.ah.dcr.state.nc.us/sections/hp/colonial/Nchr/Subjects/cumming.htm (accessed 11/17/10); Butler, "The Early Settlement of Carolina," *Virginia Magazine*, 23. Batts' survey of the lands south of the Chesapeake facilitated more settlement in the Albermarle region. By 1663, land records filed in Virginia show that as many as 500 people were living in Carolina (which at the time was still considered the south Virginia frontier).

21. William S. Powell, *North Carolina Through Four Centuries* (Chapel Hill: University of North Carolina Press, 1989), 52; Jonathan Martin, "Bertie County (1722)," North Carolina History Project, http://www.northcarolinahistory.org/encyclopedia/613/entry (accessed 9/29/12). So many people were beginning to settle beyond Virginia's southern border that in 1662 Captain Samuel Stephens was commissioned to command what Virginia leaders came to call the "southern plantation," and tasked with appointing a sheriff for the lands of the Albemarle region. When King Charles II regained the throne after the English Civil War and Cromwellian rule in 1660, he awarded Carolina to eight men who had supported him. Charles' charter ushered in Carolina's proprietary period.

22. Butler, "The Early Settlement of Carolina," *Virginia Magazine*, 26.

The execution of King Charles I left his young son, Prince Charles Stuart, a monarch in exile. The English Civil War and Cromwell's Interregnum interrupted the Stuart line until the Restoration placed the son of the dead king back on the throne.

II
Of Cavaliers and Roundheads

Charles Towne was a child of many circumstances and events that led to the voyage of John Vassall and his fellow Barbadian adventurers to Carolina. A key episode in the story was the conflict that saw the English monarchy deposed, the exodus of Royalists from England to places on the fringe of the English world, and the heir to the English throne cast into exile - a prince without a country.

The war that saw King Charles I beheaded and England ruled by the pious Oliver Cromwell actually comprised a series of conflicts that James Heath called the Wars of the Three Kingdoms in his 1662 chronicle. The English Civil War was rooted in both civil and religious issues. Involving Ireland, Scotland, and England, the wars led to the suspension of the Stuart monarchy.[1]

The wars between Royalist "Cavaliers" loyal to the monarchy and Parliamentary "Roundheads" featured three distinct conflicts, each with connections to the others. Between 1642-1646, Parliamentarians led by Oliver Cromwell clashed with Royalists loyal to King Charles I over the type of national government England would have. That conflict over royal versus parliamentary supremacy flared again between 1648 and 1649. Events would, in time, render those arguments moot. Charles Stuart was found guilty by a panel of fifty-nine judges as a "tyrant, traitor, murderer and public enemy" after Royal forces were defeated by Oliver Cromwell's

The English Civil Wars ended with the execution of King Charles I in 1649. What followed was parliamentary rule under the leadership of Oliver Cromwell.

New Model Army. The reign of King Charles I ended on the scaffold at Whitehall with a stroke of the executioner's heavy iron blade on January 30, 1649. The king was dead, but his son and heir was still alive, and anxious to avenge his father's death.[2]

Six months later the young heir to the throne, Charles II, rallied and marched at the head of a Scottish army to avenge the king's death. By June 1650, fighting had broken out in Scotland again, as supporters of the Stuarts clashed with Parliamentary forces under Oliver Cromwell. The Roundheads defeated Scottish forces under David Leslie at the Battle of Dunbar in September 1650, and captured Edinburgh by the end of the year. In 1651, the New Model Army then targeted Perth. Young Charles, taking advantage of the aggressive move, advanced with his army into southern England. Leaving future Lord Proprietor George Monck to finish things in Scotland, Cromwell gave chase. The two forces came together at Worcester on September 3, 1651. Cromwell's troops dealt a final blow to Charles Stuart's hopes to have revenge for his father's execution by defeating the Royalists. Even so, the legitimate heir to the throne managed to escape, fleeing into exile in Europe.[3]

Taking a cue from their exiled prince, people who had stood by the Stuart monarchy decided that England had become too partisan and dangerous for them. These so-called Cavaliers – at least those who could afford it – opted to leave the country and seek refuge in the English colonies of the Western Hemisphere. Barbados and Virginia especially became strongholds of Royalist sentiment, and remained so until an exasperated Cromwell sent a fleet to bring them to heel. These "transplanted Englishmen," to borrow a term from historian Larry Gragg, were among those who would infuse the Barbadian economy with money, ambition, and eventual interest in colonizing the North American mainland.

The Restoration of Charles Stuart

Oliver Cromwell became Lord Protector of England, Scotland and Ireland in 1653. With Charles Stuart no longer a threat, the way was clear for Cromwell to remake England into a reverential nation that feared God and conducted itself according to the Holy writ found in the King James Bible, one of the few things James I did that met with Cromwell's approval. Domestically, Cromwell stayed true to his Puritan beliefs and waged a campaign to impose austerity measures that were wildly different from the often bawdy, drunk, and merry-making practices that had existed under the old monarchy. The Cromwellians closed bull-baiting and cock fighting pits. Inns offering alcoholic libations and theaters were shuttered. They publicly whipped actors who persisted in practicing their art. Sundays were God's day and Cromwell's soldiers insured that the people kept it holy. Parliamentary Puritans also banned racing, gambling of any sort, and clothing that was even remotely colorful, instead of the humble, subdued hues favored by Cromwell. Mirth and laughter virtually disappeared in Cromwell's England.

Oliver Cromwell

Geopolitically, Oliver Cromwell favored a foreign policy that would enable England to challenge Spain's hegemony in the Western Hemisphere without resorting to war. Cromwell believed that Spanish holdings in the Caribbean were ripe for the plucking, convinced by the Dominican Thomas Gage, whose time and experience in the region made him something of an expert on the tropics. At Gage's urging, Cromwell and his counselors devised a plan they dubbed the "Western Design" to attack the island of Hispanola.[4]

Robert Venables

Co-commanded by General Robert Venables, a veteran of the fighting in Ireland, and General-at-Sea William Penn, eighteen warships carrying a force of 2,500 men, less than half of them combat veterans, sailed for the Caribbean in the autumn of 1654. Barbados' governor Daniel Searle accompanied the fleet as a civilian commissioner on the expedition. The flotilla made Barbados on Christmas Day and reinforced their expeditionary force with volunteers from among the indentured servants and freemen of the English islands of Barbados, St. Kitts, and Nevis. The armada then sailed toward their primary target, Hispanola. Things went badly from the start. Sickness and poor logistics, rough terrain, and inexperienced soldiers doomed the English expedition to failure. The commanders regrouped at the beach and loaded the ships for what they hoped would be an easier target at Jamaica.[5]

Back in England, people grew weary of Cromwell's religious zeal. The Protector for Life managed to keep his hold on power through sheer strength of conviction and personality, but like all mortals his time eventually ran out. Oliver Cromwell died on September 3, 1658, to be replaced by his much less charismatic son, Richard.[6]

Richard Cromwell

Modest and self-effacing, with a love of horses and the outdoors, Richard Cromwell was a poor substitute for his father. Indeed, he personally recognized his inadequacy to fill his father's shoes. "It might have pleased God and the nation too," he said not long after assuming his father's place as the most powerful man in England, "to have chosen out a person more fit and able for this work than I am." Among the troubles he inherited was a military that chafed under civilian leadership, which almost led to a renewal of the civil war. Cromwell found allies in Parliament, both moderates and conservatives alike who disapproved of a military free from civilian control. Ironically, Cromwell averted the crisis by giving in to the army's demands and dismissing the Parliament.[7]

Flexing its political muscle, the army revived the Rump Parliament in the spring of 1653. Only a quarter of the legislators that Cromwell had dismissed years earlier answered the summons, but those who did refused to concede to the army's dictates. Retired General John Lambert returned to head the army, but Parliament soon dismissed him and other officers for allegedly promoting sedition by a petition critical of the legislative body. Lambert in turn expelled the Rump and oversaw the selection of twenty-three officers to rule England without input from either house of Parliament. Recognizing his limitations, Richard Cromwell quietly retired to the continent.[8]

In Scotland, General George Monck viewed the army's moves with alarm. The elder Cromwell had left Monck to rule Scotland, while the Protector himself attended to business in England. Upon Oliver's death, the general took a wait and see approach to the administration of Richard Cromwell. Monck had been around Richard enough to doubt that he was made of the same stuff as his father. When the army appeared to be on the verge of a coup that would install what was essentially a military junta in England, however, Monck decided it was time to take action. By January 1659, the general was on the march at the head of 8,000 men, heading south for England.[9]

Gen. George Monck in London

Monck, the soldier that Samuel Pepys described as "a dull, heavy man," made it clear he would be the strong right arm of the Parliament by carrying out their orders to insure the people's call for a "free Parliament." He sent troops to remove all gates, portcullises, posts, and chains that signified London's strength. The general may have intended to show the citizens an example of how far Parliament was willing to go to protect its authority. But two days later, Monck followed up by informing the Rump Parliament that it must dissolve and issue a call for new elections. The

The newly restored King Charles II in the procession from Dover to London in 1660. Future Lord Proprietor of Carolina George Monck accompanied him on the journey.

people, weary of eleven years of dreary, solemn life under Commonwealth rule, took to the streets to rejoice.[10]

After General Monck opened Parliament to the largely Presbyterian members of the Long Parliament who earlier had been excluded because of their willingness to reach an accord with Charles I, supporters of the monarchy began openly toasting the heir to the throne, Charles II. The younger Stuart had been declared King of Scotland in 1649, but Cromwell's Interregnum and the ending suffered by Charles I left him a king in exile. When Monck shook up the power structure, perhaps Charles had a glimmer of hope that the throne might soon belong to a Stuart again.

Yet the heir to the English throne was uncertain of Monck's motives. The general might as easily be setting himself up as a new Protector, as being the catalyst for a return to an English monarchy. For his part, Monck had to move deliberately, walking a tightrope between factions that included the army, Parliament, and supporters of Charles II who were eager to see a Stuart once again on the throne in London.[11]

In the spring of 1660, the Long Parliament ended its tumultuous nineteen-year reign by dissolving itself in preparation for new elections. While it did, royalist Sir John Grenville met secretly with George Monck to consult with the general about a possible return for Charles. Monck made it known that it was his intention to reinstall Charles II as King of England, though he was cautious enough to avoid putting anything in writing. Nevertheless, the two men had a meeting of the minds, and Grenville was able to deliver hopeful news to the Scottish King at The Hague. Not long afterward, six members of the House of Lords and a dozen of their fellows from the House of Commons arrived and offered Charles the throne. When the Stuart prince arrived at Dover on May 26, the old soldier who had been most instrumental in his return greeted him on bent knee at the dock where *The Prince* tied off.[12]

With the rightful king returned to the throne, England shuffled off the leaden weight of the Interregnum and basked in the light of the new monarch. Maypoles were again erected in town squares, while inns tapped kegs of wine and ale that had been banished during the teetotalling days of Cromwell's rule. Sportsmen returned to wagering on horses and dice, and balls lit the night with gaiety that had been sorely missed. Opportunity abounded, and there were plenty who were eager to seize it. Among them were eight men who would have a great impact on the settlement at Cape Fear, the Lords Proprietors of Carolina. When the grateful monarch granted them a patent to the territory below Virginia and above Florida, they moved quickly to find people eager to populate their lands. A promising place to find such settlers lay in the Lesser Antilles, on a small, fertile island that would become the richest place in the English empire, and provide the seeds for settlement at Cape Fear.

Endnotes

1. Charles Carlton, *Going to the Wars: The Experience of the British Civil Wars, 1638-1651* (London and New York: Routledge, 1992): 7 (hereafter cited as Carlton, *British Civil Wars*).
2. Sean Kelsey, "The Trial of Charles I," *English Historical Review*, Vol. 118, No. 477: 583–616. General Thomas Fairfax, a moderate and monarchist, refused to have any part in the proceedings, and resigned as head of the army. Oliver Cromwell was elevated to command in his place. When Charles II was restored to the throne in 1660, nine of the surviving regicides still in England were executed, while most of the others were condemned to spend the rest of their lives in prison.
3. Stanley D. M. Carpenter, *Military Leadership in the British Civil Wars, 1642–1651: The Genius Of This Age* (Abingdon, UK: Frank Cass, 2005): 45.
4. David Plant, "The Western Design, 1655," *BCWProject: British Civil Wars, Commonwealth & Protectorate, 1638-1660,* http://bcw-project.org/military/anglo-spanish-war/western-design, hereafter cited as Plant, *The Western Design;* Gardiner, *Commonwealth & Protectorate*, passim.
5. Plant, *The Western Design,* passim. Hispanola is today the island countries of Haiti and the Dominican Republic. The English flotilla, as was usual for the

English military all the way through the eighteenth century, had a dual command structure, with no one officer in overall command. This was just one of many problems that led to the English defeat at Hispanola.

6. Peter Ackroyd, *Rebellion: The History of England from James I to the Glorious Revolution* (New York: Thomas Dunne, 2014): 352 (hereafter cited as Ackroyd, *The History of England*).

7. Ackroyd, *The History of England*, 358. Things came to a head with the army when it marched on St. James with their commander, Major-General Charles Fleetwood, and demanded the gathered Parliament be closed.

8. Ackroyd, *The History of England*, 358-359.

9. Ackroyd, *The History of England*, 359-360. Monck's plan was murky at best. Even he said his goal was simply to preserve the commonwealth.

10. Ackroyd, *The History of England*, 360-361. There was conjecture, even while Monck served under Cromwell, that the general was a closet Royalist. Historians continue to debate whether or not Monck was simply biding his time until an opportunity arose to at least eliminate some of Parliament's power, if not restore the monarchy outright.

11. Ackroyd, *The History of England*, 361. There were still those in England, especially among old veterans, who proudly referred to themselves as "commonwealth men." How they would react to a lessening of Parliamentary authority, much less the return of a Stuart King, was something that remained to be seen.

12. Ackroyd, *The History of England*, 363.

The island of Barbados in 1675, roughly a decade after the Charles Towne settlement failed.

III
Barbados. The Sugar Island

As the English thirst for overseas colonies grew, adventurers, mercantile interests, and politicians all cast covetous eyes on the holdings that provided a steady stream of riches for Madrid and its Portuguese neighbor. There was a strong desire for Englishmen to find a source of wealth of their own, but England never did find any gold or silver mines, or capture a portion of the spice trade, or discover the fabled Northwest Passage to the exotic Orient. Neither did they breach Spain's monopoly on American possessions that provided all of those things. The one thing the English were able to accomplish was to spread their sphere of influence and enterprise to the Caribbean, and eventually – as at Charles Towne, for example – to the forests of the North American coast. Barbados was one such place that the English took for their own.[1]

Stumbled upon by Sir William Courteen in 1625, Barbados sits in the chain of islands just southeast of Cuba, the easternmost landfall of the Lesser Antilles. Originally discovered by Portuguese and English explorers, it has known only an English flag from its discovery through its independence in 1966. England secured its claim to it when Captain Henry Powell landed there in 1627 with eighty settlers. By 1639 they had a House of Assembly, making it just the third Parliamentary Democracy ever established in the world. Barbados is not a large island, just twenty-one miles long and fourteen wide, but the argument could be made that this small oasis in the Atlantic is the fountain from which sprang much of the settlement and culture of the southeastern United States.[2]

Englishmen in the seventeenth century were a mobile people. It was taken for granted, according to historian Carl Bridenbaugh, that most Englishmen of the period "had come to look upon migration and travel, whether occasional, seasonal or permanent, forced or voluntary, as a normal accomplishment of their age." For such an itinerant people, migration to the colonies of the Caribbean and North America was the natural progression of a lifestyle that precluded staying in one place for too long. There was a growing surplus of men in the English gentry who, because of primogeniture, had no hope of inheriting family lands of their own. The gentry married earlier, lived longer, and saw more of their offspring survive to become adults in their own right than did the rest of the English population. As their numbers grew, mobility was often the only means that afforded an ambitious young gentleman the opportunity to secure estates of his own. Places like Barbados were attractive to such men.[3]

The Early Years of the English on Barbados

Outside the usual paths taken by destructive hurricanes that routinely batter the Bahamas and Bermuda so mercilessly, Barbados was uniquely situated to serve England as an outpost in the Western Hemisphere. Between five and six hundred miles separate it from the American mainland, and its proximity to the Spanish Main made it attractive for privateers and merchant shippers capitalizing on the wealth and raw materials being brought out of places like Potosi. Prevailing winds and geography made it a fairly easy place to defend. English ships could sail from harbors on the south end of the island and swoop down on any attacking enemy, while high cliffs and rocky beaches to the north would make any attempt at landing an enemy force from that direction extremely difficult, if not an exercise in futility. Attackers trying to sail in from the south would have to contend with contrary winds that would give the defenders a definite tactical advantage.[4]

Taking its name from the Portuguese phrase for "bearded ones," likely because of the appearance of its fig trees when discovered early in the seventeenth century, the island was strategically located to play a

The "bearded" fig trees native to Barbados likely account for the island's name, from the Portuguese phrase for "bearded ones."

major role in the development of the Caribbean and the North American mainland into an interdependent Atlantic world. Ships of the era sailing for the tropics and the southern parts of the Americas generally sailed south to the Azores before tacking to the west, following ocean currents that took them across the ocean in the fastest way possible. After putting Africa behind them, their first landfall on that route was Barbados.[5]

The first three decades of the colonization of Barbados witnessed the settlers there trying to remake the tropical island in the image of that other island from which they sprang, England. The hot climate did not prevent them – especially those with the wherewithal to do so – from copying the lifestyle of the Mother Country to their own tiny piece of England in the Caribbean. As swiftly as circumstances allowed, Barbadian settlers attempted to transplant as much of the English way of life to the island as they could. As a result, the first three decades of English rule found Barbadians possessed of many of the same traits as those found in England itself – a tendency towards mobility, concerns with disorder and lawlessness, faith in common law, anti-Catholic sentiment (by the mid-seventeenth century being Protestant was a requirement if one was to be properly English), and a fierce determination to preserve local autonomy.[6]

Sugar cultivation and processing (above) was hot, dangerous work, and required a large workforce of cheap labor to do successfully. As sugar became king on Barbados, slavery became the key to the great wealth the sweet crop generated.

Barbados was not precisely a vision of paradise in the early days. Until the 1640s and the introduction of sugar, a thick canopy of trees was the first thing to catch a visitor's eye upon their arrival. Richard Ligon, a Royalist who fled the English Civil War in 1647 and who lived in Barbados for three years, noted that colonists still planted potatoes and corn "between the boughs, the Trees lying along upon the ground; so far short was the ground then of being clear'd." The less savory traits exhibited by Englishmen in Barbados often took visitors to the island aback. Thomas Verney wrote in 1640 that Barbadians were "such great drunkards" that they would find money "to buy their drink all though they goe naked."[7]

Ligon wrote of an almost penal way of life in describing the Barbadian existence of the lower sorts of people in 1650. Planters depended heavily on forced labor, initially exploiting Indians, followed by indentured white servants and enslaved Africans, for its economic survival. Without them, the sugar cane that was the foundation of Barbadian wealth simply could not be harvested and processed. Brutal conditions in the sugar cane fields awaited both white servants and African slaves. It involved hard menial labor from sun up to sundown, and often pushed workers into an early grave. Yet for coerced laborers, yeoman farmers, and craftsmen alike, life was very similar in many basic ways.

Residents of the island subsisted on a diet that seemed little more than roots and mush, cooped up in low-roofed little houses "like Stoves, or heated Ovens." Poor whites in Barbados were hardly better off than the slaves or indentured. According to Ligon, they were so sluggish and depressed as to not muster the motivation to even open their doors and windows to catch a refreshing ocean breeze. Barbados had an appalling death rate, with a life expectancy of only forty-five years for white males that managed to survive to see age twenty. For females the median age of death was just thirty-six, mostly due to fatalities suffered in childbirth.[8]

The diet of Englishmen in Barbados in the early years was not very diverse. They ate sweet potatoes in a variety of forms and dishes, cassava, or manioc (a starchy root plant), plantains, guava, and a variety of citrus fruits. Brought from South America, the sweet potato was a staple of Barbadian meals. Served up after being boiled or fried, the sweet potatoes tasted to Barbadians like chestnuts, and often took the place of bread on island tables. The first settlers also made nobby, their favorite drink, from sweet potatoes. Another beverage, perino, was made from cassava. From what was left of the native – and by then enslaved – Arawak Indians, the English learned to make a sort of white bread, also from the cassava root. It was nourishing, but tasted little like what English colonists remembered from home unless precious corn flour was mixed in with the cassava before baking.

Settlers enjoyed oranges, pomegranates, guavas, plums, prickly apples and pears, custard apples, bananas, papaya, and a number of melons, including pineapple (a settler favorite). Visitors to the island were shocked to see residents doing without the traditional English fare of bread, beef, pork, mutton, cheese, fish, and vegetables when in season. As Barbadian planters became more successful, the English influence on their diets became more pronounced, as they could afford to import more and more foodstuffs from home.[9]

17th century English fashion was ill suited for life in the tropics.

Mansions in 17th century Barbados mimicked the style of the great houses colonists left behind in England.

If Englishmen in the tropics blamed the climate for the high death rate on Barbados, they could as easily have blamed themselves. Their stubborn insistence on mimicking the lifestyle of the English gentry back home crippled their ability to accommodate themselves to an environment that was decidedly *not* English. They ate too much heavy food for their own good, while their servants and slaves ate too little. Everyone, regardless of station, drank too much. Their English-style clothing became instruments of torture under tropical skies. Women wore corsets, bustles, layers of petticoats, and textured skirts that trailed the ground. Men wore periwigs, full-skirted coats, embroidered waistcoats, and long sleeves. At their necks were flowing cravats, and below their waists, beribboned knee breeches. Over time, some adjustments were made. Islanders eventually switched to linen, silk, or calico for most of their clothes, but many of their suits and cloaks continued to be made of wool. Their slaves went almost naked, the males wearing canvas drawers and the women skirts. White servants wore much the same sort of attire as their fellows in England, including Monmouth caps. Settler homes on Barbados were elaborate copies of English houses, sumptuously furnished once planters began making money from sugar, and built from brick or stone. The usually multistoried houses had glazed windows and storm shutters. The result was a residence that was hot, stuffy, and dark, requiring candlelight all day that added to the accumulated heat. By contrast, Spanish-style dwellings left on the island that pre-dated the English rush to build a little England were designed to take advantage of cooling breezes, and were much more open and airy.[10]

Barbados was organized from the outset as a place for profits. Early immigrants to the island, outside of the gentry and commercial families who sent representatives out to make their fortunes, tended to be single white males serving an indenture. Life for these contracted workers was little better than that endured by Barbados' Indian and African slaves, consisting of backbreaking labor in hot fields and too often an early death. Early Atlantic trade was a matter of commodities and links to places where they could be sold or traded. These commodities, places, and the people associated with them formed the backbone of the Atlantic world of the seventeenth century. In the 1640s, Virginia planters began shipping beef, pork, naval stores, livestock, and grain to Barbados in exchange for slaves, rum, molasses, and salt. Dutch merchant ships that, until the passage of the English Navigation Acts, traveled a circuitous route that touched on virtually every port on the American mainland or in the Caribbean basin that had something to trade facilitated the exchange. By 1690, a full tenth of all Barbadian exports went to Virginia.[11]

Barbadians imported English goods, built substantial English-style houses, and created expensive social structures and showy cultural institutions that mimicked those of England. They were a tightly knit group of people from similar backgrounds, and from this an island elite developed. These island gentry did their best to resist what they considered to be the corrupting influence of Africa introduced to the island by the slaves they imported to work their fields, and sought to live their lives as much in the English manner as circumstance would permit. Barbadians rapidly created Anglican parishes on the island, built churches, and hired clergymen to lead them. Their government and legal institutions were patterned on those in England. They sought mates and children with great zeal (though women were generally scarce), and resisted compromises in their diets, apparel, and housing that no doubt made life much more uncomfortable than it had to be on a tropical island, all for the sake of maintaining their Englishness. And they developed a real affection for Barbados, where, as one 1650 petition identified them, they were truly "Englishmen transplanted."[12]

As a result of the sugar revolution, by the 1650s Barbados had a population density greater than any comparable area in the English-speaking world except London. Barbadians became notorious for their riotous and abandoned lifestyles. The already mentioned high mortality rates and the scarcity of women contributed to the slow growth of the number of families there, despite an eagerness among Barbadian males to start them. Planters treated white labor as a disposable commodity, and as the pool of white workers began to dry up, the importation of Africans seemed a natural extension of that thought process. It resulted in the first large-scale use

As the labor force of white indentured servants began to dry up, Englishmen in Barbados turned to African slavery to secure the large, cheap labor force needed to make sugar successful as a cash crop.

of Africans and non-European laborers in any of the English colonies.[13]

Part of the rationale behind importing Africans was what was thought to be their inbred ability to withstand the heat of the tropics. Richard Ligon found it hard to believe that people from a cold climate transplanted to Barbados could "indure such scorching without being suffocated." Ligon, like most Englishmen fresh off the boat at Barbados, felt as though he was being "fricased," and experienced a "great failing in the vigor, and sprightliness we have in colder Climates." Yet Englishmen were largely ambivalent about living in the tropics. They associated the sun with riches to be had for those willing to take them. They feared the hazards of hot climates, but countered that fear with a belief that wealth awaited those who could meet the challenge of life near the Equator.[14]

Newcomers to Barbados, both African and English, were expected to endure a period of "seasoning" before taking on the hazards of labor and living in a tropical clime. This involved what they described as changing the balance of humors and thinning the blood in the body. The process of seasoning generally took up to two years, and might take its name from the most visible characteristic of the process – sweating – that bore similarities to the seasoning (or drying out) of green wood.[15]

Heat and humidity was not only unpleasant, but also irritating in that it forced Englishmen to jettison much of what they brought to the island that instilled the sense of comfort that derives from the familiar. Authorities warned prospective colonists ahead of time to give up their expectations about familiar types of food, clothing, housing, and pastimes, even though most still tried to mimic the lifestyles of their homeland to such a degree as circumstances permitted. Heat brought illness and infirmities, even in more northern places like Virginia and Carolina. Fogs and dews were thought to carry diseases, and mariners avoided places known to be susceptible to them. Their closed, dark dwellings, when the heat of the day made them more akin to stoves than homes, left Richard Ligon wondering why the inhabitants did not spontaneously combust. Only the Caribbean trade winds offered respite from the simmering orb that seemed to suck the very life from Englishmen in the tropics.[16]

Sir George Ayscue

The men who settled Barbados did not shy from the challenge presented by life there, in a place that existed in the shadow of the Spanish empire's American holdings. The island became a common link for many of the men who would become the Lords Proprietors of Carolina and who would participate in plans to settle the territory below Virginia, including at Cape Fear. Sir Thomas Modyford, who acted as agent for one of the groups seeking permission to settle Carolina, arrived in Barbados on the same ship that carried Richard Ligon in 1647. Modyford bought a five hundred acre plantation in partnership with his brother-in-law, Thomas Kendal, for £7000 (as a measure of inflation by that time, the previous owner had bought the same tract for just £400 seven years earlier). Sir John Colleton was the only Lords Proprietor to actually live on Barbados, but others owned estates there, including Anthony Ashley Cooper, 1st Earl of Shaftesbury, who owned a modest plantation in St. George's Parish.[17]

After the arrival of sugar in the 1640s, Barbados' fortunes began to rise. The island's planter elites became quite wealthy, and enjoyed the perks that deep pockets bring. But the English Civil War dampened the good times somewhat. Regular trade routes with England were disrupted by the thrust and parry of Cavaliers and Roundheads at home, forcing Barbadian planters and traders to find alternate markets. The result was a strong mercantile relationship with New Englanders, who traded lumber and other materials for Barbadian commodities. The Dutch profited as well by taking over a larger share of the inter-colonial carrying trade, since English ships became scarce because of the war.[18]

Wartime Barbados became a refuge for Royalists who saw the writing on the wall with the mounting victories in England by Parliamentary forces. A great exodus of Englishmen who supported the monarchy brought waves of newcomers to the tiny island. Their politics reflected their allegiances, and Barbados became a thorn in the side of the Cromwell Protectorate that, by 1655, required a stern reminder of who was in charge. Parliament dispatched a flotilla under Sir George Ayscue to enforce its embargo on Barbados and its inhabitants, who Parliament considered to be "notorious robbers and traitors." Roundhead rule on the island was re-established with the assistance of Thomas Modyford and John Colleton, who both enjoyed the perks their aid brought in terms of higher offices. General Robert Venables found the two men particularly useful allies during Cromwell's plan to wrest Hispanola from Spain. The island was a cauldron of political intrigue for the next five years after the reassertion of Parliamentary rule, until the restoration of Charles II to the throne.[19]

The Sugar Island

Barbados is coral, but the soil there is some of the richest on earth. Early Barbadian settlers tried to emulate the success of mainland English planters, sowing their fields with tobacco and other crops they hoped would prove profitable. But Barbadian tobacco was wholly inferior to that grown in Virginia, cotton required too much land to grow profitably, and rice cultivation required marshland and a large labor force. Other crops attempted included annatto and ginger, but the markets for those spices were much too small to warrant the effort. The answer lay in a sweeter direction.[20]

Sephardic Jews from Brazil deserve the credit for introducing sugar to the English islands of the Caribbean. Jewish control of the sugar in-

Sephardic Jews from Brazil brought the technology and know-how required to grow sugar to the islands of the Caribbean, including to Barbados.

dustry in the Dutch parts of Brazil predates any similar agricultural development in the English colonies of the West Indies. The vast country in the northeast corner of South America was an important producer of the sweet commodity during the early decades of the seventeenth century, and Jews had been there since at least the fifteenth century. They were involved in all aspects of sugar production in Dutch Brazil, and even developed plantations in Surinam when it was under the English flag. They made good lives for themselves on the South American mainland for almost two centuries before circumstances demanded they move on once again.[21]

When the Dutch took northern Brazil from Portugal in 1630, the new regime was characterized by a greater than normal degree of religious toleration. The area seized by the Dutch, from the Rio San Francisco to Maranhao, was christened New Holland, and contained a varied assortment of people who professed a number of different faiths. There were Dutch Protestants, Portuguese Catholics, New Christians (Jews who adopted the veneer of Christianity to avoid persecution), professing Jews, native Indians, and Negro slaves who brought the faiths of Africa to the new hemisphere. By 1634, a proclamation from the State General guaranteed Jews and Catholics free practice of their faith "without investigation of their conscience or home." With such a guarantee in place, Jews who had been hiding their faith stepped out into the open. They were joined by others who sailed from Holland. By 1640, Recife was said to have more Jews in its population than Christians.[22]

By 1637, the Jewish newcomers were keen to get into the sugar business. Records show they eagerly began buying up abandoned Portuguese sugar mills auctioned off by the Dutch West India Company. Jews owned some of the best plantation land in the Pernambuco River Valley, and that may have eventually led to their later troubles, as envy among their Christian neighbors was evident. By 1641, at least sixty-six Christian merchants had appealed to the Governor and Supreme Council of Brazil to curb the wealthy Jewish residents "who controlled the sugar trade, and gave all the best positions to their newly-arrived co-religionists." When Portugal sent troops to reclaim their lost province, enemies of the Jews took the opportunity to roll back Jewish gains.[23]

For their own safety, Brazilian Jews once again looked beyond the seas for refuge. Cayenne and Surinam were favorite choices for some, but many more sought a new start in the non-Catholic lands where English was spoken, including Barbados. Public opinion in England at the time was decidedly against allowing Jews to emigrate there, but a more accepting reception was found in England's colonies. Colonial officials, while not wanting the Jews on the streets of London, were perfectly amenable to their taking up residence in the English colonies of the Caribbean. For their part, Jewish immigrants with experience as traders and planters, who had both capital and slaves, were anxious to carry on the lucrative sugar trade that had been so profitable on the mainland. From Guiana to Barbados, expatriate Sephardic Jews planted roots and sugar cane in new homes and picked up where they left off when the Portuguese came.[24]

Dutch ships facilitated the Jewish migration to the English colonies of the Caribbean. Their hulls carried the displaced to their new island homes, and in the process started the sugar and plantation revolutions without realizing it. Sugar ushered in the great plantations of the Western Hemisphere. In some respects, the plantation was versatile, adaptable to whatever crops were best suited for a given location. In the Caribbean the staple was sugar. In Virginia, tobacco or indigo. Later, Carolinians would become the kings of the rice trade. But unlike tobacco, sugar could only be grown in the tropics. Sugar had much to recommend it. Unskilled

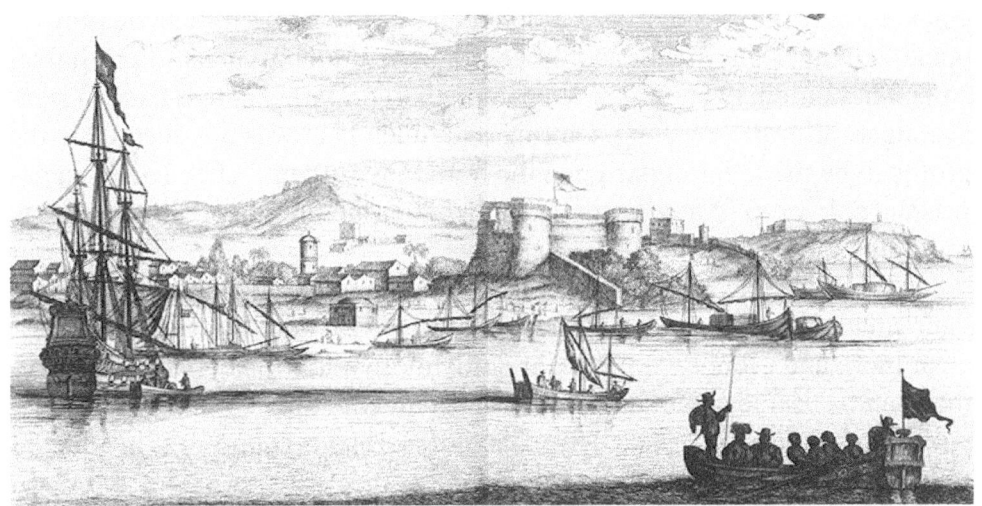

Ships of the Dutch West India Company (above) were largely responsible for the spread of technology, trade, and the movement of populations throught the Americas and Caribbean.

labor could tend it, and it could be grown for long periods of time on the same land without exhausting the soil. A seemingly insatiable appetite for sugar in Europe created steadily rising prices for it. Sugar, however, was a perishable commodity. It had to be processed soon after cutting or it would rot. Planters had, of necessity, to become both growers and processors of the cane from their fields. Dutch Jews, carried to Barbados aboard Dutch ships, brought that knowledge with them and shared it with their new English neighbors.[25]

Contemporary accounts credit Pieter Brower, a Dutch Jew from Brazil, with planting the first sugarcane on Barbados in 1637. Serious efforts to grow the sweet crop were underway by 1642, when Dutch interests provided English planters with the rollers, coppers, and other equipment required to process the cane. The Dutch provided the equipment on credit, against the first crops brought in. It was a good investment. By the 1650s, sugar was being consumed in ever-greater quantities as the price of sugar dropped, and as new beverages such as chocolate and coffee were introduced to European palates. Sugar was also thought to have curative powers. Herbalist John Gerard declared that "It drieth and cleanseth the stomacke, maketh smooth the roughness of the breast and lungs, cleareth the voice, and all sournesse and bitternesse."[26]

Barbados planters produced mostly muscovedo sugar – a wet, brown variety – and produced only a small amount of the "clayed," or "plantation white" kind. It was a rich man's crop that required a healthy purse to finance a growing and processing operation. To make it profitable, a planter's holdings had to be large enough to provide enough cane to run the sugar mills all year long. Getting that much land was not cheap, but the profits to be made far outstripped the initial investment. After 1650, sugar was the only crop of any significance in either the French or English West Indies.

Successful Barbados planters began buying up the holdings of their smaller neighbors as the price of sugar encouraged Barbadians to clear more and more land for sugar cultivation, until by 1660 almost all of the island's usable area was covered in sugarcane. Sir Thomas Modyford wrote as early as 1652 that "This island of Barbados cannot last in a height of trade three years longer, the wood being almost already spent, and therefore in prudence a place must presently be thought upon, where this great people may find sustenance and employment."

The prices of land rose precipitously (reference the earlier example of Sir Thomas Modyford's first plantation purchase and its value a mere seven years earlier). In 1676, Barbados Governor Sir Jonathan Atkins reported that land in Barbados was more expensive than that in England. Smaller planters were priced out, and those who hoped to secure land of their own once their indentures were finished soon realized no such land existed. In 1657 Richard Ligon prophesied that all plantations under thirty acres would be bought up by the great planters, and he was at least partially correct. He wrote that the ten to thirty acres "in poor mens' hands" had all been consolidated into great plantations of 500 to 700 acres in his history of the island.[27]

The consolidation of land on Barbados into the hands of wealthy elites was closely connected to a growing outflow of white men from Barbados that began in the 1650s. There was nothing left on Barbados for men of small means, unless they wished to remain as hired workers on land they until recently owned. As economic conditions improved in England, finding people willing to brave the tropics and a grueling work life as an indentured servant was increasingly difficult.[28]

Life for an indentured white servant on Barbados was nearly as brutal as that of a slave. They performed the same grinding tasks under the same pitiless sun, with masters who were often as brutal in their treatment of their workers as were the cane fields. Many times indentures fell victim to legal chicanery that trapped them in extended service contracts that set

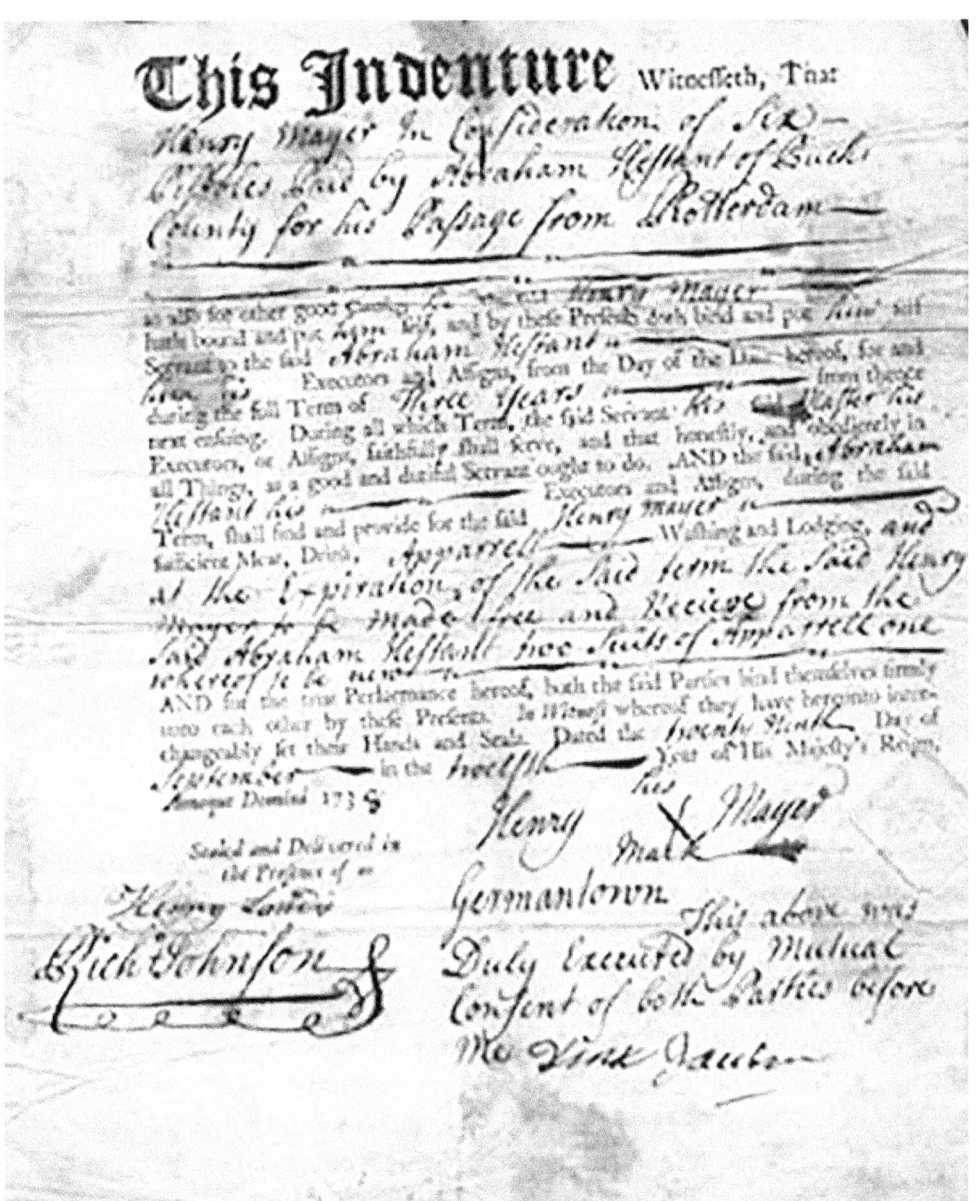

Indenture agreements like this one were legally binding contracts that set the terms of an indenture. When the English economy got better, the supply of whites willing to serve an indenture dried up.

back the time when they earned their release and land of their own.

In the beginning, indentured workers recruited from Europe provided ample manpower for the sugarcane fields. Indenture was a tried and true method of getting labor for the sponsor, and a head start on land ownership for the indentured. Typically serving for three years (in the American colonies a half century later, the average indenture was seven years), indentured servants would work the length of their contract, learning the techniques they would need for a successful farm of their own once their contract was satisfied. When that day came, the laborers received acreage of their own to plant on, thus becoming competitors of their former employers. That all changed when sugar became king on Barbados.[29]

To make up for the labor shortfall, Barbadian planters and their agents began aggressively seeking indentured workers, especially among the people of northern Germany, still destitute after the interminable destruction of the Thirty Years War. Moreover, magistrates in England with ties to Barbadian interests began sentencing criminals to hard labor in the island's sugar fields. Sometimes the poor indentured workers were guilty of nothing more than being in the wrong place at the wrong time, and found themselves pressed into servitude on trumped-up charges. Evidence of this unscrupulous practice is revealed in the phrase "barbadosed," which became part of the English lexicon. Dispossessed small planters began emigrating to other colonies in search of opportunities that no longer existed on Barbados.[30]

Through the 1650s, roughly 2,000 such newly indentured servants immigrated to Barbados each year until the restoration of King Charles II to the English throne. But work in the sugarcane fields was hot, brutal, and deadly. As the English Civil War ended and economic conditions improved, the pool of indentured servants dried up. In 1674, indentures made up only about twelve percent of the white Barbados population – far too few to satisfy the labor demands of a sugar economy that, by 1680, would account for sixty percent of England's annual sugar imports. Barbados was the richest of England's overseas colonies, but its labor shortage was becoming a threat to that success.[31]

Eventually, the lack of opportunities in the sugar fields of Barbados dried up the available pool of indentured servants, and even the illicit support of the English judiciary could not provide enough workers. No one wanted to work an indenture in a place where there was no land to be had after they satisfied their contracts, assuming they even survived to claim it.

The only viable option left to Barbadian planters was African slavery.

Barbados, the Cradle of Slavery

Barbados did not invent slavery in the Americas, but rather adopted and perfected the system first used in Virginia. The turn to African slavery became an obvious choice to Barbadian planters as indentured servants became harder and harder to find. Slavery was a much less complicated proposition than working with white indentures. For one thing, slavery was an open-ended commitment. Whereas indentures eventually ended, a slave was a planter's property for life. With slavery, there was no obligation to set the laborer up on their own plots of land and provide them the tools to work it when their contracts expired. With slavery, much needed workers could not escape their obligations to the planter by joining one of the many military and exploratory expeditionary adventures originating in Barbados. In slavery, planters had a virtually inexhaustible supply of the strong backs they needed to make sugar thrive on their island estates.[32]

African slavery provided the labor force needed for sugar in Barbados after indentures declined.

Thanks to wildly profitable sugar, Barbados became the center of England's American universe, despite its location at the periphery of the Caribbean. It was the first landfall for ships crossing from Africa and Europe, a full thousand miles closer than any other destination. Its proximity to the American mainland allowed it to establish important commercial relationships with other English and European colonies. Barbados was also wealthy, a center for capital to fund business endeavors in other colonies such as those on the mainland. Its climate and embrace

In the 1600s slavery was fed by Africans transported by Dutch merchant ships to auctions like this one in an illustration by Howard Pyle.

of slavery quickly made it a clearinghouse for the slave trade. By 1680, exports from Barbados exceeded the value of all other exports from North America to England. Between 1669 and 1700, yearly sugar exports from the West Indies to England rose from 11,700 tons to 27,400 tons. Between 1698 and 1700 alone, sugar exports – now almost exclusively the product of coerced labor - earned Barbados planters £316,000.[33]

The Dutch, such as those who brought the first slaves to Jamestown, played a major role in the success of English colonies in the Western Hemisphere during the seventeenth century. It was the Dutch who brought the technology for growing and processing sugarcane to Barbados. While the English were embroiled in civil war, Dutch merchant fleets provided a means of moving Barbadian sugar, rum, and molasses to buyers on the North American mainland and Europe. By 1690, a tenth of all Barbadian exports went to Virginia, and much of that was carried aboard Dutch merchant ships. When tobacco prices dropped in the 1630s, the Dutch bought what leaf England would not. When civil war left England's American colonies bereft of markets and sources of credit from home, the Dutch provided the commodities Barbados and the Chesapeake needed to survive, grow, and prosper.[34]

The size of Barbadian plantations dictated that one slave was required for every two acres under cultivation. Because early on slaves were in short supply plantations of more than 500 acres were unusual on the island, but slave traders did their best to meet the needs of Barbadian planters. Between 1601 and 1650, Dutch ships carried 41,000 people from Africa to lives of slavery in the Americas. Between 1651 and 1675, especially when colonial neglect caused by the English Civil War was at its peak, the Dutch transported another 64,800 Africans. Even after England's Royal African Company and new navigation laws curtailed Holland's access to English markets, the Dutch still managed to bring another 56,000 slaves to markets in the Western Hemisphere between 1676 and 1700. Caribbean sugar plantations absorbed well over two thirds of all slaves carried across the Atlantic by major European powers. Barbados, by then with decades of experience managing slaves, was at the center of that trade.[35]

The skyrocketing number of African slaves on Barbados caused concern among whites, where by 1645 more than 5,000 Africans toiled in the cane fields. By the 1660s, slaves outnumbered whites by a margin of two to one. Planters began crafting new restrictive legislation to control large slave populations there by the 1650s. The effort was carried out at the same time that they worked on laws to do likewise for their still substantial indentured population. The code that emerged in 1661 completed the evolution from servant to slave, making Africans chattel property and their bondage a lifetime state – not just for the slaves, but for their progeny, as well. The slave laws they passed became the model of most other English colonies in the years to come.[36]

Between 1650-1700, Barbados reflected the quintessential plantation-slave society. Only three years after the failure of Vassall's Cape Fear colony, Barbados contained at least 32,800 slaves, almost double the 17,950 slaves in England's five other West Indian island colonies combined (and close to six times the number of slaves in all of England's mainland colonies). Given the vast number of slaves on Barbados in the mid-seventeenth century, it seems likely that some of Vassall's *Adventurers* took Africans with them to Charles Towne. While artifacts found at the site lead archaeologists and historians to believe only a small percentage of the colonists enjoyed enough wealth to afford slaves, a few elites may have taken some with them.[37]

Certainly John Vassall was involved in the slave trade, as a promissory note exists between Vassall and his brother-in-law, Nicholas Ware of Nansemond, Virginia, in which Vassall is promised a quantity of tobacco in payment for four African slaves. African-Americans along the Cape Fear River today claim to be descended from those slaves, who they believe slipped into the surrounding woods to escape their servitude and remained behind to join local Indians when the settlement broke up in 1667. Though no document has been found to date that definitely indicates the presence of slaves with the Vassall colonists, to think that these gentlemen of means, so used to the services of slave laborers on Barbados, would undertake to build a colony without them seems naive. Outside of perhaps genetic testing, in the absence of documentary evidence, there is no way at present of proving or disproving the claim.[38]

Slavery was the engine that made the Barbados sugar machine work. It supplanted indentured servitude, and allowed planters to bring more and more land under cultivation. As large cane fields replaced the smaller holdings of less wealthy planters, and as food crops were replaced with more profitable sugarcane, Barbados began to look elsewhere for the things it needed to feed and house a burgeoning population of planters and slaves. Carolina was very attractive for those who sought to start over on the American mainland. Massachusetts mariner William Hilton, Jr. certainly found it akin to Eden, according to the accounts of it he brought to Barbados in 1663. But before any colonization effort could proceed, John Vassall and his band of would-be settlers had to first secure the blessings of the eight men that Charles II had given the vast expanse of land below Virginia to.

Endnotes

1. D.A. Farnie, "The Commercial Empire of the Atlantic, 1607-1783," *The Economic History Review*, New Series, Vol. 15, No. 2 (1962): 205-218 (hereafter cited as Farnie, "The Commercial Empire").

2. Jack P. Greene, "Colonial South Carolina and the Caribbean Connection," *The South Carolina Historical Magazine*, Vol. 88, No. 4 (Oct. 1987): 192-210, hereafter cited as Greene, "Caribbean Connection;" J.E. Buchanan, "The Colleton Family and the Early History of South Carolina and Barbados, 1646-1775," Ph.D dissertation, University of Edinburgh, 1989, hereafter cited as Buchanan, "Colleton." The small island occupies 106,000 acres, and even today seven eighths of its cultivated land is still devoted to sugar production. Though not nearly as vulnerable to hurricanes as its more northern neighbor, Bermuda, Barbados does occasionally have to deal with the giant tropical storms. In the seventeenth century, its residents also contended with periodic droughts, pests, and plant disease that threatened not just their livelihoods, but their very survival.

3. Carl Bridenbaugh, *No Peace Beyond The Line: The English in the Caribbean, 1624-1690* (New York: Oxford University Press, 1972): 5; Larry Gragg, *English-*

men Transplanted: The English Colonization of Barbados, 1627-1660 (Oxford: Oxford University Press, 2003): 3-4, hereafter cited as Gragg, *Englishmen Transplanted*; Richard Waterhouse, "England, the Caribbean, and the Settlement of Carolina," Journal of American Studies, Vol. 9, No. 3 (December 1975): 259-281, hereafter cited as Waterhouse, "England, the Caribbean, and the Settlement of Carolina."

4. J.H. Parry, *A Short History of the West Indies* (New York: St. Martin's Press, 1987), 74, hereafter cited as Parry, *West Indies*.

5. Gragg, *Englishmen Transplanted*, 1.

6. Buchanan, "Colleton," 29; Gragg, *Englishmen Transplanted*, 6-7. While Englishmen of the seventeenth century had a notion of loyalty to the Anglican Church and their monarch, their strongest ties were to the places they lived. Their communities came first, and they jealously guarded their autonomy from encroachment from the national government. This was true in all of England's American colonies, whether in New England, the Chesapeake, or the Caribbean.

7. Gragg, *Englishmen Transplanted*, 14-19. A shortage of axes early in the settlement restricted the clearing of forests to coastal areas. Clearing land for cultivation did not really take off until the introduction of sugar, when slaves were put to the task in order to prepare more land for sugarcane cultivation. In fact, so much land was cleared that finding native Barbadian wood became an almost impossible task by the 1660s, and offered another rationale for a mainland settlement.

8. Richard S. Dunn, "The English Sugar Islands and the Founding of South Carolina," *The South Carolina Historical Magazine*, Vol. 101, No. 2 (April 2000): 145-147, hereafter cited as Dunn, "The English Sugar Islands." Between 1676 and 1679, there were twice as many whites buried in Barbados as were baptized in one eighteen-month period. In a good year, the ratio dropped to three buried for every one baptized. In bad years, the figure was 5:1.

9. Gragg, *Englishmen Transplanted*, 19-22. Slave and indentured servant fare was even more constricted. The people who worked the fields for the planter families generally ate only potato and cassava roots, washed down with plain water. Father Antoine Biet noted in his writings that "there is no nation which feeds its slaves as badly as the English. . . and the English servants. . . are not much better treated."

10. Dunn, "The English Sugar Islands," 149-152; Karen Ordhal Kupperman, "Fear of Hot Climates in the Anglo-American Colonial Experience," *The William & Mary Quarterly*, Third Series, Vol. 41, No. 2 (April 1984): 235, hereafter cited as Kupperman, "Hot Climates." Climate did dictate changes in English attire on Barbados. Men opted for caps in place of periwigs, except on special occasions, for instance.

11. April Lee Hatfield, *Atlantic Virginia: Intercolonial Relations in the Seventeenth Century* (Philadelphia: University of Pennsylvania Press, 2007): 52-59, 92-96, hereafter cited as Hatfield, "Atlantic Virginia;" Gragg, *Englishmen Trans-*

planted, 109; Greene, "Caribbean Connection," 194. Barbadians who relocated to Virginia almost always maintained personal and business connections with the island. The island also served as a communications nexus between the colonists in the Chesapeake and England.

12. Gragg, *Englishmen Transplanted,* 8-10.

13. Greene, "Caribbean Connection," 194-195.

14. Kupperman, "Hot Climates," 216. Englishmen generally felt they were constitutionally better suited to survive and thrive in more temperate climates like New England or Newfoundland. But those interested in getting rich in America overwhelmingly chose southern and tropical places as their destinations.

15. Kupperman, "Hot Climates," 215, 220, 223. On average, a newcomer to the heat of the Caribbean might sweat out 1.5 liters per hour. Within ten days that amount doubles, and generally reached a height of nearly five liters and hour within six weeks. One man's punishment, of standing in the Barbados sun all day, was described as "enough to pierce his braine."

16. Kupperman, "Hot Climates," 224-225, 233-234. English settlers in Virginia, and later in Carolina, were dismayed to suffer not just the heat of summer, but also the bone chilling cold of winters on the mainland.

17. Buchanan, "Colleton," 20-21.

18. Buchanan, "Colleton," 22.

19. Buchanan, "Colleton," 16. With the Restoration, Colleton was forced to return to London to get back in the good graces of King Charles II. He already had an idea about settling Carolina in mind, as he left his sons, Peter and Thomas, on Barbados to manage his plantations and establish a base of operations for a Carolina venture.

20. Richard S. Dunn, *Sugar and Slaves: The rise of the planter class in the English West Indies, 1624-1713* (New York: Norton, 1973): 53, hereafter cited as Dunn, *Sugar and Slaves.*

21. Gordon Merrill, "The Role of Sephardic Jews in the British Caribbean Area during the Seventeenth Century," *Caribbean Studies*, Vol. 4, No. 3 (October 1964): 32-33, hereafter cited as Merrill, "Jews." Brazilian Jews originated in the Mediterranean, where the Spanish Inquisition forced them to begin migrating to the Iberian peninsula starting in 1478. It was there, in Spain and Portugal, that they became known as Sephardic Jews.

22. Merrill, "Jews," 37. In 1643 John Nieuhoff wrote of the Jews in Brazil and their enthusiasm for the sugar industry: "Among the free inhabitants of Brazil that were not in the company's service (Dutch West India Company), the Jews were the most considerable in number, who had transported themselves thither from Holland. They had a vast traffic beyond all the rest, they purchased sugar mills and built stately houses in the Recife. They were all traders, which would have been of great consequence to the Dutch Brazil, had they kept themselves

within the due bounds of traffick."
23. Merrill, "Jews," 38.
24. Merrill, "Jews," 38-39. During the Protectorate, Oliver Cromwell displayed a remarkable amount of religious toleration when he allowed some Jews to enter England. This likely stemmed from his understanding of the economic impact the nomadic Jews could have on England's economy. Cromwell dodged the political briar patch such a move could engender by simply not addressing the issue.
25. Russell R. Menard, *Sweet Negotiations: Sugar, Slavery, and Plantation Agriculture in Early Barbados* (Charlottesville: University of Virginia Press, 2006): 61, 80, hereafter cited as Menard, *Sweet Negotiations*. Dutch Jews had a powerful motive for introducing sugar to the English Caribbean. Since Dutch ships held a virtual monopoly on the carrying trade in the West Indies, any crop that could be sold at a profit in Europe was to their advantage.
26. Louis B. Wright, *The Colonial Search for a Southern Eden* (Tuscaloosa, AL: University of Alabama Press, 1953): 37; Menard, *Sweet Negotiations*, 61-62; Farnie, "The Commercial Empire," 209. Another seventeenth-century physician and wit said of it, "If sugar can preserve both Pears and Plums/Why can it not preserve as well out lungs?"
27. Ligon, 156.
28. Waterhouse, "England, the Caribbean, and the Settlement of Carolina," 267; Menard, *Sweet Negotiations*, 63-64. A 1667 report on Barbados claimed the island had "not above 700 considerable proprietors. . . 12000 good men formerly proprietors have gone off, wormed out of their small settlements by their more suttle and greedy neighbours." By 1680, a handful of big planters owned the majority of land holdings on Barbados. Of 2,639 landholders, a mere 175 planters owned fifty-three percent of the island's land. They also owned fifty-four percent of the indentured servants there, and fifty-four percent of the slaves on Barbados.
29. Dunn, *Sugar and Slaves,* 50-57.
30. Parry, *West Indies*, 54; Dunn, *Sugar and Slaves,* 69.
31. Gragg, *Englishmen Transplanted*, 57, 116; Timothy Paul Grady, "On the Path to Slavery: Indentured Servitude in Barbados and Virginia during the Seventeenth Century" (master's thesis, Virginia Polytechnic Institute and State University, 2000): 8, hereafter cited as Grady, "On the Path to Slavery." By the mid-1660s, outmigration from Barbados was such a problem that one contemporary source estimated as many as 12,000 white men had left the island for other colonies over the preceding quarter century. Barbadian officials worried there would not be enough white men left for island defense of the trend continued.
32. James Horn, *A Land As God Made It: Jamestown and the Birth of America* (New York: Basic Books, 2005): 287; Parry, *West Indies*, 65. The Dutch ship *White Lion* and the English Earl of Warwick's *Treasure* captured the Portuguese slaver *Sao Bao Batista* in the Gulf of Campeche in the summer of 1619. They took some of the Portuguese cargo of 350 Africans aboard and made for the West

Indies and Virginia to sell them. These are the slaves brought to Jamestown in the John Rolfe account . . . Englishman John Pinney, a planter on Nevis, frankly declared that "negroes are the sinews of the plantation" and "to make sugar without the assistance of negroes" was to attempt to make bricks without straw.

33. Richard S. Dunn. "The Barbados Census of 1680: Profile of the Richest Colony in English America," *The William & Mary Quarterly*, Vol. 26, No. 1 (Jan. 1969): 3-30.

34. Gragg. *Englishmen Transplanted,* 109.

35. Parry, *West Indies*, 68; Buchanan, "Colleton," 33; David Eltis. "The Volume of the Transatlantic Slave Trade: A Reassessment," *The William & Mary Quarterly* (2001): 17-46; David Eltis, "A Brief Overview of the Trans-Atlantic Slave Trade," *Emory University*, 2009, accessed 1/17/2013, http://www.slavevoyages.org/tast/assessment/essays-intro-01.faces. Slavers servicing Barbados took their human cargos primarily from Sierra Leone, the Grain Coast (Liberia), the Ivory, Gold, and Slave Coasts, the Oil Rivers of the Niger Delta, Cameroon, Gabon, and Loango in West Africa.

36. Hilary McD. Beckles, "The Hub of Empire: The Caribbean and Britain in the Seventeenth Century," in *The Origins of Empire: British Overseas Enterprise to the Close of the Seventeenth Century* (New York: Oxford University Press, 1998) 218-240; Ed Rugemer, "Making Slavery English: Comprehensive Slave Codes in the Greater Caribbean during the Seventeenth Century" (Presentation, Yale University, British Studies Colloquium, 2011): 8. Barbados legislators passed earlier versions of a slave code in 1650 and 1652.

37. See "Uncovering Charles Towne" in this work for an analysis of artifacts found at the Charles Towne site and what it means for historical hypotheses of the settlement's make up.

38. Jerome S. Handler and John T. Pohlmann, "Slave Manumissions and Freedmen in Seventeenth-Century Barbados," *The William & Mary Quarterly*, Third Series, Vol. 41, No. 3 (July 1984): 195; Lothrop Withington, *Virginia Gleanings in England: Abstracts of 17th and 18th-century English Wills and Administrations Relating to Virginia and Virginians: a Consolidation of Articles from The Virginia Magazine of History and Biography* (Genealogical Publishing Com, 1980): 90; Hatfield, *Atlantic Virginia,* 149; Thomas C. Loftfield and Lindley S. Butler, "Barbadians on the Cape Fear: The Sugar Business and Seventeenth Century Carolina" (Unpublished paper, author's collection), 58, hereafter cited as Loftfield and Butler, "Barbadians." Nicholas Ware, who married Vassall's sister, Anne, promised his brother-in-law 8,617 pounds of tobacco for the four slaves. Archaeologist Thomas C. Loftfield and historian Lindley S. Butler contend the number of slaves at Charles Towne would likely have been small, as the yeoman farmers who made up the bulk of Charles Towne's population could not have afforded them.

Charles Stuart became King Charles II in 1660, and used land in what would become Carolina to reward the eight loyal men who helped put him back on the throne.

IV
Eight Loyal Men

The return of Charles Stuart to the throne of England delivered rewards to those whose fealty to the beheaded King's heir was instrumental in the restoration of the monarchy. In as much as Charles II's treasury was short of coin, it was an easy choice for the new King to bestow grants of land in the Americas to his loyal servants. So when a group of his most loyal retainers approached him with a plan to colonize Carolana, Charles was amenable to the plan.[1]

King Charles II's government had no comprehensive colonial policy, perhaps to provide the widest possible latitude for those willing to undertake new colonies and get them on a sound footing as soon as possible. Beyond their usefulness as sources of trade and revenue, the King could have cared less about most of the particulars of their administration. Charles was painfully aware that his wealth was nothing more than the wealth of his subjects. The royal coffers depended on the efforts of the great men in England to form companies that would successfully generate wealth in commodities such as gold and slaves from Africa, fish from the northern seas, or furs from the Arctic.[2]

There was also no precedent in English history for a group proprietary, but the new monarch was willing to encourage the enterprise, especially as it involved some of his chief advisors and friends. Charles II tended to look favorably on schemes of internal improvement, and supported the commercial and colonial enterprises of the day. One of the centerpieces of his foreign policy was to support anything that weakened Dutch domination of Atlantic trade. The plans for a Carolina settlement dovetailed nicely with the King's larger vision for England's place in the world.[3]

The eight men who became the Lords Proprietors of Carolina were among the cream of English elites. One, George Monck, may have been the man most responsible for the end of the Interregnum when he marched his army into London and ended Parliamentary rule. Others brought their own various skills and connections to the table as well. Two had direct experience of living in the colonies of the Caribbean and on the American mainland. Not all of the Lords Proprietors had a strong interest in the actual development of Carolina. Some saw Carolina as an investment option (but one too risky to over invest in). Others were elderly and lacked the energy to take on the time consuming work of developing a new colony. Some would fall out of favor with the King, and some would die before Carolina had a proper chance at success. But all of them were due recompense from the Crown to reward their efforts on Charles II's behalf.[4]

Edward Hyde, Earl of Clarendon

Among the first to feel the King's generosity was **Edward Hyde**, whom Charles II made Earl of Clarendon in 1661. Hyde had served the first King Charles in the Short and Long Parliaments of the 1640s. When civil war broke out Hyde was sent to confer with the Prince of Wales. With Charles I's execution, his son fled to France while Hyde took refuge on the Isle of Jersey. From there, he declared Charles Stuart the new King, a gesture the returning monarch would remember during the Restoration more than a decade later. Hyde was the father-in-law of the King's brother, James, who had married Anne Hyde and fathered a child by her. Edward Hyde, the Earl of Clarendon, would become King Charles II's favorite minister. Later, after the disaster of Admiral De Ruyter's raid up the Thames that destroyed the British fleet at Medway during the Second Anglo-Dutch War, Hyde was made a scapegoat by his enemies in Parliament and the Church of England. The animosity towards him stemmed from his being an honest and fair man (qualities sure to meet with disfavor among the Machiavellian members of Charles' court and Parliament), and his determination to be equitable in dealing with religious groups other than the Anglicans. King Charles II convinced the Earl of Clarendon to flee to the safety of exile in France. He spent the last seven years of his life there, writing a history of the rebellion that had brought Cromwell to power and deposed Charles I. He died on December 9, 1674. Though he never touched English soil again in life, his remains are interred at Westminster Abbey.[5]

George Monck was a soldier who learned his trade as a teenager at Cadiz under the namesake grandson of Sir Richard Grenville of Roanoke fame. Monck performed so well that he received a commission as an army ensign. He fought briefly for the Dutch before ending up under English colors again in Dublin during the Irish rebellion of 1642. For sixteen months he served with distinction, and Monck's name began receiving notice in important circles in England. He refused to take the oath of allegiance to the King required of all soldiers returning from the war in Ireland, and spoke candidly to the monarch himself about mismanagement of the Irish conflict. After the defeat of the British at Nantwick in 1644, the House of Commons charged Monck with treason and jailed him for a time in the Tower of London. But when Parliament assumed control of the war effort, they sought Monck out based on his military experience against the Irish.

Gen. George Monck

No big admirer of Parliament, Monck nonetheless stayed loyal to the body that paid his salary. He fought in Ireland during the English Civil War, and obeyed the orders of Cromwell during the Protectorate. He eventually got elected to the House of Commons. When Charles Stuart was ready to resume the throne, he sent a letter to Monck trying to feel him out and enlist his support. Monck forwarded a copy of the letter to Oliver Cromwell, and stayed true to his employer. No one would accuse George Monck of treason again.[6]

When Richard Cromwell assumed his late father's role as head of the English government, he soon found himself arguing with both the military and Parliament. To get a handle on the discontent, Cromwell transferred or dismissed many officers of the army. These changes had the effect of eroding morale and the effectiveness of Monck's army in Scotland. Supporters of the exiled Charles Stuart knew the general's dissatisfaction with the civilian leadership. In 1659, they surreptitiously sought Monck's aid in restoring the monarchy in England. Monck refused. A loyal soldier, the general declined to become involved in court intrigues. Nevertheless, Monck soon found himself indirectly contributing to the King's return.

After Cromwell's Parliament began acting in ways unacceptable to the army, Monck marched on England. His troops entered London on February 3, 1660. Monck ordered the seating of those members of Parliament who had been dismissed during the civil war that saw Charles I executed and Oliver Cromwell ascend to power. The general then closed the Parliament and ordered a new one formed, along with a Council of State, headed by himself. At this point he entered into talks with representatives of Charles Stuart. Charles accepted Monck's conditions for the return of the exiled monarch almost in their entirety, and Parliament voted to invite him home to become King Charles II. The day after Charles landed at Dover on May 25, 1660, George Monck was knighted. By July he was named Duke of Albemarle. The duke's regiment, the Coldstream Guards, was retained as the King's bodyguard (and remains the bodyguard to the ruling monarch to this day).[7]

Charles Stuart lands at Dover in 1660 enroute to becoming king.

Monck returned to military duty in the Second Dutch War (1665-1667), in which he won a great sea battle before illness claimed his life on January 3, 1670. The old soldier, acknowledged for his loyalty and honor, was buried with honors in Westminster Abbey at the direction of King Charles II.[8]

If no one is exactly certain where the idea for a Carolina proprietary originated, as "kinsman" to three of Barbados' leading planters (Colleton, Kendall, and Modyford), George Monck, the Duke of Albemarle, was a good choice to head the petition for a charter. Monck was perhaps the most trusted of Charles II's advisors and the instrument of his restoration. The old soldier had worked closely with Anthony Ashley Cooper to bring about the King's return to the throne, and was a national hero.[9]

The son of the Lord Mayor of London, **William Craven** was knighted by King Charles I in 1627, after distinguishing himself as a soldier in the service of the Prince of Orange. He spent years in duty to the Queen of Bohemia, whom he first met when, as an young officer, he was sent to Germany to help restore the monarch and her husband to the throne they lost in the Thirty Years War. Queen Elizabeth was the sister of Charles I, and Craven served her for twenty-five years. His loyalty to Elizabeth went beyond what was expected of him, and he became a prominent member of her court. When Charles I's execution ended her stipend from English coffers, Craven generously covered her expenses from his own pockets. Craven's financial support also extended to the male side of the royal family. He reportedly contributed as much as £50,000 to Charles I during the civil war.[10]

William Craven

Craven offered his services to the exiled Charles Stuart while the future King was visiting Queen Elizabeth in Bohemia. Consequently, the Cromwellians declared Craven an enemy of the Protectorate. His lands and property were seized and sold, and it was not until the return of Charles II to the throne that he began to regain some of what had been taken from him. The royals anointed him Earl of Craven as a reward for his services. He died in 1697.

Brothers John Berkeley (left) and William Berkeley (right) served the cause of King Charles II, and were rewarded for it with land in Carolina. William Berkeley was one of only two Lords Proprietors with experience in the American colonies, as governor of Virginia.

Brothers **William** and **John Berkeley** also served Charles I - William as governor of Virginia, and John as a diplomat and soldier in the civil war. During the conflict, John Berkeley served as Governor of Exeter and commander of Royalist forces in Devon. Exiled to France after the defeat of royalist forces in 1651, John Berkeley paid court to Anne Villiers, the Countess of Morton, who turned down his marriage proposal. She allegedly did so on the advice of Edward Hyde, resulting in an enmity between the two men. John was made Baron Berkeley in 1658. After the Restoration, John Berkeley became a member of the Privy Council and served on the board of the Admiralty. He died on August 26, 1678.[11]

William Berkeley crossed the Atlantic Ocean early, assuming the governorship of Virginia in 1641. He was an avid agronomist, and promoted diversification of the colony's agriculture. On the other hand, he adamantly opposed Quakers and Puritans. During the English Civil War he remained firmly on the side of the royalists, and encouraged Cavaliers to immigrate to Virginia. William Berkeley may best be known for quelling Bacon's Rebellion in 1676. After the Restoration of Charles II, he briefly returned to England, where he was rewarded for his loyalty by being made one of the eight Lords Proprietors of Carolina.[12]

The future Earl of Shaftsbury, **Anthony Ashley Cooper**, was the youngest of the Lords Proprietors. Born to a titled, wealthy family, Cooper inherited his father's baronetcy, and was knighted in 1631. He became the Earl of Shaftsbury in 1661. During the civil war, Cooper originally sided with the royalists, but ultimately surrendered his appointments and joined the Parliamentarians because of his concerns about the King's policies. Cooper believed Charles I's goals would result in the downfall of both religion and government in England. Ashley Cooper stood with the Roundheads as a moderate member of Parliament, until he concluded that Cromwell was determined to rule alone. At that point, he joined the side of the exiled prince, Charles Stuart. Cooper was one of the twelve men in the House of Commons who extended the invitation to Charles to return and be crowned King Charles II. He served on the Board of Plantations, owned land in both Barbados and the Bahamas, and enthusiastically supported Carolina colonization. A friend of the political philosopher and proprietors' secretary John Locke, Cooper – by then using the appellation Lord Ashley – collaborated with Locke to write the "Fundamental Constitutions" in 1669.

Anthony Ashley Cooper

Shaftsbury fell into disfavor over his enmity with King Charles' brother James, the Duke of York. James was a Roman Catholic and heir to the throne – something which the Protestant Shaftsbury detested and feared. Ashley was accused of collaborating to overthrow the duke and imprisoned in the Tower of London. Released on bail, he fled to Amsterdam where he died in 1683.[13]

George Carteret was born on the Channel Island of Jersey, and at a young age served as acting governor in his absent uncle's stead (something the people of Jersey Island complained about, claiming that he was too young and inexperienced for the job). He saw duty with the British navy as a lieutenant aboard the *Convertive*, and participated in an expedition against North African pirates in 1637. When the civil war broke out, Carteret ardently supported Charles I, and

George Carteret

tried to raise an army for him in Cornwall. Instead, he was persuaded to become the primary supplier of arms and munitions to royal forces. From Jersey he orchestrated a commerce raiding campaign against Cromwell's navy. The island eventually became a refuge for many royalists who fled

England in 1646. When the exiled Prince Charles arrived on Jersey, he knighted Carteret. In return, after the execution of Charles I, Carteret proclaimed Charles Stuart the new King. Parliamentary forces landed in Jersey, and after three months, forced Carteret to surrender his castle home. Carteret and his family were allowed to join the exiled Charles Stuart in France.[14]

After the Restoration, Carteret became a member of the Privy Council, the treasurer of the navy, and in 1661, a member of the House of Commons. He was also one of the early supporters of the Hudson Bay Company, and (along with John, Lord Berkeley) one of the proprietors of New Jersey. He died at nearly eighty-eight years of age in 1680.

John Colleton, along with Anthony Ashley Cooper and William Craven, may have been the proprietor most enthusiastic about the settlement of Carolina. When his property in England was seized due to his support for the royalists during the civil war, Colleton moved to Barbados in 1651, and bought land there. Described variously as a financier, merchant, promoter and planter, Colleton was a relative of both former island governor Thomas Modyford and George Monck. When Charles resumed the throne, Colleton returned to England, where he was knighted in 1661. He never again set foot on Barbados, and died in 1666. There will be more about Colleton to come.[15]

The Forming of a Proprietary

Maryland had proven that a proprietary colony on the American mainland could work. By 1660, it was well-established and generating wealth for the nation and its owners. The proprietors of Carolina crafted their own charter based on the successful formula employed in Maryland.[16]

The involvement of such esteemed men as those who came together to become the Lords Proprietors of Carolina was not purely out of self-interest. Sir William Berkeley saw Carolina as a way to expand the English presence beyond Virginia's border. John Colleton recognized Carolina as a place where much-needed food, lumber, and other materials could be secured for Barbados, and as a place for the island's surplus population to relocate to. Ashley, John Berkeley, and Carteret all wanted to improve England's status as a colonial power. Edward Hyde, the Earl of Clarendon and the most important military man in Restoration England,

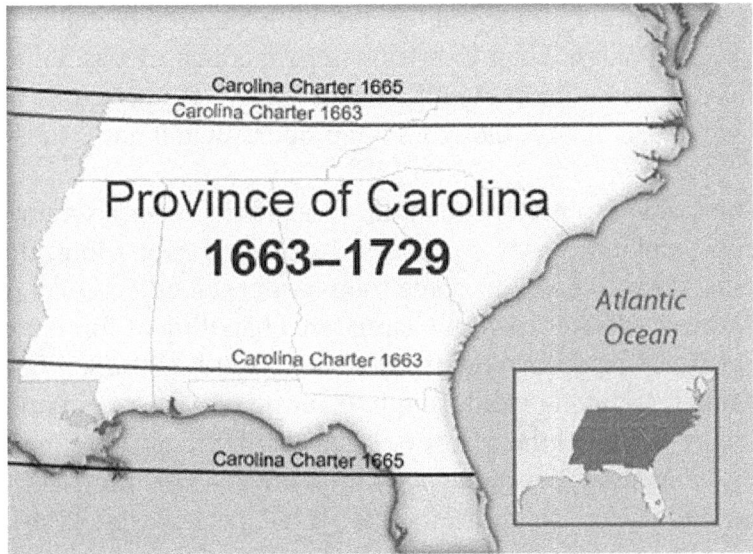

The Carolina Charter of 1663 granted a huge swath of the New World to the Lords Proprietors. It was expanded two years later to include even more territory.

was merely lukewarm to the Carolina venture, except as it served to send a message to Spain. As the proprietors themselves asserted, "ye business is yd Kings & nations more than our owne."[17]

Given the diverse natures, motives, and personalities of the eight men who joined in the Carolina venture, it is perhaps surprising that they all came together in a common enterprise. It is also likely that they took a long view regarding the potential rewards to be realized from Carolina. Francis Bacon once observed that a colony took two decades to realize any profit for its investors. That, coupled with the poor record of the previous attempts to colonize Carolina, and it was unlikely that any of the eight Lords Proprietors would ever see a return on their investment in their lifetime. Anthony Ashley Cooper was forty-three years old when the Lords Proprietors issued their 1663 charter, already older than the male life expectancy at the time. The other Lords Proprietors were even older. George Monck and Edward Hyde were fifty-five, and both suffered chronic health problems. George Carteret was the oldest of them all at age sixty-five.[18]

The group of eight men who became the Lords Proprietors of Carolina were an eclectic bunch, and in many cases shared little in common beyond their loyalty to the Stuart monarchy. In one case there was outright enmity between them. Yet these men saw Carolina colonization as a way to enhance England's power, prestige and profits, and also as a way to promote the Church of England – aims which corresponded nicely with those of their monarch, King Charles II. The fact that they stood to make substantial fortunes of their own if the colony proved successful was for the most part a secondary (though not unimportant and not inconsiderable) concern.[19]

The Lords Proprietors were, in a real sense, simply a marriage of convenience, and a means to various ends. Clarendon and John Berkeley could barely stand to be in the same room with each other. Other members of the group disagreed with Clarendon's handling of foreign policy and his harshness towards religious dissenters. William Berkeley and George Monck got along well enough, if for no other reason than the great distances that separated them. They all harbored differing notions of the relationship that should exist between England and her colonies. Ashley favored excluding the Dutch from trade with America, which ran counter to the free trade sensibilities of William Berkeley. The one thing they all seem to have agreed on is that Carolina was a means of achieving much more than just another English plantation on the far side of the world.[20]

Historians are divided as to exactly who had the idea to form the Carolina proprietary. Both Sir William Berkeley and Sir John Colleton have been suggested as likely candidates. Colleton and Berkeley each had first-hand knowledge of the colonies, the previous in Barbados, the latter in Virginia. Berkeley, as the governor of Virginia, would also have been the proprietor with the most intimate knowledge of the lands below the Chesapeake. The two may have worked closely with Anthony Ashley Cooper to put the proprietary group together. Yet there are problems with assigning the credit for the Carolina idea to either Colleton or Berkeley. Berkeley never showed much enthusiasm for a settlement south of Virginia, as such a settlement would likely become a competitor to his own colony. Likewise, Shaftesbury never exhibited much interest in Carolina until 1668. Had he been deeply involved in pulling together the men who would form the Lords Proprietors, it is likely he would have also included men like Prince Rupert or the Duke of York, who Ashley had more in common with.

The Duke of Albemarle, along with Sir John Colleton, top other lists of those most likely to have advanced the idea of the proprietary. Monck was at the center of efforts to secure the charter from the King, the eight Lords frequently met at Albemarle's home to plan their venture, and the diverse natures of the men who became Lords Proprietors all point to

Monck. Colleton likely suggested John Berkeley, and John Berkeley likely lobbied to include his brother, William, as well as George Carteret. William Craven was an intimate of Edward Hyde, and Hyde was a friend and confidant of Ashley. On the other hand, perhaps it was none of the above. The suggestion could have originated, for instance, as an idea bandied about after a meeting of the Council of Foreign Plantations that simply drew those still in the room into the scheme.[21]

However it came about, once conceived John Colleton became the workhorse of the enterprise. Charles II had barely been fitted for his English crown before Colleton was back in England lobbying for a Carolina proprietary. In the preceding ten years, he had not returned to England even to visit, except for the possibility that he may have traveled to London to petition Oliver Cromwell for reinstatement after Governor Daniel Searle stripped him of offices bestowed on him by General Robert Venables during the Interregnum. Colleton took up residence near the Church of St. Giles and lived there from 1660-1665, when he moved to St. Martin-in-the-Fields, closer to St. James and the seat of government. Once the proprietary was formed, the Barbadian planter put his decade of expe-

St. Martin-in-the-Fields church, near where John Colleton resided close to the seat of power at St. James. This church was torn down in 1720.

rience in the tropics to work handling the day-to-day business of the Lords Proprietors and administering their Carolina patent. Colleton likely hoped that a Carolina charter would abort any prospective return to a Caribbean proprietary that would work against the interests of the island's large sugar planters. [22]

John Colleton and his planter colleagues saw opportunity on the American mainland. For them the attraction lay not in siphoning off the surplus population of Barbados, but in the prospects for profit the vast expanses of unclaimed American land represented. A few small planters under financial hardship leaving the island would have had no appreciable impact on the situation in Barbados. The large planters were under no economic pressure to leave, though a recent influx of people they considered undesirable may have had some small impact on their decisions. While Colleton had no intention of swapping residence in Barbados for residence in Carolina, he did see a mainland colony there as an avenue to increased revenue.[23]

To advance the idea of a Carolina proprietary, Colleton hoped to capitalize on the reawakened interest in colonial adventures that were especially favored by the King and his brother James, Duke of York. His selection to the Select Committee for Foreign Plantations on 7 November 1660 was the first step in providing the access he needed to promote his own schemes. Fellow committee members included six of the original eight Lords Proprietors of Carolina. A second committee formed later added another. The committee put Colleton in close, regular contact with the people who were both best situated and able to influence the Crown to support a Carolina venture. The opportunity to discuss Carolina settlement presented itself when Sir William Berkeley, governor of Virginia, returned to England and was asked by the committee to use his influence to encourage further migration to the Albemarle.[24]

The eight men who would champion the settlement of Carolina began meeting as early as 1661, while William Berkeley was in England. Many of those meetings took place at the Cock Pit lodgings of George Monck, across the courtyard from King Charles' Whitehall apartments. Sir George Carteret contributed the fees to obtain the Carolina Charter, and was later reimbursed £106/11/6 on 5 January 1664 for "ye Charge of ye Patent of His Maties Grant for Carolina . . . with an Exemptyfication thereof . . ." They took advantage of the time while the question of the Heath patent was being decided to lay the groundwork for their own effort

Cockfighting, as in this 17th century print by William Hogarth, was a popular pastime that no doubt gave the building near where George Monck lived its name. The building later became a theater.

at Carolina colonization. By 25 August 1663, the Lords Proprietors were ready to unveil their "Declaration and Prospects (or Proposals)" for settlement in the territory below Virginia. [25]

Edward Hyde secured the chairmanship of the proprietors, but John Colleton had a major organizational role and was the most hands-on administrator of the group. Colleton's leadership is borne out by the fact that all of the letters written by the Lords Proprietors between 1663-1666 are all in his distinctive style. The arrangements made during those years all have Colleton's fingerprints on them and reflect his ideas. Clarendon, Ashley, and William Berkeley were relatively inactive in the Carolina venture during the early years, but the other five all took active roles in the administration of the proprietorship. The Lords Proprietors clearly intended Carolina to be a colony launched with as little a personal investment as they could get away with. Ideally, the Carolina colony would be self-funded, with Barbadian adventurers covering the initial costs of settlement mainly through contributions of sugar. To make the venture attractive to as wide a cross section of potential colonists as possible, personal and political freedoms were guaranteed in the Declaration and Proposals.[26]

Not everyone supported the effort. Governor Willoughby of Barbados disapproved of any measure or enterprise that was likely to pull white men from his island. Willoughby worried over the rapidly changing ratio of whites to blacks on Barbados, and was fearful that more white emigration would create a security risk for the whites who remained there. But Barbadian planters saw the proposed mainland colony in a different light. For them, Carolina would be a compliment to the Barbadian economy, providing the food and raw materials so badly needed on their sugarcane-covered island. The acquisition of new lands, something that had been long missing in bought-up and over-planted Barbados, was something that drew their support.[27]

The groundwork laid, the Lords Proprietors wasted no time in opening their new grant up to potential settlers, a number of whom were already queuing up to stake their claims to the Carolina lands at Cape Fear.

Endnotes

1. Daniel W. Fagg, Jr., "Carolina, 1663-1683: The Founding of a Proprietary." (Ph.D dissertation, Emory University, 1970): 2, hereafter cited as Fagg, "Carolina, 1663-1683." To facilitate colonial ventures, and to bring the management of existing colonies under one authority, Clarendon, in his office as Lord Chancellor, established the Privy Council's Committee of Trade and Plantations on 4 July 1660. Only Anthony Ashley Cooper served on this committee, but when the Council of Foreign Plantations was formed five months later, all of the future Lords Proprietors served on it.
2. Fagg, "Carolina: 1663-1683," 4-5. Wealth generated for the backers of colonial ventures meant wealth for King Charles II, too. With the profligate lifestyle of the monarch, he needed every shilling he could get his hands on.
3. George Louis Beer, *The Origins of the British Colonial System, 1578-1660* (Gloucester, MA: Peter Smith, 1959):4. Edward Hyde, Earl of Clarendon, wrote of Charles II, "Upon the King's first arrival in England, he manifested a very great desire to improve the general traffick and trade of the Kingdom, and upon all occasions conferred with the most active merchants upon it, and offered all that he could contribute to the advancement thereof."
4. Rebecca M. Seaman, "Native American Enslavement in Proprietary North Carolina: A Causality Study," (Ph.D dissertation, Auburn University, 2001): 87-89, hereafter cited as Seaman, *Native American Enslavement*. Not all historians agree that Charles Stuart granted the Lords Proprietors their charter because of a perceived debt owed them. Wesley Craven viewed the Lords Proprietors as a small, select group of highly powerful men whose schemes Charles II felt obliged to endorse. At the same time, Craven disputes the notion that Carolina was intended to be a colony of true religious freedom and increased political rights. Though such rights were included in the charter of the colony, he assigns an economic motive for their inclusion. Alan Cairnes concurs that economic motive was at the root of

the moves made by the Lords Proprietors to recruit settlers.
5. William S. Powell, *The Proprietors of Carolina* (Raleigh, N.C.: The Carolina Tercentenary Commission, 1963): 12-16, hereafter cited as Powell, *Proprietors*; Carlton, *British Civil Wars,* 65; N.A.M. Rodger, *The Command of the Ocean: A Naval History of Britain 1649 —1815* (New York: Penguin Group, 2004), 66, 77, 97, hereafter cited as Rodger, *The Command of the Ocean*; J. Rickard, "The Second Anglo-Dutch War (1665-1667)," http://www.historyofwar.org/articles/wars_anglodutch2.html, 12 December 2000.
6. Powell, *Proprietors,* 16-25.
7. Powell, *Proprietors,* 16-25; Ronald Hutton, "Monck, George, first duke of Albemarle (1608–1670)," *Oxford Dictionary of National Biography*, Oxford University Press, http://www.oxforddnb.com/index/18/101018939, accessed 6/11/11. Monck's conditions included religious tolerance, a general pardon, and the preservation of land transactions that occurred during the reign of Cromwell.
8. Powell, *Proprietors,* 16-25.
9. Buchanan, "Colleton," 46.
10. Powell, *Proprietors,* 25-29.
11. Powell, *Proprietors,* 29-33.
12. Powell, *Proprietors,* 43-47; Warren M. Billings, *Sir William Berkeley and the Forging of Colonial Virginia* (Baton Rouge: Louisiana State University Press, 2004): 89-90, hereafter cited as Billings, *Berkeley and Virginia*; Warren M. Billings, "Sir William Berkeley," 1999, http://www.virtualjamestown.org/essays/billings_essay.html, accessed 6/11/11. As well, the proprietors needed a representative on the scene in their colony to keep an eye on things.
13. Powell, *Proprietors*, 33-38.
14. Powell, *Proprietors*, 38-43; Herbert Richard Paschal, Jr. "Proprietary North Carolina: A Study in Colonial Government." (Ph.D dissertation, University of North Carolina, 1961): 67, hereafter cited as Paschal, "Proprietary North Carolina." Carteret was well remembered by his sovereign for his loyalty and service during Charles' exile. He carried a letter from Charles that read: "Carteret, I will add this to you under my own hand that I can never forget the good services you have done to my father and to me and if God bless me you shall find I do remember them to the advantage of you and yours; and for this you have the word of your very loving friend Charles R."
15. Powell, *Proprietors*, 47-49.
16. Charles Greer Suttlemeyre, Jr., "Proprietary Policy and the Development of North Carolina, 1663-1729" (Ph.D dissertation, St. Benet's Hall, Oxford University, 1991):107, hereafter cited as Suttlemeyre, "Proprietary Policy."
17. Louis H. Roper, *Conceiving Carolina: Proprietors, Planters, and Plots, 1662-1729* (New York: Palgrave Macmillan, 2004): 16-17, hereafter cited as Roper, *Conceiving Carolina.* The point being that the Lords Proprietors each had

differing motives for their association concerning Carolina. Their partnership was far from being based on mutual admiration and friendship.

18. Paschal, "Proprietary North Carolina," 97; Roper, *Conceiving Carolina,* 28.

19. Buchanan, "Colleton," 12-50; Roper, *Conceiving Carolina,* passim; Fagg, "Carolina, 1663-1683," 28. Clarendon, Craven, and Berkeley all shared exile with Charles Stuart during the Interregnum. The experience had differing impacts on them, driving a wedge between Clarendon and Berkeley, who flatly despised each other. Ashley and Albemarle each made their fortunes thanks to the Restoration. Still, the King must have needed to make an extra effort to forget about their previous allegiances to Parliament.

20. Billings, *Berkeley and Virginia,* 334. Governor William Berkeley considered free trade – including with the Dutch – as essential to grow and diversify the Virginia economy.

21. Fagg, "Carolina, 1663-1683," 31-34. Wesley Frank Craven favors the theory that Berkeley and Colleton joined Ashley in putting together the list of men who would become the proprietors. Fagg, on the other hand, finds the Monck-Colleton combination more likely.

22. Buchanan, "Colleton," 36, 41-43. John Colleton arrived back in London in 1660, having left Barbados so quickly that he may have left his children behind. He never returned to Barbados, in part because he did not like the island's governor, Sir Francis Willoughby, and in part because social changes that came with the Restoration made life much more amenable in England. Colleton and his fellow sugar planters likely preferred the island remain under royal administration, one which had proven much more amenable to Barbados' planter elites than past proprietary administrators had.

23. Buchanan, "Colleton," 39-40.

24. Buchanan, "Colleton," 43-46. The Select Committee for Foreign Plantations was tasked with overseeing the administration of the Caribee islands (including Barbados), Jamaica, and New England. Fellow members included Sir James Drax, Martin Noel, Thomas Kendall, and Thomas Middleton, all of whom had Caribbean interests. The committee asked for Berkeley's help populating the Albemarle in large part because it was the most obvious and least costly way to plant settlers there. Given Berkeley's reluctance to do anything that might conceivably weaken his own colony, little came of the plan.

25. Fagg, "Carolina: 1663-1683," 29-30; Roper, *Conceiving Carolina,* 17. The Cock Pit was an old fashioned, crenellated house that stood in front of a circular royal cockpit. Meetings of the Carolina proprietors were centered there until the death of George Monck . . . the Proprietors' Declarations and Prospects is also recorded as their Declaration and Proposals. It was quickly issued in the summer of 1663 largely because a group of prospective Puritan settlers in New England had expressed interest in a Carolina settlement . . . The final Declaration and

Proposals were certainly not all that were discussed by the Lords Proprietors. It probably underwent several drafts before finally being released for public consumption . . . The questions surrounding the Heath patent involved claims made by the Duke of Norfolk and Samuel Vassall, both based on the Heath grant.

26. Buchanan, "Colleton," 50; Fagg, "Carolina: 1663-1683," 55-60. Monck and Colleton were the unequivocal leaders of the Lords Proprietors. The guarantees of religious freedom in the 1663 Charter came in the form of the "freedom of conscience" clause, and was carried over into the 1665 revision of the Carolina Charter. It gave clear license to those who would not "conform to the public exercise of religion" according to the "ceremonies of the Church of England."

27. Buchanan, "Colleton," 62; Fagg, "Carolina: 1663-1683," 58; Hatfield, *Atlantic Virginia,* 107. Willoughby and his fellow colonial governors objected to the Carolina call for settlers enough that in 1663 the Lords Proprietors made a formal request to the governors of Barbados, the Caribee Islands, Virginia, New England, and Bermuda to not hinder free and unengaged persons from moving to Carolina.

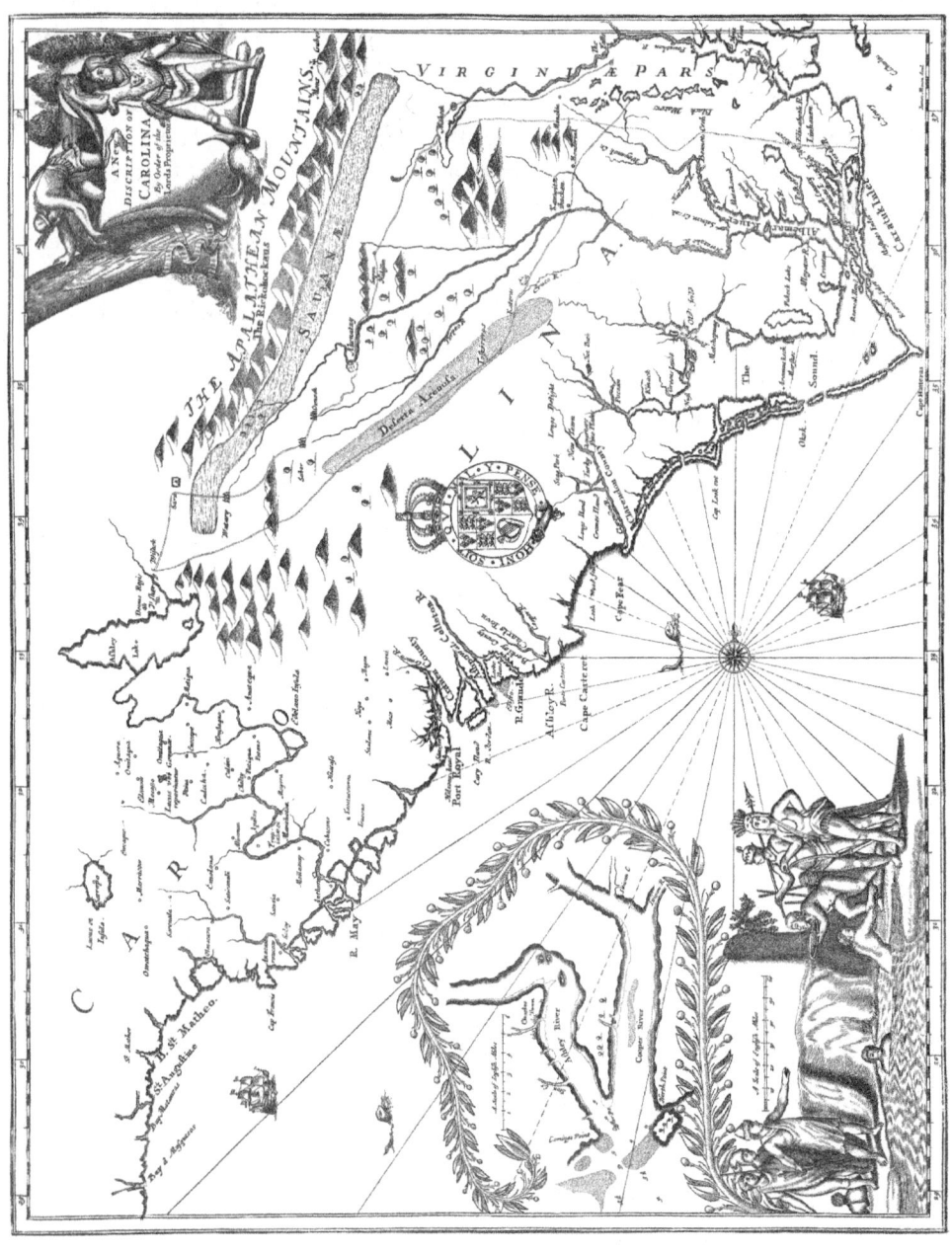

This map by Ogilby, ca. 1672, depicts Carolina shortly after the time of the Vassall settlement at Cape Fear. The map has been reoriented to more accurately reflect the geography of the coast.

V
Carolana/ Carolina

Carolina was born for mainly the same reasons as the Royal African Company, the Hudson Bay Company, and the Royal Fisheries Company – profit. English mercantilists hoped to produce wine, olive oil, silks, and other lucrative commodities in an effort to create wealth for Carolina's investors and the Crown. The settlements would produce such things ". . . as the Kinge hath not yet within his Terrytories in quantity, although his people consume much of them to the exhausting the wealth of the Kingdome."[1]

By the early 1650s, authorities in Virginia were offering land grants south of the Chesapeake. Hunters, trappers, traders, merchants, explorers, former soldiers, and farmers in search of more and better lands appeared in the area bordering the great sounds of northeast Carolina. The Lords Proprietors' earliest governing experience concerned Virginians who settled along the banks of and in proximity to the Chowan River. Virginia also played a major role in the settlement of the Cape Fear, providing both settlers and supplies, and serving as a haven when the Charles Towne settlement finally gave up the ghost in 1667. Lessons learned by the proprietors in their administration of the Albemarle settlements prepared them for later efforts. They would not be long in coming, though previous claims to Carolina had to be resolved first.[2]

The Heath Patent

Although Sir Walter Raleigh's Roanoke colony failed, it succeeded in putting Carolina on the map and in the minds of Englishmen with an eye to adventure and colonization. In 1629, two of King Charles I's most trusted friends lobbied the sovereign obtain the lands below Virginia for themselves.[3]

Sir Robert Heath, the King's attorney general, and George Calvert, first Baron Baltimore and former member of the Privy Council, each expressed interest in the territory that would become Carolina. Of the two, only Calvert had any colonial experience. Nevertheless, Heath pursued a patent on behalf of other parties in hopes of profiting by his efforts. Despite Calvert's experience, the King awarded Heath a patent on October 20, 1629.[4]

Sir Robert Heath

Heath's Carolana patent was vast, and included the island of Bermuda. Encompassing all land between 31° and 36° north latitude, or from the St. Matthew River on the south, to the "River or Rivelett of the great passe," and west "soe far as the Continent extends itselfe," there was ample room for any conceivable number of settlers to put down roots. The King's grant was contingent on Heath and his heirs building their colony according to instructions and guidelines handed down by Charles I and his secretaries. Heath incorporated the mainland portion of the grant and named it Carolana, Latin for Charles, in honor of his generous monarch. In awarding the grant to Heath, the King lauded his counselor's "pious desire as well of enlarging the Christian religion as our Empire & encreasing the Trade & Commerce of this our Kingdom." In addition to rewarding a faithful officer, Charles was also testing the Spanish monarch, seeing if Spain would allow the English claim to go unchallenged.[5]

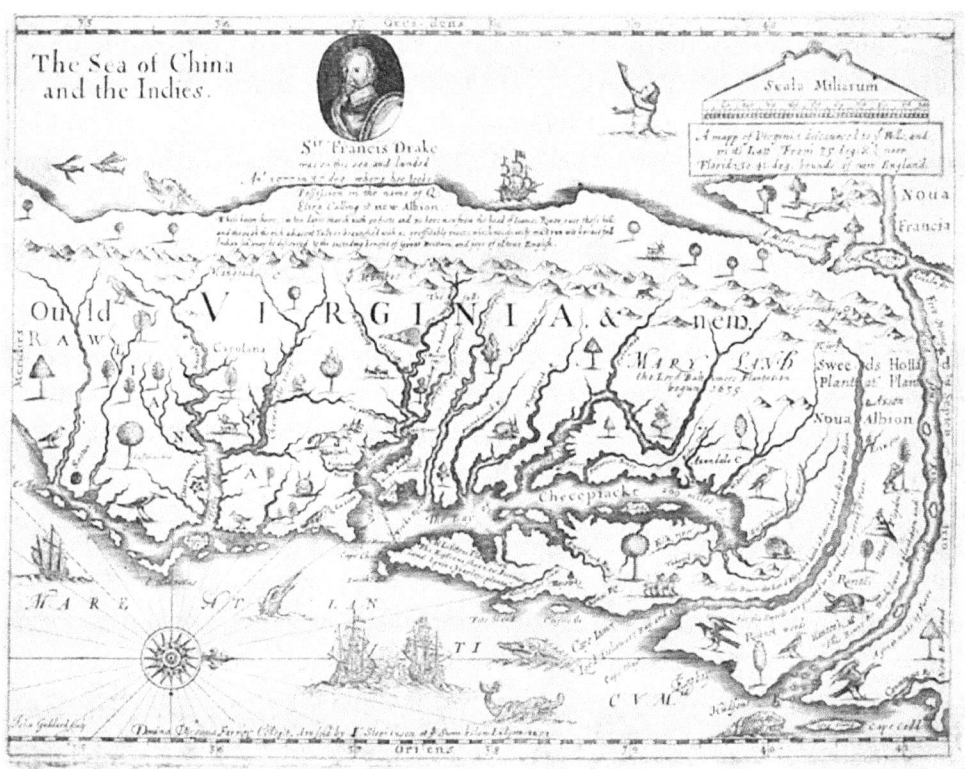

John Farrar's 1651 map also encompasses the Heath patent.

Exactly what role King Charles had in the Heath venture is unclear due to a paucity of records, but based on what is known, it seems likely that he granted the lands of Carolana to Heath on the condition that he share any profits that might accrue from the enterprise. That the King was willing to provide Heath more material support to promote the endeavor is bolstered by a letter from Heath to Edward Nicholas, secretary to the Admiralty, dated January 17, 1629. In it, Heath informed Nicholas that the King had sent a ship, the *St. Claude*, in support of the Carolana venture.[6]

Interest in Carolana seems to have originated with French Huguenot refugees who fled to London after the fall of La Rochelle on October 24, 1628. Rights granted to the Calvinist French under the Edict of Nantes had been steadily eroding in Catholic France. This eventually led to the siege of La Rochelle and the following wave of Huguenot emigration to places more tolerant of non-Catholic Frenchmen. Among the displaced Protestants was Antoine de Ridouet, Baron de Sance. De Sance had resided in England a year before as secretary to the Duc de Soubise, commander of the defense of La Rochelle during the infamous siege. He had returned to London by 1629, living off a pension of £100 per annum granted to him by King Charles I. De Sance asked Charles for a position in his Privy Chamber, and for letters of denization for both himself and his son George. In his petition, de Sance expressed his "great desire to be the means of settling French Protestants in Virginia, to plant vines, olives, and make silk and salt. . . ."[7]

As the baron and his company envisioned it, they would transport Huguenot veterans of the campaigns in Holland to a new settlement somewhere in the territories of southern Virginia or what became Carolina. The colony would also be open to English settlers, but the bulk of the colonists would be naturalized French. The Frenchmen decided on a settlement site near modern New Bern, North Carolina.[8]

At some point de Sance interested Sir Robert Heath in his idea. Articles of incorporation were agreed to between the two men on March 19, 1629. For his part, Heath saw Carolana as an opportunity to rid England of a troublesome wave of immigrants and, at the same time, to fatten his own pockets. France's religious civil wars of the 1500s pitted adherents of the Catholic Church – including the monarchy – against protestant Huguenots (who were basically Calvinists). Among the Huguenot faithful were a great many of France's artisans and craftsmen, people with valuable skills that any nation of the time would have welcomed. England was one such nation. When religious persecution in France goaded Huguenots to cast their eyes beyond French borders in search of a new home, Charles I's realm became a prime destination. By the second quarter of the seventeenth century, however, England's leaders became alarmed by what they considered an unhealthy number of the expatriate Frenchmen living in England. Heath saw his Carolana venture as the perfect solution to the social problem. For him, French Huguenots were ideal candidates to colonize the new English lands in far distant America.[9]

Heath believed the colony would solve two problems: first, sending the Huguenots to his colony in the Western Hemisphere would remove a drain on English resources and a potential source of instability for Charles' realm; second, Huguenot colonization would expand English holdings and profits.[10]

By mid-October 1629, the expatriate Frenchman de Sance was deeply involved with Heath and the Crown to place a colony in the lands south of the Chesapeake. Together they formed detailed plans for Carolana's settlement, taking care to insure that only Protestants would comprise its colonists. De Sance wrote regulations that would require French settlers to obtain certificates of their Protestant faith from their pastors in France, confirmed by their ministers in London. Once those had been acquired, Attorney General Heath would provide each Huguenot colonist with a certificate of immigration. He then entered their names and vocations in a book, as a record of those shipping out. When they arrived in Carolana, their certificates were to be collected. Anyone without a certificate was to be considered a "stranger," and returned to England. King Charles himself instructed Heath to make sure only Protestants settled in Carolana.[11]

As plans progressed, de Sance lowered his ambitious, large colonizing aspirations to a more manageable 100-150 settlers. Among the eighty-one colonists who would make the first voyage, he intended to take a minister, carpenters, shipbuilders, locksmiths, masons, bakers, cooks, a tailor, a boot maker, an apothecary, a barber, sewing men, and others to lay the foundations for their fellow Frenchmen who would follow.[12]

Samuel Vassall's bust in King's Chapel, Boston, Massachusetts

De Sance busied himself trying to find merchants and traders to underwrite the project. One such businessman may have been Samuel Vassall, a wealthy London Puritan of Huguenot descent and member of the Massachusetts Bay Company. By 1630, de Sance was consulting Vassall about the number of men needed and the amount and nature of supplies required for a successful Carolana venture. At de Sance's request, William Boswell helped to gather firearms and equipment after the baron took ill. Unfortunately, de Sance's sources of financing soon dried up. By the spring of 1630, the baron asked Boswell to present a bargain to the King in which the Frenchman would forfeit his pension from the Crown in return for arms for the Carolana settlers. De Sance's days as leader of the Huguenot colonization of Carolana ended there.[13]

Baron de Sance's Carolana dreams came to an abortive end when King Charles I issued an edict through his Privy Council critical of de

Sancé's plans for all French settlers to acquire affidavits from French pastors professing their Protestant faith. In reality, he was uneasy about the prospect of Frenchmen colonizing English lands in the Western Hemisphere. The Church of England, suspicious of the Huguenots in general, shared the King's concerns. They certainly did not want to see English lands colonized by people of a faith that did not follow the dogma of the church of the realm. With no easy means of recruiting colonists for Carolana, and with waning enthusiasm from the King, Sir Robert Heath lost interest in the Carolana enterprise. He signed over his grant to Henry Frederick Howard, Lord Maltravers, in 1638. Leadership of the venture now shifted to Samuel Vassall and a group of partners, including George Lord Berkeley.[14]

Henry Frederick Howard, Lord Maltravers

The leaders of the Carolana enterprise were men of wealth, renown, and accomplishments. George Berkeley was the eighth Baron Berkeley of the Berkeley Hundred plantation on Virginia's James River. William Boswell boasted ample connections at the court of Charles I and with the French government. Huguenot leaders Hugh L'Amy and Peter De Licques were intimately familiar with the French Protestants who would be recruited to make the journey to Carolana. Berkeley acquired an enfeoffment of land in Carolana between 34° and 36° latitude. Lord Berkeley, Boswell, Vassall, L'Amy, and De Licques sealed their partnership by signing articles of agreement on May 15, 1630.[15]

Samuel Vassall provided the link to the future settlement at Cape Fear. He was uncle to John Vassall, who planted a colony there in 1664. As early as 1617, Samuel Vassall was heavily involved in the Adriatic trade, and had pioneered the vending of Surrey-made cloth at Ragusa, Italy. His rebellious streak sometimes got him into trouble. In 1620 he resisted forced loans that landed him in prison at Battersea. Nine years later, he refused to pay the tonnage duty on 4,638 hundredweight of imported currants, so the Crown's taxmen confiscated the shipment and locked Vassall up again. The following year, Vassall landed in jail once more over a dispute concerning a shipment of tobacco. Over a sixteen-year period,

Samuel Vassall spent a considerable amount of time under lock and key at Marshalsea, the Fleet, or Gatehouse prisons. Yet London city voters elected him to both the Stag and Long Parliaments in 1640, and Vassall became one of England's foremost plantation merchants.

Because of his position and prominence, Samuel Vassall was selected in 1643 to serve on a commission headed by Robert Rich, Earl of Warwick, Governor-in-Chief and Lord High Admiral of all the plantations in America. These commissioners showed a decided preference for the Massachusetts Bay Company of which Vassall was a founding member, granting it all of the lands in Narragansett County. The commission also strengthened the Providence plantations by incorporating them.[16]

In 1632, Samuel Vassall sent Henry Taverner, master of the *George of London*, on a voyage of discovery along the Carolana coast. The Puritan merchant then set about obtaining from Sir Robert Heath that part of Carolana lying between 31° and 33° north latitude. This parcel encompassed all of the lands not granted to Lord Berkeley in his 1630 enfeoffment. Once that was accomplished, Vassall entered into yet another agreement with Edward Kingswell to provide two ships, the shallop *Thomas of London* (Henry Taverner, master), and the pinnace *Henry* (Orpheus Dunkin, master), along with a number of provisions in return for Kingswell's promise to lead a group of settlers to Carolana. At the last moment, however, Vassall was unable to provide the ships. The reason is unclear. In their stead, a party of about forty colonists went aboard the *Mayflower* for the voyage across the Atlantic.[17]

Kingswell, with his wife and family in tow, along with the remainder of the settlers committed to the voyage, sailed from England aboard the *Mayflower* with Master Peter Andrews at the helm. After a number of weeks, they arrived in Virginia in October 1633. When the ship dropped anchor in the Chesapeake, Andrews refused to complete the second leg of the voyage, that would have carried the settlers south to the lands in Carolana targeted for colonization. Kingswell and his fellows were forced to remain in Virginia over the winter of 1633-1634, "in distress. . . with no transport to take them to Carolana."[18]

Unknown to Kingswell, Vassall had already dispatched another ship, the *Thomas* under Henry Taverner, to Virginia with twenty-eight additional colonists to join those transported by the *Mayflower*. As late spring dawned on the James River, transportation to Carolana still had not materialized. Kingswell lodged a complaint about the affair with Virginia governor Sir John Harvey, then boarded the first available ship returning to England. Taverner's instructions called for him to link up with Kingswell's party in Virginia, and then proceed to Carolana. When Taverner arrived in the Chesapeake, he found that Kingswell had already departed. Plans to dispatch yet a third ship, the *Henry*, under master Orpheus Dunkin, were aborted when Kingswell arrived back home to declare the venture off.

Back on English soil by June 1632, Kingswell filed suit for breach of covenant against both Samuel Vassall and Peter Andrews. The matter eventually went high enough to involve the Privy Council, the High Court of Admiralty, and the Lords Commissioners for Foreign Plantations. The honorables found in favor of Kingswell, and ordered Vassall to pay £611 in damages.[19]

The next person to take up the banner for settlement in Carolana was Henry Fredrick Howard, Lord Maltravers, one of a circle of Crown courtiers and promoters who saw potential in a mainland colony below Virginia. Howard secured a letter from King Charles I sometime prior to 1637 that instructed the governor and council of Virginia to plot out a county in the Albemarle region for settlement. Maltravers had ambitions beyond the Albemarle, however, and set his sights on securing the dormant Heath patent. With Charles' approval, the grant transferred to Howard on December 2, 1638. To Maltravers' chagrin, plans to develop a colony were derailed when the English Civil War erupted.[20]

Then there was Spain...

Even as Sir Walter Raleigh organized an expedition to plant Elizabeth I's flag on North American soil, English privateers, including Sir Francis Drake, raided Spanish settlements in the Caribbean and along the littoral regions of Central and South America. By the time the Virginia Company of London established Jamestown in 1607, Madrid had accepted the fact that the Spanish Crown would have to compete with England for control of North America.[21]

Spain greatly impacted English settlement efforts during the seventeenth century. As Englishmen planned and schemed to establish a presence below the Chesapeake in tidewater Virginia, none of them seemed to take into account that the area was technically already claimed by Spain. Indeed, Spanish colonial authorities considered everything from their stronghold at St. Augustine to the Chesapeake Bay to be under their flag,

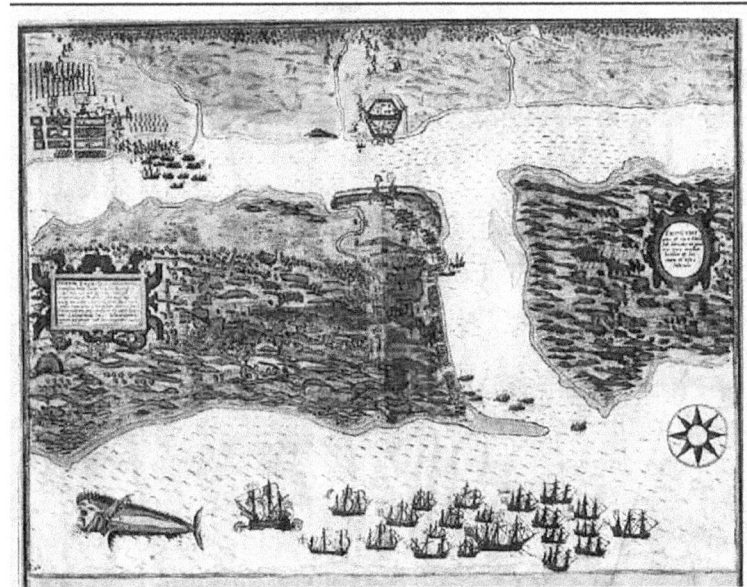

Baptista Boazio's 1586 map of Spanish St. Augustine, with Sir Francis Drake's raiding fleet closing in off the coast.

all of it a part of Florida.[22]

During the Cromwell Protectorate, English leaders began to eye the Carolina territory as a bulwark to protect the increasingly wealthy settlement at Jamestown from potential Spanish raids. As early as 1650 E.W. Gent advocated a Carolina colony. He pointed out the "apparent danger all the Colonies may be in if this [Carolina] be not possessed by the English."[23]

Spain claimed all of North America by "right of discovery." England contested their claim based on the principle of "effective occupation." Spain correctly interpreted the English efforts to settle Carolina as a challenge to its sovreignty. In the seventeenth century, the validity of territorial sovereignty was largely contingent on a nation's ability to put colonists on the ground and keep intruders out. Once a rival nation managed to plant its own colony, and keep it for a period of time, then its argument for ownership took on a degree of legitimacy. In short, if Spain could not keep England out of territory it claimed as her own, then she stood to lose it. During the troubles and disarray in England between 1664-1670, Spain was able to bolster its forces at St. Augustine to enforce its title. Before then, however, Englishmen were able to plant their flag along the coast between Jamestown and modern Georgia almost with impunity.[24]

When the Lords Proprietors were granted their first Carolina charter in 1663, the boundaries of their patent ended just north of the Saint

Mary River and Cumberland Island. The charter issued two years later moved the English claim much farther south, to a point well below St. Augustine. The earlier charter had been based on the inaccurate coordinates of the Heath patent drawn up more than thirty years earlier. Despite their claim to territory much farther north, in reality the boundary Spain honored north of St. Augustine was at Cape San Romano, or Cape Fear. The Lords Proprietors realized that their patent could only be legitimized by putting colonists in Carolina, and then only if those settlers were defended against potential Spanish moves to oust them.[25]

Cognizant of the limitations of Spanish power along the east coast of the American mainland, the Lords Proprietors had nothing to lose by extending their claim further south than Cape Fear. In 1664, an English diplomatic mission was dispatched to Madrid to settle the differences between Spain and England over issues of trade and territory in an effort to open Spanish markets to English trade. The Lords Proprietors gambled that even if they had already established a settlement below Cape Fear before the treaty was signed, a negotiated compromise boundary line would likely leave the area from Port Royal north intact. In the meantime, plans for a Carolina settlement had to be considered with the threat of Spanish interference always in mind.[26]

William Hilton's 1663 voyage of discovery along the Carolina coast confirmed the Spanish presence in the area, and by extension the potential for trouble with them. Hilton's journal entries record that on a Wednesday near "Saint Ellens, in the lat. of 32 deg. 30 min.," off the coast of Florida, the crew found strong evidence of a continued Spanish presence. Local Indians came aboard the *Adventure* and surprised Hilton by speaking to him in Spanish. Perhaps more revealing, the Indians were not in awe of the English ship's cannon and firearms. That Spanish influence was confirmed when Hilton accepted help from Spanish officers in securing the release of four English prisoners held captive by local Indians. That the Spaniards were able to act as intermediaries speaks to their relationship with the Florida natives.[27]

Carolina was part of the long American east coast chessboard on which Spain and England engaged in a geopolitical tug-of-war to see who was going to possess the fertile lands south of Chesapeake Bay. In truth, Spanish desires to possess the American mainland stemmed more from a need for strategically placed outposts to help protect their treasure fleets, traveling from Central and South America to Havana and Madrid, than from any real desire to colonize there. When the Lords Proprietors encouraged settlement at Cape Fear, it was motivated in part to see how far they could intrude upon Spanish claims without Iberian authorities pushing back. A settlement at Cape Fear had the added benefit of acting as a tripwire for any Spanish move against Jamestown. Testing Spain's resolve would also be a motive for the Lords Proprietors' endorsement of the plans put forth to establish new English colonies in Carolina.

The First Carolina Voyage of William Hilton

The man who made the most exhaustive surveys of the Cape Fear's potential as a settlement site was William Hilton, Jr., master of the ship *Adventure*, from Massachusetts. Hilton made two separate voyages to the region in the employ of both New England Puritans and Barbadian adventurers between 1662-1663. A brief visit by Edward Bland in 1650 had already resulted in favorable impressions of the lands around the cape, where he reported "a pleasant country of temperate Ayre, fertile soyle," and "a place so easie to be settled in." Bland's good impressions spurred potential colonizers to investigate further. William Hilton was the instrument of their examinations.[28]

William Hilton, Jr. (1617-1675) is something of a mystery to historians, but genealogists have pieced together some information about the Hilton family whose sea-going son played such an integral role in the early exploration and settlement of the Cape Fear. The future explorer arrived in Massachusetts as a six-year-old with his mother aboard the *Anne* sometime in 1623, sailing from Northwich, Cheshire, England. His father, also named William, resided in New Plymouth, having arrived in 1621. Some time after, the family moved to Piscataqua. The Hilton family adhered to the tenets of the Church of England, something highly unusual for settlers in Massachusetts at the time. The fact that they lived in the heart of Puritan country is highly suggestive that Hilton the younger may have been at least acquainted with Samuel Vassall, the secretary of the Massachusetts Bay Colony. It was during the years the Hiltons lived in Massachusetts that Vassall became deeply involved in the Heath patent and its claims to Carolina. That Hilton undertook a 1662 voyage of discovery on behalf of Massachusetts Puritans, followed a year later by a trip for John Vassall's group of Barbadians, lends at least some credence to the theory.[29]

William Hilton, Jr. apparently also crossed paths with Captain

Nicholas Shapley during his formative years. At one point the Hilton family lived in a house owned by Shapley at Kittery Point, Massachusetts. William Hilton, Sr. had a license to operate an inn there, but circumstances forced the family to give up the house when Shapley sought to enlarge and improve it. From there the family moved to York, where the elder Hilton operated a tavern and ferry.[30]

William Hilton became a mariner well acquainted with the Atlantic world of the seventeenth century. He went to sea at an early age, sailing from his home port of Charlestown, Massachusetts. Records indicate that he sailed to the far corners of the ocean - from New England, to London, to Surinam and Barbados. Hilton appeared to be the ideal man to find a place for people eager to start their own colony. His chance to prove it came when the "Committee for Cape ffaire at Boston" sponsored his first expedition to Carolina. The expedition sailed from Charlestown on August 14, 1662.[31]

Massachusetts in the mid-seventeenth century was a place of growing population and diminishing land. Earlier settlers had already been granted the prime open parcels, and subsequent generations were left bereft of good plots on which to establish their own estates and plantations. These people, along with merchants intrigued by the possibility of establishing new markets, were the ones who chartered Hilton to scan the southern coasts for likely places to plant a settlement. Hilton's voyage in the *Adventure* suffered from cartographic inaccuracies that created confusion. At the time, the three capes below Cape Hatteras along the North Carolina coast did not carry the same names they have on modern maps. In 1662, Cape Lookout was labeled Cape Fear (after its original Latin name, *Promontorium Tremendum*, or fearful headland, or cape). Modern Cape Fear was labeled Cape San Romano. The third cape was identified as Sandhoeck on at least one period map. Hilton managed to miss Cape Lookout entirely, and instead mistook the next cape as the one dubbed Cape Fear. It has carried that name ever since. The cape that contemporary charts identified as Sandhoeck Hilton renamed Romana, which became the modern Cape Romain.[32]

Accompanying Hilton on that 1662 voyage were a number of men whose names historian Louise Hall has managed to cull from a variety of colonial records. Hilton named geographical features in the Cape Fear region for them, as noted on the Shapley map. Long Island was named for Anthony Long, and Blower Ile for New England merchant and sailing master Pyam Blower. A river bearing his name honored crewmember Peter Fabian. Shapley's map bears the names of other members of Hilton's expedition – Winslow, Goldsmith, Hory, Borges, Brown, Crane, Green, and Greenless. Though these names appear in several contemporary manuscript and printed maps of the region, over time the names fell into disuse. The only names given by Hilton that are still used in the modern era are Turkey Quarter, Rocky Point, and Stag Park.[33]

The Shapley map also pinpoints what may have been a large Indian village south of Indian River (Town Creek), not far from where the Vassall settlement would establish its central compound on the north side of the tributary feeding int the Cape Fear River. Labeled "Sachom's P[lantation]," speculation is this may be the same village referenced in Barbadian descriptions of the Charles Towne settlement as Necoes. Hilton found little to admire about the local Indian population, describing them as poor, simple, and thievish. Hilton and his crew observed roughly 100 Indians on their first visit to the Cape Fear, many of them aged and living on the west bank below the forks of the river. Despite their apparent poverty, the locals treated Hilton and his men well. The Englishmen visited their village of Necoes, and eventually purchased the surrounding lands from the Indians.[34]

What Hilton found for his employers at Cape Fear was impressive. Their accounts speak of having ". . . ranged through very spacious tracts of rich Oake land . . ." interspersed with a dazzling variety of flora and fauna that would provide ample sustenance for any colony planted plant there. Hilton christened the river the Charles, for the new King, and after three weeks of exploration weighed anchor for Massachusetts. Hilton's glowing report spurred the Puritans in Boston to mount an expedition to settle in Carolina.[35]

William Hilton ferried his Puritan charges, mostly from Newbury and Charlestown, to the Cape Fear early in 1663, his passengers sharing space with cattle and hogs to fill their larders and smokehouses. Accompanied by another ship captained by Anthony Long, who participated in Hilton's earlier voyage of discovery, they arrived at the Cape Fear by February. But within two months something occurred to preclude a Puritan beachhead taking hold in Carolina.

Historian Louise Hall and others suspect that the decision to abandon the Cape Fear had something to do with the New Englanders being

Nicholas Shapley's map of the Cape Fear based on William Hilton, Jr.'s explorations.

seen as interlopers by the Lords Proprietors. As the New England expedition was getting under way, King Charles II and the eight loyal nobles on the receiving end of his gratitude were putting the final touches on the first Carolina Charter. The charter provided the terms for settlement of Carolina, and gave the Lords Proprietors great latitude in the administration of the province. Just as the New Englanders arrived in the Cape Fear, proprietor William Berkeley returned to Virginia to serve a second term as governor. Upon learning of the "Two hundred ffamilies (sic) from New England, we hear are seated a little to the South of us," Berkeley expressed concern that the settlers on the Cape Fear might be a hindrance to the proprietors' own plans for colonization. It is not unreasonable to speculate that the Lords Proprietors would have taken steps to subvert the Puritan settlement before it could take hold.[36]

The Lords Proprietors were the most fervent of Royalists, men whose position was closely tied to their loyalty to the monarchy and the Anglican Church of England. To them, Puritans shared entirely too much in common with Cromwell's Commonwealth men. Sir John Colleton especially would not have been eager to see Puritan New Englanders plant a colony within the Lords Proprietors' domain.[37]

Another possible explanation is that the Puritans learned of another group from Barbados who had petitioned the Lords for the same land. Perhaps assuming that the islanders' proposal would more likely find favor than their own, they quickly abandoned the Cape Fear. Speculation also centers on the possibility that the Lords Proprietors refused to grant to the New Englanders the same lenient terms for settlement that had been offered to their fathers in Massachusetts. Still others blame the New Englanders themselves, one investor's account complaining that they had ". . . come back again without so much as sitting down upon it [the Charles River]; and for the better justification of themselves in their return, have spread reproach both upon the harbor and upon the soil of the river." Indeed, the Puritans allegedly posted a warning at the mouth of the river as they departed, offering a less than flattering assessment of what lay north of the inlet bar.[38]

The decision on the part of the New Englanders to abandon the Cape Fear was apparently not unanimous. Some determined adventurers voted to stay and try to make a go of things, but the unwilling majority overruled them. Whatever their reasons for leaving, the Puritans released their livestock to range free on what is now Bald Head Island at the mouth of the river, refilled their water casks, and sailed back to Massachusetts Bay.[39]

Even as the Puritans' ships put Cape Fear behind them, their supporters in England were presenting the Lords Proprietors with formal notice of the colony, proposing concessions by which the New Englanders would shape their settlement into one they would find most acceptable. The sponsors made their petition to the Lords Proprietors unaware that the Puritan colony had already been abandoned at Cape Fear. The most significant concessions they hoped to secure were (1) – that the New Englanders be granted ownership of the land they settled without encumbrances, and (2) – that the Lords Proprietors confer upon them the status of an independent, autonomous government.

They would get neither. The Lords Proprietors rejected both proposals out of hand. Religious and loyalty issues aside, the primary objective of the proprietary venture was to generate revenues for the eight men who held the rights to the Carolina lands. There was little chance that they would assent to a colony that planned to offer them nothing for the privilege, and one that selected their own leaders without the consent of the Lords Proprietors.

In response, the New Englanders argued in a letter dated August 6, 1663 that they had equitable interest in the land at Cape Fear, since they had purchased it from the local Indians. Knowing that the Lords Proprietors needed settlers to populate their grant if they hoped to profit from it, the Puritans also frankly declared that no one from New England would transplant to Carolina without a guarantee of independent self-government in both the executive and legislative branches. Nor would settlers suffer encumbrances of any sort on the titles to the soil they tilled. Clearly the "Committee for Cape ffaire at Boston" envisioned a colony with a form of self-government that would make them effectively independent of the Lords Proprietors. Unwilling to concede such terms of settlement, the Lords Proprietors did not even bother with a reply to Hilton's group.[40]

In the view from the Lords Proprietors' Cockpit offices, the Indians never owned lands to sell in the first place, rendering the New Englanders' claim of equitable interest meaningless. If the proprietors recognized the Indians' sale of the land at the Cape Fear to the Puritans, it might call into question their authority to convey territory in Carolina at all. Granted sole rights to virtually all of the lands between Chesapeake and Florida by royal favor, the Lords Proprietors made it clear that they considered themselves both land agents and rulers of Carolina.[41]

Perhaps the Lords Proprietors dismissed the New Englanders out of hand, as Carolina began to attract the keen interest of other parties. Another group of Englishmen, who also hailed from an over-crowded American colony, were making plans to succeed at the Cape Fear where the New Englanders had failed.

Endnotes

1. Fagg, "Carolina: 1663-1683," 6. Duke of Albemarle to Gov. Lord Francis Willoughby of Barbados, 1663.
2. Suttlemeyre, "Proprietary Policy," 107; J.D. Lewis, "A History of Clarendon County – One of the Three Original Counties in Carolina," http://www.carolana.com/Carolina/Settlement/clarendon_county_original.html, accessed 6/17/2009, hereafter cited as Lewis, "Carolana." Like Barbados, Virginia in the mid-seventeenth century suffered a period of declining economic opportunities. In 1665, Carolina surveyor and interpreter Thomas Woodward noted that to attract Virginians to land below the Chesapeake, Carolina needed to offer better opportunities for land ownership. Woodward's letter to Lords Proprietor Sir John Colleton went on to state that most Virginians resented the small land grants offered by the Lords Proprietors, and that "the very rumor of them discourages many who had intentions to remove hence from Virginia." Woodward suggested the Lords Proprietors learn from the experience of Lord Baltimore in Maryland, who found that "men will remove from Virginia" only if offered easier conditions for acquiring acreage, "it being only land they come for." Virginians later resented the 1663 New England settlers at Cape Fear, as they thought their claim to land there pre-dated the Carolina charter.
3. Paschal, "Proprietary North Carolina," 10.
4. Paschal, "Proprietary North Carolina," 10-11. King Charles I likely awarded the patent to Heath because he was a silent partner in Heath's plan.
5. Paul E. Kopperman, "Profile of Failure: The Carolana Project, 1629-1640," *North Carolina Historical Review* 59 (1982): 1-23, hereafter cited as Kopperman, "Profile of Failure"; Colonial and State Records of North Carolina, http://docsouth.unc.edu/csr/index.html/document/csr01-0002, accessed 9/1/12-9/30/12; Fagg, "Carolina, 1663-1683," 35; Paschal, "Proprietary North Carolina," 18-19. In modern terms, Heath's grant extended from today's Jacksonville, Florida to the Virginia border, and west to the as yet undiscovered Pacific Ocean.
6. Paschal, "Proprietary North Carolina," 19-20.
7. Paschal, "Proprietary North Carolina," 14-15. Denization is an obsolete pro-

cess by which foreigners could petition the Crown for some of the rights enjoyed by natural born citizens.

8. E. Lawrence Lee, *The Lower Cape Fear in Colonial Days* (Chapel Hill: University of North Carolina Press, 1965): 25, hereafter cited as Lee, *Lower Cape Fear*; Kopperman, "Profile of Failure," 1-29.

9. Chris Nickson, "Tracing Huguenot History in England," http://www.exploregenealogy.co.uk/tracing-huguenot-history-england.html, accessed 11/17/10; Lee, *Lower Cape Fear*, pp. 16, 24.

10. Lewis, "Carolana," http://www.carolana.com/Carolina/Proprietors/1629to1665.html, accessed 10/12/10.

11. Paschal, "Proprietary North Carolina," 21-24. While Heath was the public face of the Carolana venture, he had no intention of making the journey to Carolana himself (Paschal says Heath was too happy with the creature comforts at home to go off adventuring on the other side of the world). Baron de Sance was the real leader of the Huguenot émigrés . . . On April 20, 1630, King Charles I instructed Heath to be certain that no aliens settled in Carolana without special permission, and that not even Protestants be allowed there unless they subscribed to the disciplines of the Church of England.

12. Paschal, "Proprietary North Carolina," 24-25.

13. Paschal, "Proprietary North Carolina," 24-25; Lewis, *Carolana*, http://www.carolana.com/Carolina/Proprietors/1629to1665.html. William Boswell was the secretary to England's ambassador in Paris.

14. Kopperman, "Profile of Failure," 1-29; Fagg, "Carolina, 1663-1683," 55. The Heath grant presented an obstacle to colonizing efforts by the Lords Proprietors until the 1629 patent was declared void on August 12, 1663 because the grantees failed to colonize the province. As a result, the Crown ordered the Attorney General to vacate all previous claims to Carolina.

15. Paschal, "Proprietary North Carolina," 26. This enfeoffment granted Berkeley a fief, or lands, within the Heath patent.

16. Carl Bridenbaugh, *Vexed and Troubled Englishmen, 1590-1642* (New York: Oxford University Press, 1967): 425-426. Vassall's inclusion on Warwick's commission is understandable, as the Puritan merchant had also served previously as a Navy Commissioner. The favor shown to the Massachusetts Bay Company, to the exclusion of petitions from other potential colonizing groups, would set the stage for troubles later on.

17. Paschal, "Proprietary North Carolina," 28-30. Taverner made landfall at Virginia, then turned south to explore as far as St. Helena Sound. The information he gathered helped cartographers create a new map of the region a year later . . . Edward Kingswell was likely the heir of Sir William Kingswell, of Shalden.

18. William Lawson Grant and James Munro, *Acts of the Privy Council of England: Colonial Series*, Vol. 1 (London: HM Stationery Office, 1908): 205; Paschal, "Proprietary North Carolina," 30-31. Peter Andrews, master of the

Mayflower, was the brother-in-law of Samuel Vassall. The *Mayflower* mentioned here is not the same ship that carried the Plymouth colony to Massachusetts Bay in 1620. Andrews' *Mayflower* had previously been known as the *Christopher and Mary*, a ship of about 400 tons burden.
19. Paschal, "Proprietary North Carolina," 32. Kingswell died before he received monetary damages from Vassall. His executors, Robert and Dorothie Wingate, petitioned the Privy Council to secure the judgment on behalf of the Kingswell estate. Wingate had also been a member of the ill-fated voyage to Carolana in 1632.
20. Paschal, "Proprietary North Carolina," 32-39. Maltravers' ownership of the Heath patent presented an obstacle to future settlement efforts a few decades later, when the Lords Proprietors were compelled to petition Charles' heir and successor to vacate the previous title in order to implement their own plans for colonization below Virginia.
21. Grady, "Vomit," 32.
22. Grady, "Vomit," *SCHA*, 37. Spain's settlement at St. Augustine in 1565 was the first European presence in North America.
23. Grady, "Vomit," *SCHA*, 36. Gent feared the Spanish were much closer to Virginia than they actually were, and that it was a certainty that the Spanish King would "no doubt vomit his fury and malice upon the neighbor Plantations, if a prehabitation anticipates not his intention."
24. Daniel W. Fagg, Jr., "Sleep Not with the King's Grant: A Rereading of Some Proprietary Documents," *NCHR*, Vol. XLVIII, No. 2 (April 1971): 172 (hereafter cited as Fagg, "Sleep"); Seaman, "Native American Enslavement," 85. The Spanish governor increased the repartimiento demands in Florida to build stronger fortifications at St. Augustine, although Spain was slow to add strength to its defenses.
25. Fagg, "Sleep," 172. The 1665 Carolina Charter revised the earlier boundaries set in 1663, moving the line two degrees further south, an encroachment well into Spanish territory in Florida.
26. Fagg, "Sleep," *NCHR*, 173. The treaty signed in 1667 addressed only trade issues. The boundary dispute was not settled until three years later. The Lords Proprietors' wager paid off and the line of demarcation between Spanish and English territory was set at the point of effective occupation, just south of Port Royal.
27. Grady, "Vomit," *PSCHA*, 39. The Spanish were cordial with Hilton and his men, even providing them with fresh meat before mediating the dispute over their captured countrymen.
28. Buchanan, "Colleton," 57-58. Edward Bland led a trade expedition to "New Brittaine" in 1650, and explored the mainland between 35° and 37° parallels. Bland's voyage took place not long after Sir John Colleton arrived in Barbados, and may have influenced his thinking regarding the prospects of Carolina as a possible site for settlement.

29. Louise Hall, "New England at Sea: Cape Fear Before the Royal Charter of 24 March 1662/3," *The New England Historical and Genealogical Register*, Vol. 124, No. 2 (April 1970): 90 (hereafter cited as Hall, *New Englanders at Sea*); Suttlemeyre, "Proprietary Policy," 34; John A. Garraty, and Mark C. Carnes, eds., *American National Biography, Volume 10, William Hilton, Jr.* (New York: Oxford University Press, 1999): 331, hereafter cited as Garrity, *American National Biography, Vol. 10*; "Hilton," http://freepages.genealogy.rootsweb.ancestry.com/~mainegenie/HILTON.htm, Ancestry.com (accessed 31 January 2015) (hereafter cited as "Hilton," *Ancestry.com*.) The Hilton's Anglican faith may account for their departure from Plymouth. Difficulties arose over Richard Hilton's baptism by a Puritan minister (the baptism was challenged because the Hiltons were not members of the Puritan church). The elder Hilton sailed for America aboard the *Fortune*. Samuel Vassall was John Vassall's uncle. The Vassalls had trade, religious, and familial connections in New England and Barbados that would have made William Hilton known to them.

30. "Hilton," *Ancestry.com.;* Hall, "New Englanders at Sea," *The New England Historical and Genealogical Register,* 90. Captain Nicholas Shapley (Shapleigh) drew the first map of the Cape Fear based on William Hilton's explorations. Shapley was the Clerk of Writs in Charlestown, Massachusetts.

31. "Hilton," *Ancestry.com.*

32. Kathleen Burk, *Old World, New World: Great Britain and America from the Beginning* (New York: Grove Press, 2009): 70; E. Lawrence Lee, *The History of Brunswick County, North Carolina* (N.p., n.d.): 11-12 (hereafter cited as Lee, *Brunswick County*). Hilton anchored near what he called Indian River (modern Town Creek) on October 4, 1662, and spent three weeks exploring the environs as far as seventy-five miles upriver, to what he thought were the headwaters of the Charles (Cape Fear) River. For a reading of Hilton's findings at Cape Fear, see the appendix in this document.

33. William P. Cumming, "Naming Carolina," http://www.ah.dcr.state.nc.us/sections/hp/colonial/Nchr/Subjects/cumming_htm, accessed 11/17/2010, hereafter cited as Cumming, *Naming Carolina*.

34. Stanley South, "The Unabridged Version of Tribes of the Carolina Lowland: Peedee – Sewee – Winyaw – Waccamaw – Cape Fear – Congaree – Wateree – Santee," Research Manuscript Series, Book 16 (1972): 35 (hereafter cited as South, "Tribes of the Carolina Lowland").

35. Hall, "New Englanders at Sea," *The New England Historical and Genealogical Register,* 92-94. For more detailed information about the men who accompanied Hilton on this first voyage of discovery, and the namesakes of those first landmarks, see the listing in the appendix.

36. Lee, *Lower Cape Fear*, 33; Hall, "New Englanders at Sea," *The New England Historical and Genealogical Register,* 94. Accounts of the New England settle-

ment attempt suggest that as the settlers were about to unload their belongings, a "young man" came aboard Captain Long's ship and went into a conference with the expedition leaders. When they emerged, the settlers had obviously been given bad news, as one of them wrote "wee have nothing to doe but to goe (sic) home." The "young man" could easily have been a messenger sent by Berkeley to warn off the New Englanders, making them aware of the imminent signing of the Carolina Charter by the King and the Lords Proprietors.

37. Suttlemyer, "Proprietary Policy," 27.

38. Suttlemeyre, "Proprietary Policy," 34; Lee, *Lower Cape Fear*, 34. The warning the Puritans left on a tree near the river bar indicated that, if indeed the land belonged to the Lords Proprietors, it would be unsuitable for their needs as a religiously tolerant community that did not discriminate against those who were not Anglican (showing that they had no prior knowledge of the religious freedoms guaranteed in the Lords Proprietors' charter). The Massachusetts Bay Colony differed from the Carolina colony in that the New England endeavor was a private enterprise. The terms of settlement were established between the Puritans and the Massachusetts Bay Company's stockholders and directors. The Carolina venture was to be governed by terms set out by the Lords Proprietors. Accounts of the failed Puritan settlement attempt at Cape Fear can be found in numerous historical works, including those by Lawson, Lee, Sprunt, Hall, and others. See attached bibliography for a list of further reading.

39. Suttlemeyre, "Proprietary Policy," 27.

40. Suttlemeyre, "Proprietary Policy," 27-29, 34. The terms sought by the New Englanders from the Lords Proprietors included a 1000-square-mile territory. The plan was similar to the one put forth by Roger Williams and Samuel Vassall for the Providence, Rhode Island plantations. The Cape Fear proposition was a non-starter. The Lords Proprietors had made it clear from the outset that they intended to keep tight control over settlement in Carolina, and would shape settlement there according to their own ideas.

41. Suttlemeyre, "Proprietary Policy," 28-29. Proprietary intransigence aside, it may also have been the case that the New Englanders may have learned that Peter Colleton, the son of proprietor John Colleton, also proposed to plant colonists at Cape Fear.

By the mid-seventeenth century, Barbados was given over almost entirely to sugar production. That meant all of the other things necessary to support civilization on the island had to come from somewhere else. Because of that, Carolina became a candidate for settlement. The picture above is an aerial view of Drax Plantation on Barbados from 1971.

VI
The Barbadian Adventurers

A Crowded Island

Seventeenth century England witnessed considerable turmoil and restlessness. Large portions of the English poor willingly grabbed any opportunity to escape the bleak prospects they faced at home. Among the gentry, the sons who would not inherit family holdings sought new places where they could build their own estates. Mercantilists looked to the periphery of the empire for new markets. For the lesser sorts – traders, craftsmen, farmers, fishermen, the ditch diggers and menial laborers of the English world – survival was a daily struggle. They too sought a haven and relief from their toils and struggles.

Barbados was just such a place in its infancy, until the arrival of sugar made the price of the island's limited tillable land too costly to own for small and middling planters. Roughly a half million people left England in hopes of better lives elsewhere during the seventeenth century, and 400,000 of those landed in the Americas. Of those, servants outnumbered free emigrants by a margin of almost four to one, and a great many of them ended up on Barbados. By the time King Charles II reclaimed his

English throne in 1660, the population problem on Barbados had reached critical proportions. John Vassall, John Yeamans, and their supporters believed that a colony on the American mainland might solve a number of the most serious economic and social problems confronting the tiny island. To that end, they dispatched William Hilton to again survey the potential of the Cape Fear region as a place to plant a settlement.[1]

Two days after Hilton left Speights Bay on his second scout of the environs at Cape Fear, The Corporation of Barbados Adventurers presented a petition to the Lords Proprietors seeking permission to settle there with the same rights as an English municipal corporation. The corporation tendered its application perhaps knowing that a group of New Englanders also desired approval from the Lords Proprietors for the same piece of real estate. Acting as agents for the group, Sir Thomas Modyford, a former governor of Barbados, and Peter Colleton, the son of Sir John Colleton, forwarded the Barbadians' petition to the lords. It seems likely that the Barbadians may have had prior knowledge of the terms sought by the Puritans from Massachusetts, and adjusted their own proposal to reflect a model more in line with what the lords envisioned for their proprietary.[2]

Sir John Yeamans

The group of influential Barbadians may have given the impression they were speaking with one voice, but that was not the case. While all of the members agreed that Carolina seemed a likely place to sow the seeds of mainland plantations, not everyone agreed on the particulars of such a settlement. John Vassall headed a faction that differed from the group lead by Sir John Yeamans. Both came to the West Indies from somewhere else. Both were wealthy men who made their fortunes in sugar, trade, shipping, and slaves. And both (especially Vassall) were deeply connected to colonization efforts in New England, Barbados, and Carolina.

Benjamin Berringer's Nicholas Plantation in Barbados, where John Yeamans also lived. The estate is now a modern distillery on the island.

The Meteoric Rise of John Yeamans

The man who would become proprietary governor and landgrave of Carolina came into the world of much humbler origins. Born in 1611 in Bristol, England, John Yeamans was the son of a brewer. His first marriage, to a "Miss Limp," provided him with the five sons who would carry on the family name, and three daughters. Yeamans' aspirations took him to Barbados in 1638, where he entered into a partnership with planter Benjamin Berringer, a fellow militia officer.

Yeamans and Berringer set about making their fortunes through land speculation in St. Peter and St. Andrew Parishes, and through the popularity of sugar in Europe. By 1641 they shared the same lodgings at Berringer's Nicholas Plantation in St. Peter Parish. The partnership lasted about seven years, before dissolving in 1648. Yeamans was ready for bigger things.[3]

Barbados offered many opportunities for a man like John Yeamans. He became rich as a successful planter, and as such took advantage of the entrée his purse provided to rub shoulders with the island elites. Yeamans gained a seat on the island's council, and secured a judgeship on the court of common pleas. Sir John Colleton formed a friendship with the ambitious Yeamans that would impact the maneuvering for Carolina later.

In 1661 Yeamans married the widow of his former business partner, Benjamin Berringer. The union of Yeamans and Margaret Foster Berringer increased Yeamans' status and personal wealth, as his bride inherited her deceased husband's estates on Barbados. Before settling the estate, island officials held an inquest to determine the truth of an unsavory rumor regarding Berringer's demise and the role his wife and Yeamans may have played in it.[4]

Berringer and Yeamans jointly owned two plantations as early as 1643, one containing 195 acres, and a second of 170 acres, both in St. Andrew Parish. The deed to the latter plantation listed both men as tenants in common instead of joint tenants. The legal arrangement effectively barred them from inheriting the whole estate in the event of the untimely death of either. Whether he planned it or Fortune merely smiled on him, the property found its way into Yeamans' open hands. According to island lore, Yeamans and Margaret Berringer became enamored with one another. Their attraction created a rift between the two partners that resulted in the dissolution of their business together. Barbadians claimed that as a result, Yeamans began plotting the death of his business and romantic rival.[5]

The cause of Benjamin Berringer's death has been clouded by time and a scarcity of records. By some accounts, Benjamin's anger over Yeamans' romantic overtures to his wife provoked a duel, in which Yeamans fatally wounded his former business partner. Other versions suggest that Yeamans hired someone to poison Berringer. Either way, Berringer died intestate. His estates and property passed to his wife of questionable fidelity. Soon afterward, she tacked on another surname to become Margaret Foster Berringer Yeamans. Yeamans and his new wife managed to persuaded authorities at the inquest that Benjamin Berringer had made a verbal will leaving his estate to his wife. When Margaret accepted John Yeamans' proposal, Berringer's properties became the property of John Yeamans. Yeamans had come a long way from his childhood as a brewer's son in Bristol, but even greater heights awaited thanks to his friendship with John Colleton and his involvement in Carolina.[6]

The Vassalls of Massachusetts, Barbados, and Carolina

The earliest known John Vassall emigrated from Normandy to England in the mid-sixteenth century, although the family has been traced as far back as the eleventh century. He distinguished himself chiefly by

Samuel Vassall outfitted two ships to help defeat the great armada sent by King Philip II of Spain to punish England for Elizabeth's persecution of Catholics in her realm.

outfitting two ships, the *Samuel* and the *Little Toby*, on board which he helped face down the great Spanish Armada in 1588. His courage and support earned him a grant in arms from Queen Elizabeth I. John and his wife, Anna Russell, had three children: Judith, born in 1582; Samuel, born in 1586; and William, born in 1592. The elder brother grew to become a politically connected Member of Parliament for London, serving on a number of influential committees between 1639-1646. He and his younger brother, William, both became influential men, though in different spheres and parts of the world.[7]

Samuel and William Vassall both had ties to the Massachusetts Bay Company. William was the first to sail to the Americas during the great Puritan migration of the 1630s. In the summer of 1635 William and his family, including a young John Vassall, departed England aboard the ship *Blessing* (Jo. Lecester, Master). William was an early patentee of New England lands, and served as an assistant with the company. He took up residence at Scituate, but William proved to be a poor fit with the other residents and consequently left for Barbados in 1648. He died there in 1655, leaving his estate to be split evenly among his three children, including John.[8]

Samuel Vassall remained in England, using London as the base of operations for his mercantile and colonial interests. Under the terms of the

Heath patent, he hoped to plant a colony of French Huguenots in Carolana in 1633. Records indicate that Samuel had experience as a textile worker in Surrey and York, which may help explain his earlier mentioned efforts to sell cloth in Ragusa, Italy[9].

The Kingswell expedition proved to be unsuccessful. Nevertheless, Samuel Vassall took part in several significant colonial and mercantile ventures. He was a signatory to the patent under which Roger Williams secured the incorporation of the Providence plantations that eventually became Rhode Island. He served on the Parliamentary Committee for Trade and Plantations during the years of Cromwell's Interregnum. He also established himself as a trader with Amsterdam, Gibraltar, and Zant. Samuel Vassall's Guinea Company traded slaves from West Africa to planters on Barbados. His son Henry joined him in his mercantile affairs when he came of age.[10]

Roger Williams, founder of the Providence Plantations. Samuel Vassall signed the same patent Williams did creating the colony.

William Vassall's son, John, is the member of the family most closely linked with the colony at Cape Fear. A scan of his family's pedigree, political, and social connections makes it easy to understand how he became intrigued at the possibility of settling a colony at Cape Fear. John Vassall was born in Stepney, Middlesex County, England, and moved to Massachusetts with his father, mother, and siblings in 1635. The family settled at Scituate, and John remained there until selling off his lands and moving to Barbados in 1661. After the failure of the Charles Towne settlement at Cape Fear, John Vassall first traveled to Virginia, where stayed for a time with his sister and her husband, Nicholas Ware. He eventually returned to Barbados, where he was a successful merchant. John also served as an envoy and commissioner at large charged with troubleshooting in the Caribbean, particularly on Jamaica. He died on that island in 1688.[11]

The Vassall family were no strangers to risk taking. That John Vassall would gamble his fortune on the chances of successfully colonizing the wilderness at Cape Fear is not particularly surprising given the history of the family. By 1663, Vassall and his fellow adventurers on Barbados

This is a modern replica of the ketch **Adventure***, sailed by William Hilton, Jr. to explore the territory at Cape Fear where Barbadian settlers would settle soon after.*

were ready to toss the dice again.

Hilton's Second Voyage to Carolina

William Hilton was a vexed man. The abortive attempt at settlement made by the New Englanders just months before, and the disparaging words they consequently spread about the Cape Fear region, cast his reliability as a scout and explorer into doubt. The mariner made for Barbados, where he contracted with John Vassall's group of investors to return to the river and confirm his earlier glowing impressions. The results of his voyage to the Charles River (Cape Fear River) would weigh heavily on the plans of those in Barbados seeking a mainland colony.[12]

The *Adventure* sailed from Speights Bay in the early days of August 1663, caught the trade winds, and tacked north by northwest for the American mainland. Hilton made landfall at Port Royal, where he spent a short time exploring, then continued up the coast to the entrance of the Charles at Cape Fear. It was mid-October by the time the *Adventure* dropped anchor near modern Town Creek, where Hilton remained until early December. This time he was determined to make an exhaustive assessment of the lands and their potential for settlement.[13]

Hilton and his men again traveled up the northeast branch of the river, still mistaking it for the main channel. On this second visit, however, Hilton also ventured a full fifty miles up the northwest branch. As on their previous visit, the Englishmen failed to encounter any Indians on the northeast branch, leading them to suppose none lived there. The northwest branch was another matter. There, Hilton and his men spotted many Indians, including a party of forty warriors. They also revisited the village of Necoes along Town Creek, and Bald Head Island. One disagreeable incident occurred when a lone warrior fired an arrow at the white men as they explored the northwest river passage. Hilton named the place where the attack occurred as Mount Skerry, believed to be in the vicinity of modern Columbus County.[14]

With the exception of the one bow-wielding antagonist, the Cape Fear Indians were as hospitable on Hilton's second visit as they had been on the first. During a parley with the group's warriors and their cassique, Chief Watcoosa, the Englishmen pointed out the arrowhead still embedded in their longboat, evidence of their less than welcoming encounter with the lone warrior at Mount Skerry. According to Hilton's journal, his account of the attack so distressed the Indian leader that in a long speech he assured the visitors that he would see to it the offender was dismembered as punishment. He then gave beads to Hilton and his men as compensation for the affront. The Indians even presented the Englishmen with two maidens to seal their friendship.

The Massachusetts explorer seemed somewhat bemused by the gift of two Indian maidens, who he took to be daughters of Chief Watcoosa. ". . . And for a farther Testimony of their Love and Good-Will towards us, they presented us with two very handsome, proper, young Indian Women," Hilton wrote, "the tallest that ever we saw in this Country; which we suppos'd to be the King's Daughters, or Persons of Distinction amongst them." Hilton apparently had a hard time declining the offer of the two women: ". . . Those young Women were so ready to come into our Boat; that one of them crowded in, and would hardly be persuaded to go out again. We presented the King with a Hatchet and several Beads, and made Presents of Beads also to the young Women, the chief Men, and the rest of the Indians, as far as our Beads would go. They promis'd us, in four Days, to come on board our Ship, and so departed from us." Gifting young women as acts of diplomacy was not unheard of among Native Americans of the early colonial period and later. From the Spanish explorations of

Hernando de Soto, to John Smith's relationship with Pocahontas, to Lewis and Clark's nineteenth-century helpmate Sacagawea, Indian women have a long history of serving as ambassadors helping white men in their interactions with Native Americans.[15]

Hilton's 1663 account of his second exploratory trip to the Cape Fear is much more detailed than the first, no doubt to refute allegations made by the disgruntled New Englanders who had abandoned their settlement there. His report reconfirms his initial findings in all respects, describing ". . . good Tracts of dry, well-wooded, pleasant, and delightful Ground, as we have seen any where in the World, with abundance of long thick Grass on it, the Land being very level, with steep Banks on both Sides the River, and in some Places very high, the Woods stor'd every where, with great Numbers of Deer and Turkies, we never going on Shoar, but we saw of each Sort; as also great Store of Partridges, Cranes, and Conies, in several Places; we like-wise heard several Wolves howling in the Woods, and saw where they had torn a Deer in Pieces. Also in the River we saw great Store of Ducks, Teal, Widgeon; and in the Woods, great Flocks of Parrakeeto's." The explorer's encounters with the local Indians, whom he apparently named the Cape Fears, were also encouraging. Hilton again proffered payment to King Watcoosa and "bought" 1,000 acres of land from them for the Barbadians. The *Adventure* weighed anchor soon afterward and returned to Barbados, arriving in early January 1664. As Hilton's longboat pulled for shore, an eager contingent of would-be colonists awaited him.[16]

Endnotes

1. Grady, "On the Path to Slavery," *PSCHA*, 7-8. The planters who would become Adventurers in the Carolina venture each invested 1,000 pounds of sugar for every 500 acres granted by the Lords Proprietors.
2. Suttlemeyre, "Proprietary Policy," 29-30. The Barbadians proposed planting a colony that would operate in a manner modeled after the City of Exeter. Rather than having a governor, council, and judiciary, the colony would function as a civil subdivision. Such a structure would keep ownership and control of the Cape Fear settlement firmly in the hands of the Lords Proprietors.
3. "Owner's History," *St. Nicholas Abbey*, http://www.stnicholasabbey.com/Learn/Owners-History, accessed 15 January 2013; E.M. Shilstone, "Nicholas Plantation and Some of Its Associations," in *Chapters in Barbados History*, Peter F. Campbell, editor (Bridgeport: Barbados Museum and Historical Society,

1986): 120-124 (hereafter cited as Shilstone, *Nicholas Plantation*). When John Yeamans eventually bought his own plantation on Barbados adjoining Berringer's, disputes about where the property lines fell created discord between the two men. Berringer's parcel, plus Yeamans' Greenland plantation, encompassed more than 365 acres – quite a large amount of acreage on such a small island. Other accounts speculate that Yeamans' alleged affections for Berringer's wife created the rift between the two men.

4. Lindley S. Butler and Herbert R. Paschal, "Yeamans, Sir John," *NCpedia*, http://ncpedia.org, 1996, accessed 1/15/2013. Apparently Miss Limp had passed away by the time Yeamans emigrated to Barbados.

5. Shilstone, "Nicholas Plantation," 120-121. Berringer returned to England on business in 1656, creating an opening for Yeamans to woo Margaret.

6. Shilstone, "Nicholas Plantation," 121-122. Militia Sergeant Major John Hawkesworth's testimony confirmed the claim of a verbal will and its terms.

7. Charles Maclear Calder, *John Vassall and his Descendants*, n.p., 1921 (reprint): 5-9 (hereafter cited as Calder, *John Vassall*).

8. Calder, *John Vassall,* 7-8. Reasons for William Vassall's departure from Scituate include the baptism of his son, Richard, by a Puritan minister without the Vassall family being a member of the church. Another account says William was asked to leave for "trying to expand the franchise," though no further details are presented as to what exactly that means.

9. Calder, *John Vassall,* 7.

10. Suttlemyre, "Proprietary Policy," 32-33. Henry Vassall was John Vassall's cousin, and acted as his agent in dealings with the Lords Proprietors regarding the Charles Towne settlement.

11. Calder, *John Vassall,* 8-9. John Vassall inherited 1,000 acres near the mouth of Jamaica's Black River on Luna Bay sometime after the end of his Carolina colony. For the remainder of his life, John Vassall was a successful merchant in the carrying trade, shipping goods between the Caribbean, the North American mainland, and Europe.

12. Buchanan, "Colleton," 65. Unknown to Hilton, Sir Thomas Modyford and Peter Colleton (the son of Lords Proprietor Sir John Colleton) had been given proprietary authority to act on whatever information Hilton's new report revealed.

13. Lee, *Brunswick County*, 14. Hilton crossed the bar at Old Inlet on October 16, 1663, six days after leaving Barbados.

14. Lee, *Brunswick County,* 12-13. The Englishmen tracked the Indian back to a hut where they assumed he lived. They destroyed it in retaliation and as a warning to other like-minded Indians to remain friendly.

15. William Hilton, Jr., "William Hilton Explores the Cape Fear River (1663)," *Learn NC*, published 2008, accessed 12/6/09, http://www.learnnc.org/lp/editions/nchist-colonial/1899; Clara Sue Kidwell, "Indian Women as Cultural Mediators,"

Ethnohistory, Vol. 39, No. 2 (Spring 1992): 97-107.
16. See Hilton's account of his second voyage and exploration of Cape Fear in 1663 in Appendix IV.

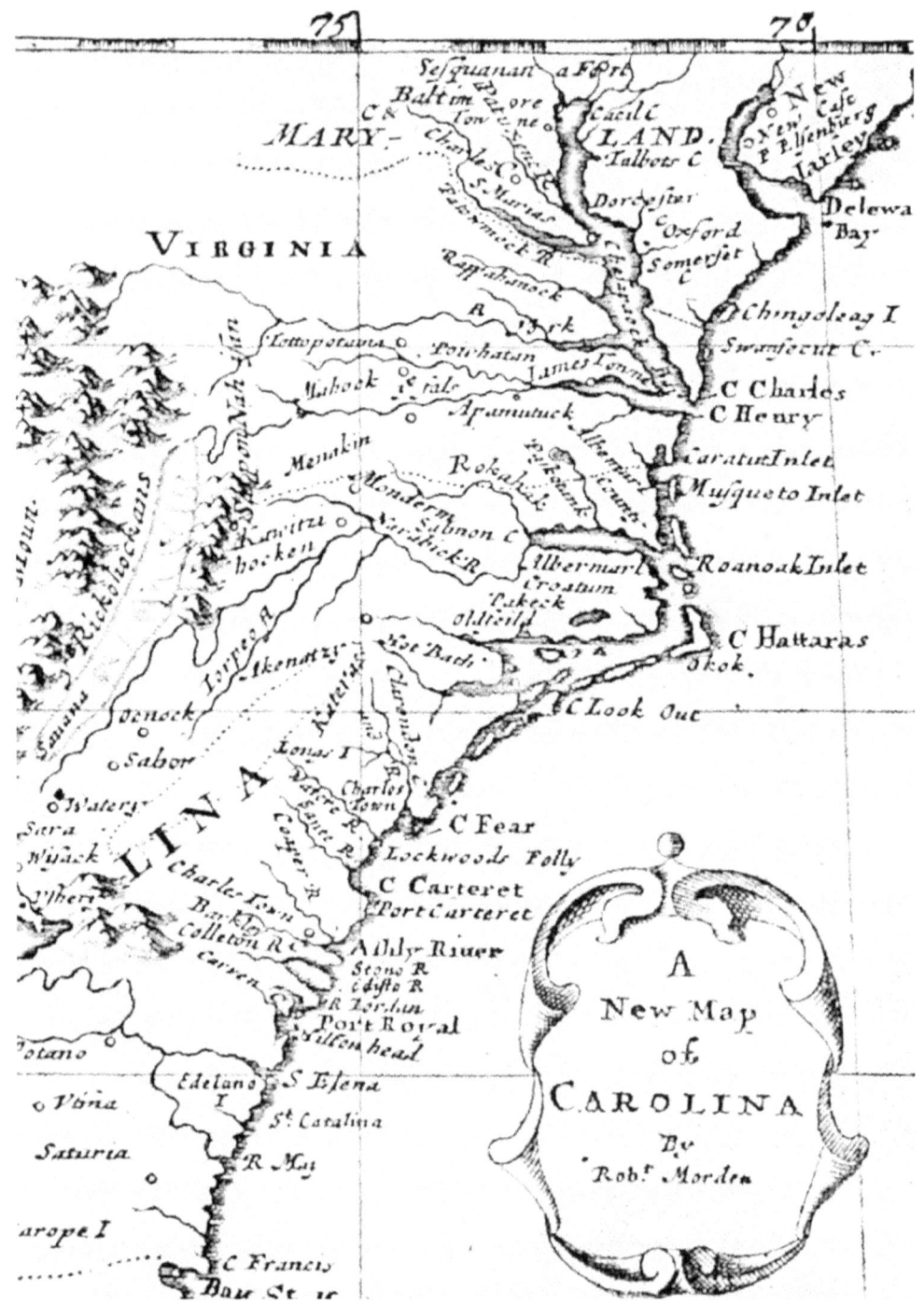

Robert Morden's map of Carolina showing Cape Fear, where the Vassall settlement was established, and Port Royal, the site fvored by the Yeamans group.

VII
On the Cape Fear

Competing Colonial Corporations

The Barbadians who received Hilton's report on the suitability of the Cape Fear region for settlement were not all of like mind. The source of the rift between the two groups, headed by John Vassall and John Yeamans respectively, is unknown, but likely stemmed from the desire of the Vassall faction to settle at Cape Fear, versus the Yeamans group's willingness to beard the Spanish by planting a colony nearer to Florida. The Vassall group, whose ranks were more heavily laden with Puritans, likely preferred the safety that Cape Fear's proximity to Jamestown and distance from St. Augustine afforded. Another source of friction may have been rooted in the Vassall faction's desire for a corporate style of government, as opposed to the preferred City of Exeter subdivision model suggested to the Lords Proprietors by the Yeamans group. Whatever the cause of the differences of opinion, the two groups split and followed their own paths to obtaining the blessings of the eight lords in London who were key to any Carolina enterprise.[1]

Vassall entered into an agreement brokered by Sir Thomas Modyford and Peter Colleton that essentially replicated all of the salient points of the Declaration and Proposals, except that it specifically exempted the payment of quitrents, and the governor and council were to regulate the manner of taking them up once again at a later date. In entering into the agreement, Modyford and Colleton exceeded their brief from the Lords Proprietors. This overstep created difficulties later for the Vassall colonists at Charles Towne. That done, John Vassall contracted with William Hilton to provide transportation for his group of settlers to the Cape Fear, where they were joined not long after by a contingent of Puritans from New England.

Vassall and his colonists landed at Cape Fear on May 29, 1664. By November, the group had established a central compound that functioned as the company's headquarters just north of modern Town Creek. Three months after setting down at Cape Fear, Vassall dispatched his cousin, Henry Vassall, to London to present the group's petition to the Lords Proprietors as a fait accompli. Vassall based his belief on the understanding that Thomas Modyford and Peter Colleton were authorized to act on the Lords Proprietors' behalf. A "Mr. Sampson" (actually Robert Sandford, or Sanford, depending on which text you read), accompanied Henry, and they managed to meet at least once with the Lords Proprietors to discuss settlement plans for the Cape Fear. Enough encouragement was proffered to

John Yeamans' group sailed for Port Royal aboard a flyboat like the one in this model of a Dutch version of the ships. They were usually between 150 - 200 tons, and served both mercantile and military roles.

Vassall and Sandford that the two men came away from a dinner meeting with the impression that their petition had met with the Lords' approval, although nothing was put in writing beyond the already published Declaration and Proposals.[2]

The Yeamans group embarked on their voyage of settlement the following year, leaving Barbados in October 1665 with a flotilla consisting of the 150-ton flyboat *Sir John*, a small frigate owned by Yeamans, and a sloop purchased for the trip by his Barbadian backers. A violent storm drove them off course, sending them north of their intended landfall at Port Royal. Instead, they reached Cape Fear at the end of the year and joined John Vassall's colonists at Charles Towne. It had not been a smooth crossing. While the three ships weathered the storm that turned Yeamans' flotilla away from Cape Romain, the flyboat *Sir John* wrecked as it attempted to cross the bar at the mouth of the Cape Fear River. Going down with her were badly needed supplies that could have made the difference in the fate of Charles Towne. Yeamans dispatched a ship bound for Virginia to obtain replacement supplies, but it foundered off Cape Hatteras on the return trip. Yeamans' stay at Charles Towne was short (mercifully so, in the opinions of some of the Vassall settlers), as he returned to Barbados in January 1666. The colonists he left behind at Charles Towne believed that the new governor had abandoned them to their fate. It was a pattern he would repeat some years later at Port Royal.[3]

Yeamans' unpopularity with the Vassall group was understandable, as he had arrived at Charles Towne without advance notice. Robert Sandford was not far behind, bearing commissions naming himself secretary for Clarendon County, Yeamans as governor, and for John Vassall as deputy-governor and surveyor-general. No one in the first wave of settlers expected this turn of events, least of all John Vassall. It soon became clear that Yeamans' priorities centered on his proposed colony at Port Royal. The settlement at Cape Fear was a secondary concern at best. Yeamans seemingly enjoyed wielding his authority, and presented an additional burden to people trying to carve out a life for themselves in the secluded Carolina wilderness. Perhaps most of all, Yeamans brought with him terms of settlement radically different from those agreed to by the settlers at the Cape Fear. Many settlers of the Vassall group wondered how they had been undermined.[4]

Yeamans, the Lords Proprietors, and the Art of Political Maneuver

When Henry Vassall sailed for London with his cousin's proposal for a settlement, representatives for John Yeamans' group also headed to England to pitch a colony in Carolina to the Lords Proprietors. The schism between the Barbadians had not dampened the enthusiasm of the faction lead by Yeamans. Nor did the fact that Vassall had already departed for the mainland curb the ambitions of his former partners. Yeamans dispatched his own envoy, his son William, to the Lords Proprietors with a proposal of his own for settlement in Carolina.[5]

The Yeamans plan called for a settlement at Port Royal near Cape Romain, but also closer to Spanish Florida than the proposed colony at Cape Fear. The Lords Proprietors preferred a site further to the south for geopolitical reasons, as England and Spain had competing claims to the lands between St. Augustine and the Chesapeake Bay. When William Yeamans, a major in the Barbados militia, spoke on behalf of his father's interests, it undermined the efforts of Henry Vassall and the group at Charles Towne he represented.[6]

The Lords Proprietors realized that the competing factions jockeying for the right to colonize Carolina below Albemarle, and their own inconsistency regarding terms and concessions, had resulted in a muddled

This illustration from an 1890s history book depicts the Yeamans group of settlers landing in what would eventually become South Carolina.

and confusing state of affairs that could hamper efforts to recruit settlers. They found the proposal made by William Yeamans at his father's request advantageously appealing. Nevertheless, the Lords Proprietors set about revamping their policy for Carolina not long after Robert Sandford departed England for Charles Towne. The 1665 Concessions and Agreement between the proprietors and the Yeamans faction was the result of those changes. In it they sought to establish a comprehensive proprietary government that would satisfy all the interested parties and still feature all of the components the Lords Proprietors thought necessary for a successful colony. They also determined to craft a document emphasizing settlement in the southern regions of their grant. With no binding, written agreement between themselves and the Vassall colonists, they enjoyed a free hand to make such changes as they saw fit. The first settlers at Cape Fear possessed little recourse to stop them.[7]

That had not always been the case. Only months earlier, eager to see settlement in Carolina get underway, the Lords Proprietors offered generous colonization terms. Based on communications with the Barbadians, the Lords Proprietors issued the Declaration and Proposals for the settlement of Carolina at Cape Fear that would affect the Vassall colonists. The Lords Proprietors recognized the desire of the Barbadians to settle at Cape Fear, and stipulated only that they should occupy the "larboard," or west, side of the river.[8]

After setting aside 20,000 acres for their own use, the Lords Proprietors provided for the colony's security, tax exemptions on certain imports, the selection of a proprietary governor and council, and the establishment of quitrents (to be paid at the rate of a half-penny per acre). Those provisions notwithstanding, a headright system for land allotment was the centerpiece of the terms. The Lords would grant 100 acres to every male freeholder who settled at Cape Fear. Servants and freewomen also received grants of 100 acres. Fifty acres was allotted for lesser and "weaker" servants (including slaves and children over age fourteen), provided that the freeholder made sure there was a man armed with a musket, shot, and powder for each fifty-acre plot granted. Another fifty acres was allowed for freeholders who brought indentured servants in order to provide them with land of their own when their contracts were fulfilled. Nowhere in the document did the Lords Proprietors insist that parcels be adjoining. The Lords Proprietors issued their Declaration and Proposals on August 25, 1663. Under the auspices of this document, John Vassall and his group set sail for Carolina.

The Lords Proporietors released their Declaration and Proposals to London propagandists, who began spreading the word of Carolina to potential colonists in England and the West Indies. Their reports were glowing. One such missive issued in 1666 aimed to attract persons of gentility. "Is there any younger Brother who is born of Gentile blood, and whose spirit is elevated above the common sort," it beckoned, "and yet the hard uasage of our Country hath not allowed suitable fortune; he will not surely be afraid to leave his Native Soil to advance his Fortunes equal to his Blood and Spirit, and so he will avoid those unlawful ways too many of our young Gentlemen take to maintain themselves according to their higher education, having but small Estates; here, with a few Servants and a small Stock a great Estate may be raised, although his Birth have not entitled him to any of the Land of his Ancestors, yet his Industry may supply him so, as to make him the head of as famous a family."

The pamphlet also addressed the lower classes that might find in Carolina a means to better their station with a little hard work and initiative.

"Such as are here tormented with much care how to get worth to gain a Livelyhood, or that with their labour can hardly get a comfortable subsistence, shall do well to go to this place," the proprietors promised, "where any man what-ever, that is but willing to take moderate pains, may be assured of a most comfortable subsistence, and be in a way to raise his fortunes far beyond what he could ever hope for in England. Let no man be troubled at the thought of being a servant for 4 or 5 year, for I can assure you, than many men give mony with their children to serve 7 years, to take more pains and fare nothing so well as the Servants in this Plantation do. Hence it is to be considered, that so soon as he is out of his time, he hath Land and Tools, and Clothes given him, and is in a way of advancement. Therefore, all Artificers, as Carpenters, Wheel-rights, Joyners, Coopers, Bricklayers, Smiths, or diligent Husbandmen and Labourers, that are willing to advance their fortunes, and live in a most pleasant healthful and fruitful Country, where Artificers are of high esteem, and used with all Civility and Courtesie imaginable."

The Concessions and Agreement also encouraged women, always in short supply in the colonies, to accompany their menfolk or hire on as indentured servants themselves. Their presence would naturally increase the colony's numbers. "If any Maid or single Woman have a desire to go over," the pamphlet assured, "they will think themselves in the Golden Age, when Men paid a Dowry for their Wives; for if they be but Civil, and under 50 years of Age, some honest Man or other, will purchase them for their Wives."[9]

Despite the Lords Proprietors' best efforts put into the Concessions and Agreement, it did not find much favor among the colonists themselves. The Vassall faction was perhaps the most aggrieved, as the document superseded their own terms of settlement set out in the earlier Declaration and Proposals. Other colonists and potential colonists also found the Concessions and Agreement disagreeable, too. For example, land was accordingly distributed via a lottery system. The proprietors set aside land for towns, with the balance divided into lots ranging in size from 2,200 to 22,000 acres. Development plans called for each of these to be subdivided into eleven equal parcels. The Lords Proprietors would retain one plot in each parcel. They would grant the remaining properties to colonists based on their draw in the lottery, depending on when they arrived in Carolina. Land grants would be contiguous, and each parcel had to be filled up before settlement would be allowed in the next parcel. They also limited frontage along the waterways to prevent anyone from monopolizing direct access to the vital rivers and creeks. In prescribing this method, the Lords Proprietors hoped to insure compact communities such as those found in New England.[10]

John Locke

The Concessions and Agreement's terms also favored settlement further south. Settlers who planted at Cape Fear received a more generous land allotment than those who opted to settle in the Albemarle. Colonists who chose to join the Yeamans colony at Port Royal would be awarded more land than Cape Fear settlers. Not only were the Charles Towne settlers upset at this development, but the colonists already established in the Albemarle were also angered by it. By 1669, the Lords Proprietors again changed their conditions for settlement, this time in favor of the famous Fundamental Constitutions of Carolina penned by John Locke.

John Vassall and his group of original settlers had no choice but to accede to the authority that Yeamans' commission as governor granted him, and try to make the best of the situation. Yeamans' relationship with Sir John Colleton likely made him privy to information denied to John Vassall, and allowed him to craft his proposition to the Lords accordingly. Hence they viewed Yeamans' plan to settle at Port Royal instead of at Cape Fear more favorably than Vassall's plan. The revamping of settlement terms for Carolina, from those established in 1663's Declaration and Proposals to those of the Concessions and Agreement of two years later, essentially undercut those who settled at Charles Towne. Despite gathering omens that all was not well at Cape Fear, the combined Vassall and Yeamans groups set about establishing the first Charles Towne in Carolina.[11]

On the Ground at Charles Towne

John Vassall first saw the Charles River (today's Cape Fear River) on May 29, 1664. Cape Fear, with shoals that stretched southeasterly for eighteen miles into the Atlantic, may initially have seemed forbidding, but once over the bar the colonists delighted in the rich flora and fauna on both sides of the river. It certainly was an isolated place. The nearest Englishmen, few as they were, resided far away to the north in Albemarle. To the south, the Proprietors had created Craven County (where the Port Royal settlement would be located some years later), but at the time only Indians inhabited the area. Even further south, the Spanish kept a wary eye on English movements from their outpost at St. Augustine.[12]

The Charles Towne settlement differed from most English colonies of the period. The favored method of colonization in the seventeenth century centered on the establishment of a compact central town or urban center, in which settlers could find mutual support against external threats. Usually the English would create one, two, or three such towns, depending on the size of the colony's coastline. Those small enclaves would sometimes struggle for years before finding a staple product that would generate an income for them. At Charles Towne, while the Vassall party established a central compound for trade and defensive purposes, no town ever evolved. Settlers instead spread up and down the Cape Fear River and its creeks and tributaries to stake out their plantations. While the long leaf pine would later become the backbone of a robust naval stores industry, it played a much smaller role at the time of the Vassall colony. Still, the

An aerial view of the Charles Towne site just north of the mouth of Town Creek. The white area along the Cape Fear River in the picture is tilled fields where the settlement's compound was located. With as many as 800 people comprising the Charles Towne settlement at its peak, the Vassall group spread up the rivers and creeks to stake a claim and homestead. Today the property where the compound was located is privately owned by the Hugh MacRae family of Wilmington. No settlement remains are visible today, as archaeologists covered their excavations up again to protect the integrity of the site.

colonists eventually created several revenue streams from the surrounding natural bounty.[13]

Seventeenth-century Englishmen saw towns in different lights. For Puritans, the town was the hub of a self-sufficient, organic, social corporation. For others they served as a marketing nexus between European (or in the case of Charles Towne, Barbadian) markets and colonial production areas. As such, towns were considered crucial for a successful colony. The Lords Proprietors put the thinking of English colonizers very succinctly: "We must assure you that it is your and our concern very much to have some good towns in your plantations for otherwise you will not long continue civilized or even be considerable or secure, there being no place in the world either of these without them." Colonization followed a monopolist model, channeling capital and colonists into a single, centrally located port town. This allowed investors to avoid the redundancies and resource inefficiencies of a scattershot approach with multiple settlements competing for finite support. Concentrating settlers in a few well-planned sites in North America kept colonization efforts organized and manageable.[14]

Colonists also became environmental agents. As Englishmen inhabited the wildernesses of North America, they both developed and destroyed the natural resources they discovered. Swamps became fields for planting. Forests were cleared for settlements. Flora and fauna were adapted to the needs of the newcomers whose requirements differed vastly from those of the Indians, who both sustained and renewed the ecosystem. English settlers tried to transplant Old World practices to the new land, as it was crucial to their goals. They believed the land must be reclaimed from Mother Nature, and fallow lands turned productive in order to be successful. Productive lands turned settlers into stakeholders in a colony's success. Landowners could secure their family's survival and turn their holdings into something that created valuable goods for transatlantic markets in Barbados and England. The Barbadian Englishmen who settled at Charles Towne, while opting not to build a compact, tightly knit municipal unit, shared these other traits with their fellow English colonists.[15]

Vassall and his colonists wasted no time in relieving the land of its "burthens," turning the plentiful long leaf pines along the river into marketable commodities. Trees became the first real staples in Carolina, as a source of tar, pitch, and turpentine. Naval stores were vital to a maritime power. Hardwood trees – oaks, cypress, and cedar –provided planks for building, spars and masts for shipping, and shingles for rooftops. Coming

Naval stores derived from the abundant long leaf pine trees of coastal North Carolina were Carolina's first staple product, and would remain so until the advent of steam made sailing ships obsolete. This turpentine distilling operation from the 1880s was typical of the industry.

from Barbados, the Vassall settlers were well aware of the value of the Carolina woodlands as a source of food, fuel, and building materials, especially in the West Indies where all three were in short supply.

Settlers felled the largest trees in the surrounding swamps and pocosins for planks "of the lasting kind" preferred in home construction. The first byproducts of their field clearing efforts were used by the settlers themselves to build their own homes, but any excess was sold as a trade product. Carpenters favored watertight cypress for shingles. Cabinetmakers also valued cedar for its fine wood grain. Coopers sought out the plentiful white oak for barrel staves. There seemed to be an unlimited supply of wood in the pristine forests on both sides of the Cape Fear River's tannin-laden waters.[16]

The Charles Towne residents favored land along creeks and rivers above all other, as in a virgin wilderness the waterways provided the only means of transportation for both people and material. Tracts with "good Oake Land" were both desirable and scarce. They existed only in scattered clusters among the ubiquitous long leaf pines. Everyone – white and black – spent long days during that first summer felling trees, clearing fields, sleeping under the stars or beneath shelter halves that did nothing to protect them from gnats and mosquitoes, until they could erect "good Houses." Charles Towne farmers planted potatoes, tobacco, corn, indigo, cotton-wool, and a variety of fruits, as well as other plants brought with them from their places of origin. Within two years modest but sturdy wooden dwellings dotted the landscape for as many as sixty miles up and down the Cape Fear River and its tributaries. The colonists, their numbers bolstered by a contingent of New England Puritans who again ventured south from Massachusetts, reportedly numbered as many as 800 people according to one promotional pamphlet distributed in London.[17]

In addition to food harvested from the ground and gathered from surrounding waters, deer, turkey, cattle, and hogs supplemented the settlers' diets. The Indians had gladly taken ownership of the livestock released by the aborted Puritan settlement of 1663, but the Barbadians undoubtedly brought their own when they set sail for Cape Fear. The livestock – both Indian and English – was allowed to range free in the forests, with only temporary holding pens erected to keep them close at hand for slaughter, salting, and shipping to markets in the Caribbean.

Open range cattle herding was rooted in the practices of the sixteenth-century highlands of the British Isles, Andalusian Spain, and the sub-Saharan steppes of West Africa. Early settlers adopted Old World methods in the Caribbean, beginning with Columbus in 1492, to evolve into the distinctive Antillean systems seen on Barbados and elsewhere. The Charles Towne residents transplanted that system of herd management to the Cape Fear upon their arrival in 1664. The cattle were likely a mix of breeds, imported Barbadian steers mating with abandoned leftovers from the New England settlement. Herders called their ranches "cow pens," but also raised pigs in "crawls" on grasslands near the river. Feral cattle ranged untended, until gathered in a spring roundup for branding and castration, with the calves kept over the summer in pickets woven with vines to protect them from predators, and to lure their mothers in for milking. The settlers gathered the manure from the livestock to use as fertilizer.[18]

The people who settled at the Cape Fear were not neophytes, unused to the climate they found in Carolina. That was certainly true of the slaves who accompanied their owners from Barbados, the slave capital of the western world. While clothing styles followed current English trends, concessions were made as to the materials they were constructed from. Lightweight cotton, linen, and canvas replaced wool for wear during the warm months. If women were part of the colony, what they wore at

The settlers at Cape Fear would have dressed much as these historical re-enactors from Charleston's Charles Town Landing historic site, in a mix of styles representing working class and upper class Englishmen.

Charles Towne likely would have dispensed with at least some of the undergarments they might have worn in cooler climes. Slaves would have dressed much as they did back on Barbados, and there often did not seem to be much difference in station between whites, blacks, and their Native American neighbors as far as fashion or labor in the fields. It was not the heat that surprised the English settlers, but the often bitter cold in Carolina that was such a contrast to hot temperatures during the summer.[19]

    The people who came to Cape Fear – records seem to indicate they were all, or at least mostly, men – were not all poor farmers, craftsmen, and bondsmen. A number of prominent Barbadians also comprised the group. While the Vassall group boasted far fewer names of note among them, the Yeamans group that joined them at Charles Towne in 1665 contained members of the gentry in Barbados. In 1673, Peter Colleton identified ten men of Yeamans' group as prominent planters from Barbados, including three officers from St. Michael's Church. Eight had served in the Barbados assembly by 1665, and nine more served in that body after the Charles Towne settlement collapsed. Both Edward Reade and Sir John Yeamans counted themselves members of the Barbados council. William

Sharpe, Simon Lambert, and John Gibbes were also each nominated to that body. The judiciary was also well represented among those with a stake in Charles Towne. Robert Hacket and Thomas Lake served as assistant judges in Barbados, and Yeamans a judge in the court of common pleas.[20]

A goodly number of those involved either as backers or settlers at the Cape Fear came from old, established families on Barbados. A survey of the surnames of the men who signed on as members of the two companies of adventurers in 1664 and 1665, reveal that forty of ninety-four match those of families who settled in Barbados before 1642. Eleven more were either members of the Barbados assembly or council, or among the most prominent planters on the island, according to Peter Colleton. Most came from the Barbados parishes of St. Peter, St. Andrew, St. Lucy, St. Joseph, and St. James. They were neighbors and fellow congregants, people close enough to one another to witness each other's wills. [21]

Other than Vassall and, for a short time, Yeamans, no one knows how many if any of these distinguished men chose to accompany the expeditions to the Cape Fear and plant at Charles Towne. But the very fact of their involvement speaks to conditions on Barbados at the time. Overpopulation and depressed sugar prices had left them frustrated, although far from impoverished. In most cases the reason they had braved the hard-

Settlers dressed for work in a Carolina environment with weather that varied wildly.

ships of life in the tropics to begin with was to make money. They pursued this goal to the exclusion of virtually all else. During a period of economic stagnation on Barbados, the appeal of a new revenue stream from colonization of the mainland was enticing.[22]

And Carolina was appealing. William Hilton's descriptions painted the picture of a place ripe for trade, commerce, and profit. Carolina offered things Barbados lacked. Its fields could supply the provender to feed the island's elites and chattels alike. Its forests would provide a steady stream of lumber with which to build and repair homes, outbuildings, and windmills for the processing of sugar. Pipe staves crafted from Carolina trees would channel fresh water to thirsty cane fields and plantations removed from accessible sources of irrigation. The long leaf pine's tar and pitch would seal sugar barrels and the seams of the ships that carried them to market. Livestock raised in Charles Towne's benign climate needed neither winter shelter nor fodder, given that they were allowed to range free and forage in the surrounding forests. Being closer to the Caribbean than New England suppliers, the items produced in Carolina could be purchased for considerably less than what northern merchants charged. The advantages of settling at Cape Fear were impressive. It is little wonder that Barbadian movers and shakers reacted enthusiastically to the notion of an expedition to colonize there. But Carolina was not Barbados, and to survive the English would need the cooperation of their Native American neighbors.[23]

The Cape Fear Indians

Vassall's colony began their adventure on good terms with those Native American neighbors, the Cape Fear Indians. William Hilton had noted the village of Necoes on the opposite side of the Indian River (modern Town Creek) from Charles Towne's compound to the north. When the English first arrived in Carolina they identified thirty Indian nation groups, ranging in size from just a few to a few hundred. They spoke different languages, but all of the dialects derived from one of three root linguistic groups – Algonquian, Siouan, or Iroquoian. The Cape Fear Indian's language was Siouan.[24]

The Siouan speaking groups of North Carolina resided on a swath of territory from the Cape Fear River Valley in the Piedmont to the coast, in between lands occupied by both the Tuscarora and Cherokee. Prehistor-

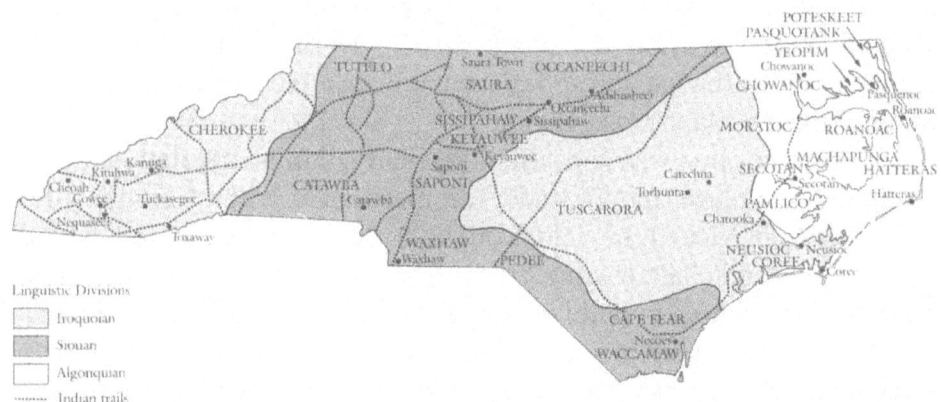

The territories and linguistic groupings of North Carolina's Native American tribes.

ic remains found in northeastern South Carolina and the Cape Fear suggest that they lived in a region outside the main area of Mississippian cultural characteristics. Historical documents pertaining to the area seem to support this, as Indian groups in the region seem to have possessed fewer chiefdom traits than among those of the Piedmont.[25]

The Charles Towne colonists were not the first to make contact with local groups. Verrazano encountered them when he made landfall along the Cape Fear in 1524. If De Ayllon's cavalry explored the region two years later as some historians believe, they doubtlessly came into contact with the Native Americans who inhabited the area. William Hilton interacted with the Cape Fear Indians along the Cape Fear River during his voyages to the region, including only weeks before the Barbadians arrived to claim Cape Fear as their own (Hilton described them as "very poor and silly [simple] creatures").[26]

Hilton saw Indian dwellings at Port Royal that matched descriptions left by Oviedo. The master of the *Adventure* described a structure there as a "great house" of no small dimensions: "That which we noted there, was a fair house built in the shape of a Dove-house, round, two hundred foot at least, completely covered with Palmeta-leaves, the wal-plate being twelve foot high, or thereabouts, and within lodging Rooms and forms; two pillars at the entrance of a high Seat above all the rest." Hilton never mentioned such structures in relation to the Cape Fear Indians. The only Indian shelter he described at all was the one he tore down in retribution for being shot at by the lone Indian bowman at Mount Skerry during his voyage to the Cape Fear in the autumn of 1663.[27]

The Cape Fears greeted the Barbadians warmly. When Hilton made his second exploration of the area in 1663, the locals made sure the crew of the *Adventure* were well stocked with mullet, bass, shad, and other fish. The Indians subsisted by seasonal hunting and gathering, along with agriculture. The explorers discovered that the Cape Fears gathered large quantities of acorns and grew fields of corn with stalks as large as any they had seen anywhere. They practiced animal husbandry using the livestock left behind by the Puritans. Any surpluses they accumulated were stored for leaner times. The English settlers came to depend on the Indians to supplement their own provender, sometimes to the point of depleting the Native Americans' own resources. But at Cape Fear the Indians willingly shared their food (at least at first), eager to show friendship with the strangers who began settling along the tributaries of the river.[28]

As English settlement spread in later years, the Cape Fear nation earned a reputation as "the most barbarous of any in the province," due to their treatment of shipwreck survivors along the coast. This persisted until they submitted to South Carolina authority in 1690. The Vassall settlement may also have encountered that fierceness as relations between the English and Indians soured.[29]

Endnotes

1. Fagg, "Carolina: 1663-1683," 92; Fagg, "Sleep," *NCHR*, 176. The agreement between Vassall and Sir Thomas Modyford and Henry Vassall was that the group would find a place to land south of "Cape St. Romana," but for security reasons the Barbadians opted for Cape Fear. Whether or not Modyford and Henry Vassall knew of the change in plans before they sailed for England to petition the Lords Proprietors is unclear. Another factor muddying the water is the fact that Hilton had renamed the region from Cape San Romano to Cape Fear on his third trip there. Whether Modyford, Vassall, or the Lords Proprietors were all talking about the same place at the early stage of negotiations may be something worthy of conjecture.
2. Fagg, "Carolina: 1663-1683," 75; Suttlemyre, "Proprietary Policy," 35; Buchanan, "Colleton," 71; Fagg, "Sleep," *NCHR*, 177-178. In August 1664, the Lords Proprietors' account book notes that the Lords Proprietors paid £1/4 ". . . for a diner, at a meeting with Mr. Sampson (Sandford) and Mr. Vassall about a treaty with them Concerning Carolina." The twenty-eight articles listed in the agreement signed between Vassall, Modyford, and Colleton later appeared in the 1664 pamphlet published by Modyford and Colleton, describing the two as representatives "who are empowered by the Lords Proprietors to treat on their behalf

. . ." As for John Vassall's speed in mounting his expedition, it would come back to haunt him when Yeamans' proposal received the blessings of the Lords Proprietors instead of his own.

3. Suttlemyre, "Proprietary Policy," 37. When the *Sir John* sank, it took with it cannons, a magazine of muskets and gunpowder, and equipment for the colony sent by Sir John Colleton. Whether he did so on behalf of the Lords Proprietors or by his own initiative is unclear. For a facsimile of the lone surviving account book of the Lords Proprietors that has an inventory of the materials sent to Carolina, see Appendix VI.

4. Buchanan, "Colleton," 71-72. The Vassall settlers were not even sure if Yeamans' commission applied to them or just the proposed settlement at Port Royal. The new terms of settlement laid down by the Lords Proprietors in the 1665 Charter and Agreement created two differing sets of land acquisition and allotment at Cape Fear, with the Vassall settlers operating under the terms of the earlier Declaration and Proposals, and the Yeamans group assigning land according to the latest system from the Lords Proprietors.

5. Fagg, "Carolina 1663-1683," 77. Henry Vassall dubbed the Yeamans' proposal the "Contrary articles," but their actual title was "Concessions and Agreement between the Lords Proprietors and Major William Yeamans." Dated January 7, 1665, the original document resides in the Shaftesbury Papers. See Appendix II.

6. Fagg, "Carolina 1663-1683," 77. Sir John Yeamans may have obtained inside information that helped him craft a favorable proposal for a Carolina colony as a result of his friendship with Sir John Colleton. Colleton would have been privy to the thinking of the Lords Proprietors, inasmuch as he was one of them. The proposed placement of the Yeamans group at Port Royal, for instance, may have stemmed from a tip from Colleton that the Lords Proprietors were eager to see a colony placed where it would push back the Spanish border as much as possible.

7. Fagg, "Sleep," *NCHR*, 178.

8. "A Declaration and Proposals of the Lords Proprietors of Carolina (1663)," *LearnNC.org*, accessed 8/14/2013, http://www.learnnc.org/lp/editions/nchist-colonial/1666, hereafter cited as "Declaration and Proposals." Instructions to the colonists to occupy only the west bank of the Cape Fear River may have been intended to establish a dividing line between the new Clarendon County of Vassall's group and the already well established Albemarle County to the north.

9. Lee, *Lower Cape Fear*, 42-43.

10. Lee, *Brunswick County*, 17-18.

11. Lee, *Lower Cape Fear*, 43. Henry Vassall blamed the Yeamans group for the failure of the Vassall settlement, accusing them of having intercepted Vassall's offer to the Lords Proprietors and making their own offer more attractive.

12. Lee, *Lower Cape Fear*, 41-53.

13. Carville V. Earle, "The First English Towns in North America," *Geographical Review*, Vol. 67, No. 1 (January 1977): 35-36 (hereafter cited as Earle, "English

Towns"). Charles Towne went against the norm for English settlements on the American mainland. Between 1585 and 1682, the establishment of a colony was synonymous with the founding of an urban place or chief town. Not only did towns serve commerce and security functions, they also served to reinforce the social contract and structure of civilization. The danger of settlers "going native" in the isolation of the North American wilderness was apparently thought to be very real, based on English experiences in Ireland.

14. Earle, "English Towns," 36-42; Mattie Erma Edwards Parker, et. al., eds., *Colonial Records of North Carolina: Colonial Records Project, Vol. 1* (Raleigh, N.C.: North Carolina Colonial Records Project and North Carolina State Department of Archives and History, 1964): 229 (hereafter cited as Parker, *Colonial Records*).

15. Max S. Edelson, "Clearing Swamps, Harvesting Forests: Trees and the Making of a Plantation Landscape in the Colonial South Carolina Lowcountry," *Agricultural History*, Vol. 81, No. 3 (Summer 2007): 382-383 (hereafter cited as Edelson, "Clearing Swamps," *Agricultural History*).

16. Edelson, "Clearing Swamps," *Agricultural History,* 390-391. Colonists marveled at Cape Fear's "divers sorts of lasting Timber that England hath not," and tree trunks "big enough to Mast the greatest Ships." While the produce of the long leaf pine, cedar, and oak trees became the main staple of the colony, deerskins obtained in trade with local Native Americans were also among the most important early exports.

17. Lee, *Lower Cape Fear*, 41-42, 158. The term "cotton-wool" in this instance refers to raw, minimally processed cotton. There are a variety of uses for it. Cotton-wool is raw cotton that has been combed to remove impurities and then cleaned. Tufts of raw cotton look rather like hunks of wool, thus the name. The texture is generally silky and soft, depending on how it is processed. According to Lee, the cotton was of the short staple variety, imported from Turkey, and of fine quality. It was allowed to grow wild, as few settlers were willing to do the weeding and other things that proper cultivation required. One frustration was the fondness of local bears for the young plants. At maturity, the fiber had to be picked from the plant and the seed removed from the fiber. Since no machines had yet been invented to do the job, it had to be done by hand – a tedious task that probably explains why cotton was not a more prominent staple crop.

18. Andrew Sluyter, "The Role of Black Barbudans in the establishment of open-range cattle herding in the colonial Caribbean and South Carolina," *Journal of Historical Geography*, Vol. 35 (2009): 333-347.

19. Herbert L. Osgood, "The Proprietary Province as a Form of Government," *The American Historical Review,* Vol. 2, No. 4 (July 1897): 679 (hereafter cited as Osgood, "Proprietary Province"); Kupperman, "Hot Climates," 235. Osgood maintains that the settlers from Barbados brought with them a number of slaves to provide the basis of an agricultural labor force.

20. Waterhouse, "England, the Caribbean, and the Settlement of Carolina," 266-267. Among the Vassall party, Humphrey Davenport and John Vassall himself were men of some consequence. Both had served as vestrymen of St. Michael's Parish. John Nevinson also served in that capacity when he returned to Barbados after the Cape Fear settlement failed.
21. Loftfield and Butler, "Barbadians," 53.
22. Waterhouse, "Settlement of Carolina," 272-275. The pursuit of lucre on Barbados was such that the Englishmen who went there paid scant attention to developing community and building institutions like church and family that sustained permanence and stability within English society.
23. Waterhouse, "Settlement of Carolina," *Journal of American Studies*, 277-278.
24. Herbert R. Paschal, "The Tragedy of the North Carolina Indians," in *The North Carolina Experience: An Interpretive and Documentary History*, Lindley S. Butler and Alan D. Watson, eds., (Chapel Hill: University of North Carolina Press, 1984): 4, 8 (hereafter cited as Paschal, "Tragedy"); South, "Tribes of the Carolina Lowland," 1. The Siouan Indian groups of North Carolina had ties with the Siouans of the Dakotas and Great Plains. Other Siouan nations that lived in North Carolina include the Catawbas, the Keyauwee, Saponi, Eno, Tutelo, Sissipahaw, Occaneechi, Shakori, Sugaree, Waccamaw, Woccon, Waxhaw, Saura (or Cheraw), and the Adshusheer. The Woccon, in particular, who lived in an area north of the Cape Fears, were definitely Siouan, and according to Stanley South provide a clue to the likelihood of the Cape Fears sharing that distinction.
25. South, "Tribes of the Carolina Lowland," 1.
26. South, "Tribes of the Carolina Lowland," 34.
27. Hugh Chisolm, ed.. Entry for "Gonzalvo Oviedo Y Valdes," Encyclopedia Brittanica (1911), http://studylight.org/encyclopedias/bri/view.cgi?number=13540, accessed 2/2/2015; South, "Tribes of the Carolina Lowland," 4-10. Gonzalvo Fernandez de Oviedo y Valdes (August 1478-1557) was a Spanish historian and writer. He is commonly known as "Oviedo" even though his family name is Fernandez. He participated in Spanish New World colonization.
28. South, "Tribes of the Carolina Lowland," 7-9, 23-24. The friendliness of the Cape Fears, who were relatively few in numbers compared to their enemies, may have stemmed from a desire to co-opt the English as allies and protectors.
29. South, "Tribes of the Carolina Lowland," 35-36.

Dwellings such as these reconsructions at Charles Town Landing State Historic Site in South Carolina are typical of the sort likely built by John Vassall and the settlers at Cape Fear.

VIII
Victims of the Times

Afflicted by Troubles Not of Their Making

John Vassall's hardy band of colonists must have brimmed with optimism that first year as they set down stakes in the rich soil, cleared fields, and built homes along the Cape Fear. That cheer did not last. Vassall's impetuousness in departing Barbados for Carolina before obtaining a firm agreement with the Lords Proprietors would return to haunt the settlers. Machinations among those with interests both in Carolina and on the world stage combined in a set of circumstances that ultimately spelled Charles Towne's doom.

In 1665, Sir John Yeamans' second group of settlers joined the Vassall colonists at the Cape Fear. The new contingent comprised Barbadians, New Englanders, Bermudans, and people from other Leeward Islands. To Vassall's dismay, Robert Sandford brought news that the Lords Proprietors had appointed Yeamans governor of Carolina. The proprietors favored Yeamans' proposal to settle at Port Royal over the Vassall site at Cape Fear. John Vassall had to content himself with the position of deputy-governor and surveyor-general. He began a long struggle to get the Lords Proprietors and his Barbadian backers to make good on their promises of support for the suddenly secondary colonization effort.[1]

The problems stemmed from a new set of terms for settlement in Carolina. Yeamans brought with him to Charles Towne the Concessions and Agreement from the Lords Proprietors, which made radical changes to the terms under which Vassall and his settlers had established their colony. The lack of a concrete acknowledgement of the terms of settlement negotiated between Vassall, Thomas Modyford, and Peter Colleton with the Lords Proprietors created much anxiety among the Charles Towne residents. The new terms sent by the Proprietors required land be parceled out by drawing lots. It left it to the luck of the draw to determine whether the land someone received was good, fertile acreage, or swampy, sandy, and useless. Add the fact that under the new terms, someone who already spent the better part of a year building a plantation might find themselves losing it to someone else based an unlucky lottery, and it is easy to see how the Charles Towne colonists might become alarmed. In August 1666 John Vassall wrote the Lords, urging them to address the issue. Henry Vassall presented the letter to the lords on his cousin John's behalf.

"It is now a considerable time since I had the honer to treat with a Committee of your Lordsps chosen from among yourselves conserning the settling of a Colony at Cape feare," Vassall pointed out, "and although there was no absolute accord and fineall agremt yet severall consessions were then offered by the sd Committee, and by me dispatched to the Barbadoes Adventurers there who did intrust me, who immediately returned anser that they would accept them and accordingly gave me power to conclude with your Honers. But in the Interim comes one Mr. now Sir Jno Yeamans and by his sonne offers other contrary Articles to wt the Adventurers did desire and made such spetious pretences that your Honers made an absolute agreement with him and refused to confirme those concessions formerly offered me..."[2]

Vassall's pique is understandable. The new terms for settlement made a big difference for the people who accompanied John Vassall to the Cape Fear. He related to the proprietors his colonists' dissatisfaction with the Concessions and Agreement, and that they had been all but abandoned by their backers in Barbados. "The Adventurers and present planters (are) highly dissatisfied," he lamented, "that they should not have these concessions at least which were tendered, and upon which they went, confirmed unto them; they thought those concessions hard enough, but those other (the new terms brought by Yeamans) intolerable." Vassall lobbied for a meeting with as many of the Lords Proprietors as possible to discuss both

Swampy low country mixed with sandy patches and fertile plots made settlement by lottery a risky proposition. For the Barbadians at Cape Fear, being able to search out and claim good lands on their own was essential to success.

old and new terms of settlement. He believed that the meetings might well determine the fate of Charles Towne.[3]

The points of contention regarding the Concessions and Agreement were threefold. One, the original agreement between the colonists, Modyford, and Peter Colleton relieved the settlers of any obligation to pay quitrents. The new terms required them to pay a halfpenny per acre when they received their deeds, ". . . and in lieu of all, and all manner of Rents, Services, Fines, Taxes and Impositions whatsoever, one Ear of corn for every hundred acres . . . if lawfully demanded." Two, the agreement signed by Modyford and Colleton allowed the settlers to take up land wherever they pleased, subject only to the approval of the proprietary governor and council. The new Concessions and Agreement imposed rules for land acquisition that simply did not work given Cape Fear's inconsistent geography; that is, favorable ground on the river's west side, but sandy soil unsuitable for growing crops on the east side. The third point, admittedly less troubling than the first two, regarded the requirement to place an armed man on every 100 acres of claimed land. The settlers argued there were many places in the Cape Fear that would not support an armed man.

The Cape Fear region was peppered with low, swampy areas that offered little in the way of resources to sustain them.[4]

When rescuers fished John Yeamans from the ocean after the sinking of the *Sir John*, they saved him from a watery grave, but compelled him to spend the next month at Charles Towne on the Cape Fear. It turned out to be his lone visit to the lands he was charged with administering. As soon as transportation could be arranged, he returned to Barbados, where global developments further distracted Yeamans and the Lords Proprietors from the welfare of the Cape Fear colony.[5]

Yeamans found the Charles Towne colonists in bad straits. A year into their settlement, they desperately needed resupply. While the surrounding area provided much of their food requirements, they depended heavily on imports from Barbados for sustenance. When the *Sir John* went down on the shoals at the mouth of the Cape Fear River, more than just military stores went down with her. Essential provisions and equipment - nails and tools for construction, medicines, cloth, furniture – were also lost. Without them, life became harder for the Charles Towne settlers, including John Vassall.

The two groups at Cape Fear were definitely at odds. Sir John Colleton was keenly aware of the differences of opinion between them. The Lords Proprietors knew the Vassall family history well, so that when Henry Vassall approached them to propose planting a colony in Carolina they believed the group would be largely Puritan. Despite the divide between the Vassall and Yeamans groups, the Lords Proprietors treated them as though they comprised one body that shared the same objectives. They informed the Vassall men at Cape Fear that Yeamans' "injenuity" had persuaded them to support his plan, and surrender more concessions to him. The agreements came despite what the proprietors viewed as the Vassall group's presumption in planting at Cape Fear before arriving at an understanding with them, "of which we doe noe wayse repent considering your forwardness to settle neare Cape Faire before you had an assurance of any consitions from us, and your resolution to make another settlement to the southward or westward of Cape Romania which we much desire."[6]

Yeamans delegated Robert Sandford to travel on board Captain Edward Stanyon's sloop to find a suitable location to plant a settlement at Port Royal. He also devised a contingency plan with Stanyon to resupply the Carolina colonists in the event the ship failed to return (a move that proved quite prophetic, given what happened to the vessel on her way back from Virginia). Yeamans put Stanyon under contract to make a roundtrip voyage between Barbados and the Carolina settlements. When Robert Sandford returned from his reconnaissance to Port Royal, Sir John Yeamans boarded the ship for the final leg to his island home. His departure left John Vassall and the Charles Towne settlers to their own devices.[7]

Sandford found the Indians around Port Royal fully aware of the troubles between the Cape Fears and the Charles Towne colonists when he made contact with them. According to his report, they " knewe wee were in actuall warre with the Natives att Clarendon and had killed and sent away many of them." The fighting took a toll on both sides. As more and more settlers fled the danger and uncertainty of life at Charles Towne, the odds for the Indian warriors began to level out. Before leaving Port Royal, Sandford left Dr. Henry Woodward behind to more fully explore the area and improve the relationship with the Indians there. Woodward was enthusiastic to learn about the Indians around the Ashley and Cooper Rivers. Sandford's visit set the stage for the return of Barbadians to Carolina in 1670.[8]

Even though Sir John Yeamans neglected Carolina, he still showed enough concern for the Cape Fear colonists to send Stanyon's ship to Barbados for supplies and reinforcements. Any hope that the expedition might bring relief to Vassall and his settlers was quashed when, after weeks of being beaten about and driven off course by wicked seas, Stanyon went mad and threw himself overboard. A young boy had to take the helm then manage to find his way back to the Cape Fear, although the storm had prevented the ship form reaching the island. Another relief ship apparently embarked from Massachusetts, but it, too, failed to reach the Puritan brethren at Cape Fear. By mid-1666, John Vassall had given up hope of receiving any relief, despite Yeamans having posted a £1000 bond to insure his return.[9]

Robert Sandford's report on the Port Royal region created even more dissension among the beleaguered Charles Towne colonists. Two factions soon emerged, with Vassall urging his companions to stay true to the settlement, while the other, led by a man named Galpin, argued for abandoning the colony. Vassall expended much of his own money to bolster the faltering colony at the Cape Fear. He also sent an urgent plea to the Lords Proprietors for aid and assistance, but the request never reached them, as the Dutch, now at war with England (March 1665 – July 1667), captured the messenger en route to London. Henry Vassall may have met the same fate, as the sea claimed him in 1667.[10]

John Vassall labored to keep Charles Towne together through the summer of 1667, but after a no confidence vote he disbanded the group and departed Cape Fear for Nansemond, Virginia, where his sister and brother-in-law lived. Other settlers returned to New England or Barbados. When Yeamans established a settlement at Port Royal in 1670, some of the Charles Towne settlers returned to try their hands at colonizing Carolina again. But the experiment on the Charles River was over.

Charles Towne. A Victim of Global Events

Pestilence, war, famine, and death are listed in the Book of St. John as the Four Horsemen who herald the coming of the Apocalypse. For many of the settlers along the Cape Fear River, the Biblical prophecy seemed to be coming true, as global events were conspiring to create a perfect storm of misery and failure at Charles Towne.

First, there was the matter of the Lords Proprietors themselves. Disarray due to a variety of factors diminished the leadership of the lords with regards to the Charles Towne settlement. Within five years of the start of the Carolina venture, three of the eight original Lords Proprietors were no longer in the picture. Because of his advanced age, George Monck, the Duke of Albemarle, retired from public life. The King and Parliament made Edward Hyde a scapegoat over the war with Holland. As a result, Hyde fled to exile in France. Sir John Colleton, the proprietor with the greatest interest in and enthusiasm for Carolina, died in 1666. Their successors and survivors concerned themselves with more pressing matters than the fate of the far-flung Carolina colonists.[11]

The root of all three English wars with the Dutch stemmed from England's desire to supplant the Netherlands' dominance of world trade. The Dutch provinces in North America stretched from the modern Delmarva Peninsula to Cape Cod, with the capital at New Amsterdam (renamed New York by the English). The Anglo-Dutch War of 1665-1667, the second of three seventeenth-century conflicts between the English and the United Provinces, began when King Charles II determined to conquer New Netherland. In the summer of 1664, he provoked the Dutch into a retaliatory action that he used as a pretext for war.[12]

By March 1665, a full-blown war had ensued, and continued

The Dutch raid on the Medway was a disaster for the English navy.

through July 1667. In 1664, Dutch ships sailed up the James River in Virginia and destroyed six ships of the English tobacco fleet at Jamestowne. In April 1665, Admiral Michiel de Ruyter took a Dutch fleet into Carlisle Bay in Barbados and sank several English ships before being driven off by the guns of Charles Fort. A crucial event in the war that affected the Lords Proprietors and the Charles Towne settlement was Dutch Admiral de Ruyter's raid on the Medway. In June 1667, de Ruyter's fleet sailed up the Thames, destroyed three major ships, and burned ten lesser English vessels. To make matters worse, the Dutch captured the flagship of the English navy, the *Royal Charles*, and the *HMS Unity*. As the Lords Proprietors performed other duties for the English government, the Second Anglo-Dutch War proved most distracting. In fact, George Monck, Duke of Albemarle, assumed an active command as Admiral of the English fleet during the greatest naval battle of the war, the Four Days Battle, in the summer of 1666.[13]

Charles Fort, Barbados

The war also affected events in the West Indies. Between 1665 and 1667, the islands of the Caribbean fell to the Dutch, leaving only Nevis and Barbados in English hands. By the time John Yeamans returned from his brief sojourn to Carolina, France had entered the fray on the side of Holland. That made traversing the Atlantic between Barbados and Charles Towne a much riskier proposition. Even if anyone on Barbados had spared a thought to resupply the hapless settlers on the Cape Fear River, securing seamen and ships to do the job would have been difficult given the ongoing war.[14]

More than 13,000 of London's houses perished in the Great London Fire of 1666.

If the second Dutch conflict and the demise of almost half the original Lords Proprietors represented the horsemen of War and Death, perhaps Pestilence and Famine accounted for the dual disasters of 1665-1666 – England's Great Plague and the Great Fire of London.

London was no stranger to deadly epidemics. Sanitation habits in London in the seventeenth century were awful on the best of days, with city streets doubling as both routes of transportation and open sewers. Carried by bubonic plague-infected fleas that infested the many thousands of rats in the city, the resulting epidemic eventually claimed the lives of at least 100,000 people in the English capital – a full 20 percent of the population. Thirty years had passed since England's last outbreak of the pestilence. When another came in 1665, it first appeared on the overcrowded docks of London. People with money and resources soon evacuated the city, including the King and his ministers. Yet some leaders remained, among them the Duke of Albemarle, George Monck. He and fellow proprietor William Craven were credited with keeping as much order as could be expected in the chaotic city, while also helping quell the flames of the Great Fire in 1666.[15]

The conflagration that consumed London proved to be a terrible tragedy, but ironically, also helped bring an end to the Great Plague. For three days in September 1666, monstrous flames swept through the medieval city within the old Roman City Wall. While the fires never reached the wealthy environs of Westminster, the Palace of Whitehall, or most of the suburban slums, it nevertheless destroyed 13,200 houses, 87 parish churches, and many government buildings. Some accounts claim that as many as 70,000 of the city's 80,000 homes burned down. Even though the official loss of life was low, the huge number of people left homeless in the wake of the conflagration was staggering. As ministers to the King and government officials, the Lords Proprietors were deeply involved in helping to contain the flames and then responding to the terrible tragedy of those left bereft of even simple shelter in its wake.[16]

Preoccupied as they were at home, the Lords Proprietors simply neglected their isolated colonists along the Cape Fear River.

The End of the Beginning

To John Vassall and the Charles Towne settlers, it must have seemed as if Providence itself had conspired against them. More maddening, perhaps, Vassall believed that even a small amount of aid would have allowed his ". . . poore Company of deserted people little regarded by any others and now way able to supply ourselves with clothing and necessaries" to endure, if not flourish.

Bubonic plague struck London in 1665, killing citizens by the cartload.

Destitute and disappointed, Vassall wrote that had the colony received as little as £200 worth of clothing in 1667, the colonists might have made a successful go of things on the Cape Fear. But it was not to be. Only Vassall's powers of persuasion kept the settlement going as long as it did. The Charles Towne colonists became victims of neglect by the Lords Proprietors and Governor Sir John Yeamans, but internal conflict and trouble with the Indians also eroded their strength of purpose and community.[17]

Puritans from Massachusetts had a long history of selling Native Americans into slavery, dating back at least as far as the Pequot War of the 1630s. After winning, the colonists sold hundreds of the losing Pequots into slavery on West Indian sugar plantations.

The settlers soon found themselves in an all-out war with the Native Americans around the Cape Fear after newcomers from New England began abducting their children, ostensibly to educate them and introduce them to the Christian faith. In reality the Puritans, who had a long history of seeing the Native American peoples as inferiors, were far more interested in slave labor. Indian slavery had a long history among European colonists. Christopher Columbus began enslaving Indians on the Caribbean islands almost from the moment he planted Spain's flag on a sandy beach in what came to be known as the West Indies. White settlers in the Western Hemisphere had long purchased Indian slaves, usually prisoners taken in wars between differing Native American groups. Especially among evangelical Puritans, Indian slaves were often justified on the premise that the whites were introducing them to the civilizing effect of the Christian faith. In reality, Indians were slaves to the white colonists just as surely as their African counterparts.[18]

As a result, the Cape Fear Indians began taking bow and arrow shots at the English as they tended their livestock in the woods surrounding their homes. The arrows would not have been a match for the settlers' firelocks in a stand-up fight had the English been able to mass their firepower, but they were effective enough in guerrilla-style warfare that demoralized the colonists and killed off most of their livestock. The rate of fire of the Indian bows was far superior to that of the colonists' firelocks in the isolated settings in which the English often found themselves. The enmity between the Indians and the settlers reached such a pitch that it became common knowledge among other Native American groups in Carolina. When the Indians began killing livestock and making it unsafe for the English to venture into the woods to hunt or farm, financial backers in London and Barbados became less willing to invest in the colony. A massive hurricane that swept by the Cape Fear before make landfall along Carolina's Outer Banks and the Chesapeake in September 1667 finished off Charles Towne.[19]

The policies of the Lords Proprietors also played a role in the colony's demise. On August 25, 1663, the Lords Proprietors issued their Declaration and Proposals for the settlement of Carolina. The document offered fairly liberal terms to those who would accept the challenge of building a home there. It guaranteed religious freedom, allowed for the construction of fortifications to protect the settlement, and specified that the Lords Proprietors would appoint the colony's governor from among thirteen candidates chosen by the settlers, giving them a measure of self-government. Moreover, six residents would be selected from the thirteen candidates to serve as the governor's council. It also allowed for voting rights and self-government insofar as granted by the King in the Carolina Charter, offered tax exemptions and land grants for settlement, established quitrents, and established the headright system with regards to land allotments.[20]

The particulars of the headright system changed in 1665, when the Lords Proprietors issued the Concessions and Agreement to John Yeamans. The Declaration and Proposals accepted by Vassalls' group at Charles Towne was the same as had been offered to, but rejected by, William Hilton's Puritan expedition of 1663. The generous land allowances, which applied to both men and women, came from the urgent desire of the Lords Proprietors to populate Carolina as quickly as possible. The land was to be laid out by the surveyor-general of the colony, and quitrents paid to the Lords Proprietors accordingly. By 1665, that arrangement had been altered. It was these changes that became a millstone around the necks of those who settled at Cape Fear.

The Concessions and Agreement, signed by the Lords Proprietors in 1665, was the precursor to the Fundamental Constitutions of Carolina written by John Locke and Shaftesbury a few years later. It codified the terms of settlement more concretely, and offered written guarantees to those who chose to settle in Carolina. The Concessions and Agreement created three distinct counties in Carolina: Albemarle (just below Virginia), Craven (south of Cape Fear), and Clarendon (between the northern and southern counties, including Cape Fear and the Charles Towne settlement). It also provided varying amounts of land to settlers depending on where they chose to establish their homesteads. As the Lords Proprietors by this time had a decided preference for the Port Royal settlement, colonists who chose to go there received larger grants than those who chose to settle in Clarendon or Albemarle counties. But the most contentious issue for the Charles Towne settlers was the land distribution policy.[21]

Sir John Colleton, himself a Barbados planter, greatly admired the efficacy with which land grants had been designed and distributed on the island colony since the 1620s. Barbados lands were cut into a uniform grid pattern, making administration and taxation easier (a system also adopted by New England colonies like Massachusetts). But the Cape Fear was not Barbados, and none of the Lords Proprietors possessed first-hand knowledge of Carolina's geography. The Concessions and Agreements of 1665 tried to transpose the Barbadian and New England method of land allotment to Carolina, with disastrous results for many colonists who had been living along the Cape Fear River, some for as long as one year.[22]

There were no neat, uniform plots of land at Cape Fear that fit together like so many pieces of a patchwork quilt. Many of the Charles Towne settlers contended with sandy, fallow parcels, interspersed with pocosin and swampy lowlands. The west side of the Cape Fear River boasted high ground with rich soil and good timber, but not in one huge, contiguous swath as on Barbados. Thus members of the Vassall expedition reportedly spread out for as much as sixty miles up and down the river and its tributaries. The grid system of land allocation dictated by the Concessions and Agreement simply proved to be impractical for the Cape Fear. Under its strictures, people who had labored to build homes and productive plantations found themselves denied the fruits of their labors. In many cases, sheer luck alone determined whether their new, neatly parceled allotment consisted of good land, swamp, or sand. Moreover, the requirement of an armed servant staying on each 100 acres of land was an imposition to settlers who were already struggling to fend off hostile Indians. Defensive efforts were compromised by the dispersal of the colonists' firepower. The Concessions and Agreement constituted a major source of the unrest that plagued John Vassall's efforts to make Charles Towne a success. The settlers immediately began petitioning the Lords Proprietors to exempt them from the unreasonable new system of land allocation, but they never received a reply.[23]

Reduced more by faction than necessity

By the early autumn of 1667, John Vassall bowed to the seemingly inevitable demise of his settlement on the Cape Fear River. Charles Towne, torn apart by internal strife and conflict, deprived of even the most basic necessities by the Lords Proprietors, and represented by an indifferent governor whose primary Carolina interests lay farther south, stood little chance of success. The failure of the settlement prompted John Vassall to write to Sir John Colleton from Nansemond, Virginia on October 6, 1667 (Vassall was unaware that Colleton had recently died). Vassall believed that had just twenty men stayed with him at Charles Towne, the colony could have survived. In the end no more than six agreed to remain. The settlers contracted with a ship from Massachusetts to take them away from the Cape Fear, most of them to make a fresh start in Virginia or New England. Some eventually went south to join Sir John Yeamans' new colony at Port Royal. Charles Towne on the Cape Fear River, however, was finished. According to the governor of Virginia, the settlement had been "reduced more by faction than necessity."[24]

Vassall blamed the Lords Proprietors for the demise of his colony. In a letter to Colleton he cited ". . . the hard termes of your Consetions" that ". . . made our friends sett us out from Barbadoes to forsake us, soe as they would neither supply us with necessaries nor find shipping to fetch us away."[25]

It is unlikely the Lords Proprietors would have consented to additional aid. By the end of March 1665, the trust fund they had established for the Carolina venture was empty. Sir John Colleton's account book recorded expenditures of £600/08/03, the largest single outlay spent on the gunpowder magazine and weapons for the settlement's defense (£284/12/03 for the magazine and cannon, £52/19/08 for 100 firelocks to be resold to the colonists). Colleton encountered problems securing money from his fellow Lords Proprietors. By 1664, only six had paid the £25 they had pledged a year earlier. When the 1665 Concessions and Agreement was signed, they each promised another £50 in support of Charles Towne, but only John Berkeley, Craven, Colleton, and Albemarle actually paid it. An additional £25 contributed by April 1666 brought six of the Lords Proprietors up to £100 each toward the support of their Carolina venture. William Berkeley and Lord Clarendon never contributed anything to the common fund. When the accounts were balanced in April 1666, the Lords Proprietors likely considered that they had invested quite enough in their Carolina patent.[26]

Even though John Vassall ended up temporarily broke and broken as a result of his Cape Fear adventure, the lessons learned from it benefited those who followed him into the Carolina wilderness. By the time Yeamans' Port Royal settlement was established, the founders of Charles Towne on the Ashley River were better prepared than their Cape Fear counterparts. In the spring of 1668, the Lords Proprietors repealed the contentious land allocation system of the Concession and Agreement, replacing it with one more amenable to the vagaries of coastal Carolina geography. The system of supply also greatly improved. As for the colonists, they also made a concerted effort to improve relations with their Indian neighbors. Better recruitment of fresh settlers kept a steady flow of new blood for Port Royal, and the boundaries of English settlement slowly, but surely, expanded ever westward. The process became, if not easier, at least less painful, by the lessons learned from that first, aborted settlement at Carolina's first Charles Towne.

Many of the original Lords Proprietors – including Sir John Colleton, perhaps the most enthusiastic proponent of the Carolina adventure – were dead by the time Port Royal began to flourish. Of those who lived on, Anthony Ashley Cooper, later the first Earl of Shaftesbury, became Carolina's biggest advocate. Cooper eventually engaged the talents of the noted political philosopher John Locke to codify the rights and obligations of both the Proprietors and settlers in the Fundamental Constitutions of Carolina (1669). That attention from the Lords Proprietors came too late for the Cape Fear colony, but the Yeamans settlement planted on the Ashley River in 1670 most certainly profited by its example.[27]

Endnotes

1. Lee, *Lower Cape Fear*, 44.
2. John Vassall et. al. to the Lords Proprietors, 15 August 1666, in *Colonial Records of North Carolina*, http://docsouth.unc.edu/csr/index.html/document/csr01-0052.
3. Buchanan, "Colleton," 72-73.
4. Fagg, "Carolina: 1663-1683," 96-97. The colonists put their concerns in a letter during a meeting of the assembly, presided over by Sir John Yeamans. The plea to the Lords Proprietors concluded with the colonists imploring the Lords Proprietors to return to the terms ". . . which your Honors once descended to with us and in us with the adventurers of ould and New England . . . y^t Your Possession of their Province may not bee utterly lost, and with it all hopes of subjecting it to an English Government . . ."
5. Lee, *Lower Cape Fear*, 46; Sprunt, *Chronicles of the Cape Fear River*, 32-34.
6. Fagg, "Sleep," *NCHR*, 181.
7. Lee, *Lower Cape Fear*, 42-50; Sprunt, *Chronicles of the Cape Fear River*, 33-34; Salley, *Narratives*, 82-108. Sandford sailed for Port Royal on June 16, 1666. Apparently, settlers in Massachusetts took up a collection to aid Charles Towne in 1667, but it was too little, too late.
8. Lee, *Lower Cape Fear*, 50; Waterhouse, "England, the Caribbean, and the Settlement of Carolina," *JAS*, 265. John Lawson, forty years later, wrote of the "irregular Practices of some of that Colony [Clarendon] against the Indians, by sending away some of their Children (as I have been told) under Pretence of instructing them in Learning and the Principles of the Christian Religion."
9. Buchanan, "Colleton," 71; Fagg, "Carolina, 1663-1683," 92; Suttlemyre, "Proprietary Policy," 38. The Vassall family's background, the attitude of the staunchly Anglican Sir John Yeamans towards the earlier colonists, the desire of the Vassall group for a corporate style of government, alterations to the original charter, and the preoccupation with separate counties suggests to Daniel Fagg that the Charles Towne settlement was mostly Puritan.
10. Lee, *Lower Cape Fear*, 42-51. Vassall may have found some satisfaction that the ship transporting Galpin away from Charles Towne was captured by the Dutch off Virginia in May 1667. In the fall of 1666, John Vassall paid to send an emissary to the Lords Proprietors to make them aware of the deteriorating situation at the Cape Fear and to appeal for relief, but the messenger never made it. Henry Vassall, also dispatched to London on the colony's behalf, failed to return to Charles Towne, either. Henry may have died when his ship was lost to bad weather or privateers. John Vassall later lamented, "had it pleased God to bring my Cauzen vassal safe hither wee had been yet in flourishing condition."
11. Roper, *Conceiving Carolina*, 20; Powell, *Proprietors*, 12-49. See individual

names for a summary of deaths and post-Charles Towne activities.

12. Rodger, *The Command of the Ocean,* 8-16; National Maritime Museum, *The Second Dutch War: Described in pictures & manuscripts of the time* (London: Her Majesty's Printing Office, 1967), 4-43, hereafter cited as NMN, *The Second Dutch War*; Ralph Davis, *English Merchant Shipping and Anglo-Dutch Rivalry in the Seventeenth Century* (London: Her Majesty's Printing Office, National Maritime Museum, 1975), 1-36.

13. David F. Marley, *Wars of the Americas* (Santa Barbara: ABC-CLIO, 1998), 166; NMN, *The Second Dutch War*, 4. A second, perhaps more significant, attack by the Dutch came on June 11, 1667. Admiral Abraham Crijnssen sailed up the Chesapeake Bay and captured a Carolina-bound shallop, before advancing on Jamestowne and annihilating the 46-gun frigate, *HMS Elizabeth*, refitting there. On the return trip down the bay, he took seventeen English prizes.

14. Fagg, "Carolina: 1663-1683," 93-94.

15. A. Lloyd Moote and Dorothy C. Moote, *The Great Plague: The Story of London's Most Deadly Year* (Baltimore: Johns Hopkins University Press, 2004), 225-226 and 254-255; Powell, *Proprietors*, 27. Craven's horse was said to be able to smell smoke from a great distance away. During the fire, Craven galloped all over the city to direct firefighting efforts. He also did great service during the plague that ravaged London.

16. Neil Hanson, *The Great Fire of London: In That Apocalyptic Year, 1666* (Hoboken, New Jersey: John Wiley and Sons, 2002), 78; Adrian Tinniswood, *By Permission of Heaven: The True Story of the Great Fire of London* (New York: Riverhead Books, 2003), 4, 101. The fire burned for three long days, September 2 – September 5, 1666. Officially, only six people died in the fire, but that number has been contested on the grounds that the extreme heat of the fire would have cremated the remains of many more, leaving no trace of their deaths. Moreover, poor and middle-class deaths went unrecorded.

17. Lee, *Lower Cape Fear*, 51-52. By the spring of 1667, John Vassall stopped a passing ship and related the news that he and the remaining Charles Towne settlers were ready to be picked up and transported away from the Cape Fear, asking for other ships to come and assist in the evacuation.

18. Alan Gallay, *The Indian Slave Trade: The Rise of the English Empire in the American South, 1670-1717* (New Haven: Yale University Press, 2002); Gary B. Nash, *Red, White, and Black: The Peoples of Early America* (Engelwood Cliffs, N.J.: Prentice-Hall Publishers, 1982). For further reading, both Gallay and Nash offer excellent treatments of the interactions between whites and Indians in the colonial period.

19. James E. Hudgins, "Tropical Cyclones Affecting North Carolina since 1566 – An Historical Perspective" (Blacksburg, Virginia: National Weather Service, 2000): 3; Lee, *Lower Cape Fear*, 50; Salley, *Narratives*, 82-108. When Robert Sandford explored Port Royal and Saint Helena Sound in the summer of 1666

on the orders of Sir John Yeamans, the local Indians "knewe wee were in actuall warre with the Natives att Clarendon and had killed and sent away many of them."

20. For a complete reading of the Declaration and Proposals of the Lords Proprietors, see http://www.learnnc.org/lp/editions/nchist-colonial/1666.

21. Roper, *Conceiving Carolina,* 18-20; Lee, *The Lower Cape,* 44-45; Harvard University Law School, *The Avalon Project: Documents in Law, History & Diplomacy.* http://avalon.law.yale.edu/17th_century/nc03.asp, accessed 11/27/10; Lewis, "A History of Clarendon County." Clarendon County encompassed all of modern New Hanover, Brunswick, Pender, Onslow, Columbus, Duplin, Bladen, Robeson, Sampson, and Cumberland Counties, and roughly half of Hoke and Scotland Counties.

22. Lee, *Lower Cape Fear*, 43-48.

23. Lee, *Lower Cape Fear*, 48-53; Roper, *Conceiving Carolina*, 20; Lee, *Brunswick County*, 16-19.

24. John Vassall, "Letter From John Vassall to John Colleton." From *Documenting the South: Colonial and State Records of North Carolina*, http://docsouth.unc.edu/csr/index.html/document/csr01-0061, accessed 9/1/12-9/30/12, herefter cited as Vassall, *Colonial and State Records*; Lee, *Lower Cape Fear*, 52. Vassall wrote, "yet had wee had but 200£ sent us in Clothing wee had made a comfortable shift for annother yeare, and I offered to stay there if but twenty men would stay with mee till we had heard from your Lordships, for wee had come enough for two yeares for a farr greater number and tho' the Indians had killed our Cattle yett wee might have defended ourselves but I could not find 6 men that wold be true to me to stay."

25. Vassall, *Colonial and State Records,* http://docsouth.unc.edu/csr/index.html/document/csr01-0061.

26. Fagg, "Carolina: 1663-1683," 102-103.

27. Powell, *Proprietors*, 20; Roper, *Conceiving Carolina*, 20; Fagg, "Carolina, 1663-1683," 111, 311. Anthony Ashley Cooper, in particular, took a much more hands on approach to the administration of the Lords Proprietors' Carolina ventures once colonists established a settlement at Port Royal.

This pile of bricks was located at the site of James Moore's House in 2010. Moore's house was built where the main compound of the Charles Towne settlement had been at Town Creek.

Dr. Gerald Shinn of the University of North Carolina at Wilmington. Shinn was a professor of philosophy and religion, but also an avid amateur archaeologist.

IX
Uncovering Charles Towne

For centuries, people who called southeastern North Carolina home knew of the site of Charles Towne, at least in a general way. James Moore built his home, which he named Old Town Plantation, on the site in the eighteenth century. Dr. Stanley South conducted minor archaeological investigations there with promising results in the early 1960s, while at the same time engaged in excavations at the site of the colonial port of Brunswick (1725-1776), seven-and-a-half miles below Town Creek. Concentrating on the colonial town that played a key role in the American Revolution, South's exploration of Charles Towne was cursory at best. That changed when Dr. Gerald Shinn, Garry W. Stone, and William R. Henry led excavations on the Moore House ruins with UNC-Wilmington students in April 1969 and September 1970. Then in May 1978, Dr. Thomas C. Loftfield's group of archaeology students from UNC-Wilmington discovered many seventeenth-century artifacts in a field adjacent to the Moore house. A decade later, Loftfield led a more thorough excavation of the site, searching for evidence of Charles Towne.[1]

Dr. Gerald Shinn, in his trademark sailor's cap (top), leads UNCW student archaeologists and volunteers in excavating the site of James Moore's colonial home north of Brunswick Town in 1970 (left). The Moore house was built on the site of the old Charles Towne settlement, and in the course of excavations, Shinn and the students discovered evidence of the earlier Barbadian compound.

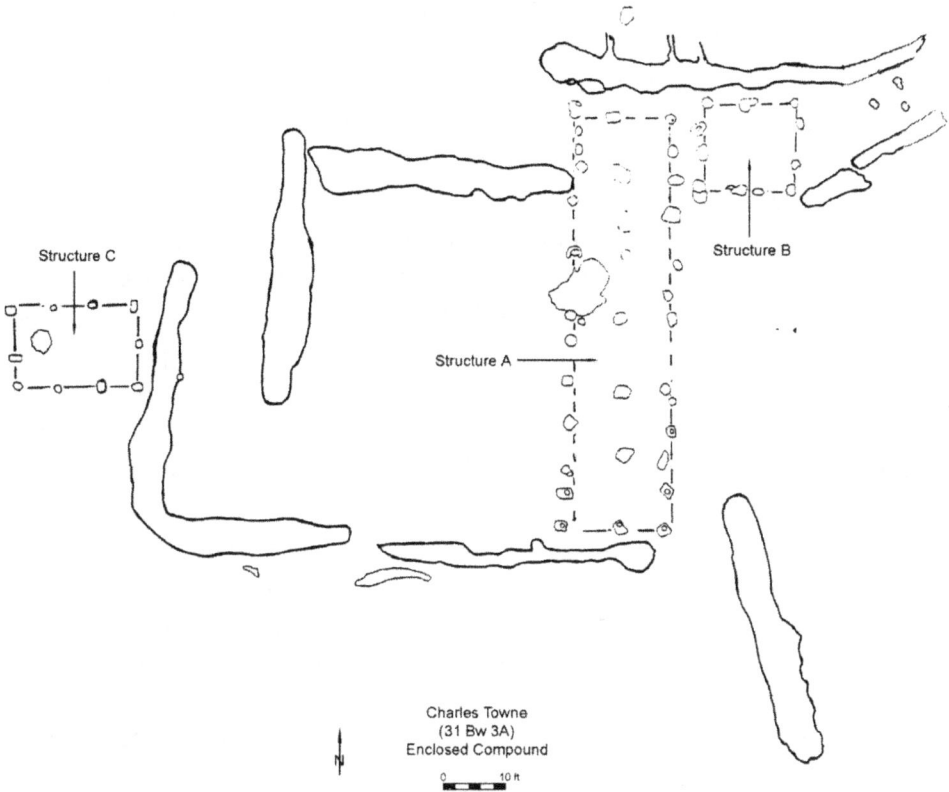

This archaeological map of the Charles Towne site shows the layout of the compound north of Town Creek. For orientation purposes, the Cape Fear River woud run along the bottom of the map, and Town Creek would be to the left.

Loftfield's digs revealed a palisaded compound with a small interior that measured approximately fifty-feet in diameter, with at least one fortified emplacement that most likely supported a cannon, and a sturdy, two-story earthfast blockhouse complex to the west of the fences that paralleled the Cape Fear River. The orientation of the site seems to indicate that the settlement's main defenses were arranged to repel attacks from the riverside. The design of the compound has striking similarities to fortifications found on Barbados. A large number of ceramic artifacts collected at the site led Loftfield to conclude that, at least among those of Vassall's party living proximate to the Town Creek site, there were a high number of affluent settlers. These were likely second and third sons of wealthy Barbadian planters, who immigrated to Carolina to make their own fortunes. It also appears that at least some African slaves accompanied the English adventurers.[2]

The soil at Charles Towne is loamy near the surface, but underpinned by a bed of hard clay that is difficult to penetrate even with modern excavation equipment. For the Vassall colonists, it would have been extremely difficult to dig into the clay substrata. Archaeologists believe that the shallow ditches surrounding the military/trading compound were not defensive moats, but instead dug to provide fill dirt to elevate the ground where palings were placed, in order to provide a secure anchor for the stockade fence. Investigations conducted by Loftfield determined that the workers sank palisade posts at least three feet deep, and raised the ground level sufficiently. Colonists used the clay to make bricks and pottery.[3]

The buildings at the Charles Towne site were post-in-ground, or earthfast, constructions, according to Loftfield's findings. They seem to consist of one large, central building that served as both a warehouse and administrative center, a smaller windowless structure that likely served as a powder magazine and barracks, and a north-facing elevated gun platform for the cannon reportedly lost when the *Sir John* sank at Old Inlet in 1665. Archaeologists suspect a second artillery platform may have been oriented to the south. The area of the enclosed compound is not very large – only 45 x 50 feet – but its design as a defensive work is almost a certainty. A third structure, its purpose as yet unknown, lay just outside the fence to the west.[4]

Colonists accessed the compound by at least one, and likely two, entryways. One wide aperture between the west fence and the main building indicates an opening large enough to accommodate wagon traffic. A smaller opening in the south fencing was probably a pedestrian gateway. Loftfield speculated the existence at least one more entrance, probably located in the wall of the main structure, facing east and providing access from the river.[5]

Artifacts excavated inside the compound showed a heavy concentration of musketballs, slags of lead, gun flints, and debris that lead archaeologists to speculate with confidence on its defensive function, especially of the smaller structure. A survey of English and Barbadian defensive works reveal similarities to those found at Charles Towne. Elements of features found at Charles Towne reflect English military engineering practices that date back to the Tudors.[6]

Loftfield thought it likely that the enclosed compound represented the entirety of the effective occupation of Charles Towne, although the colonists themselves reportedly spread out as far as sixty miles up the

Vassall and his Barbadians built a compound that was likely similar to the one at Wolstenholme in tidewater Virginia.

river and its tributaries. According to one English pamphlet promoting the settlement, as many as 800 settlers populated the area. The military compound and administrative center were advantageously located on high ground that was already largely cleared and easily defended. Indians had previously occupied the Town Creek site, which was bordered by marsh on two sides. The English compound resembled similar constructions found at Flowerdew Hundred or Wolstenhome Town at Martin's Hundred more than anything found in Barbados, Massachusetts, or the Chesapeake.[7]

Material culture excavated at Charles Towne makes it clear that at least some of the settlers were people of substance and wealth. A high percentage of expensive Delftware china shards found attest to their affluence. A small amount of porcelain, comprising only 1.1 percent of artifacts found at the site, are indicative of the very wealthiest settlers. Rhenish fragments, ball clay pipe stems and bowls, and everyday pottery were also among the items discovered. Some pottery fragments, made from a very sandy paste typical of local clays, were seemingly made by coiling. Coiling pottery was a common practice among African craftsmen, suggesting the presence of at least some Africans at Charles Towne.[8]

The Charles Towne site uncovered by Dr. Thomas C. Loftfield in 1970 (above), clearly showing where palisade walls and post holes were located. In the fall of 2010, the excavation site was covered by a cornfield (below).

The discovery of a large number of Spanish olive jar fragments was puzzling to archaeologists, as they far exceeded the amount generally found at other seventeenth century North American sites. Given the political friction between Spain and England at the time, the presence of Iberian vessel shards was unexpected. Loftfield speculated that the inter-island trade in the Caribbean accounted for the higher than normal percentages. It might also be attributable to trade with Spanish ships that traded at Charles Towne, or ships of other European countries that docked there after having visited Spanish ports.[9]

More than 2,000 glass bottle fragments indicate the presence of such vessels in considerable numbers. Pieced together, some of the fragments were enough to reassemble eleven case bottles, and five round wine bottles. Round bottles were a relatively new development in glassmaking at the time, and hence the ones found at Charles Towne represent another sign of affluence. Two bottle seals signifying ownership of bottles were also found, although a specific owner remains unidentified. Thinner glass shards are indicative of medicinal or cosmetic bottles.[10]

Firearms at the site were probably modern for the seventeenth century, likely early English dog-locks. Though first impressions might suggest this as another sign of affluence, it was not uncommon to find cutting edge weapons in frontier settings where having the best firelocks could mean life or death. That being the case, settlers often demanded them, and good planners made sure to obtain them. In addition to their defensive purposes, the guns were also used in gathering provender. Small cast shot found at Charles Towne indicates its use in hunting small animals and fowl.[11]

The preponderance of high status material at the Charles Towne compound indicates that administrators and elites comprised the majority of the settlers there, while less affluent colonists struck out for plantations and homesteads of their own further up the river and its tributaries. Yet evidence of this is elusive, as to date archaeologists have found no seventeenth-century structures anywhere other than at the mouth of Town Creek that can be definitively associated with the Charles Towne settlers. Perhaps successive settlers built their homes atop the remains of the Charles Towne plantations. Cross-contamination would make it difficult to pinpoint the dwelling places of Charles Towne-residents. Seventeenth-century shards have been discovered at the Brunswick Town/Fort Anderson State Historic site, an eighteenth-century colonial port town 7.5 miles south of Town

Creek. Whether those shards are evidence of a Barbadian occupation, or simply heirlooms of a family that settled Brunswick after 1726, is unknown.

Archaeological evidence suggests some trade between the English and their Indian neighbors, although it may not have occurred as often or as successfully as the settlers may have hoped. Small squares of cut copper, as well as trade beads, found during excavations attest to the Barbadians' intent. In return for the baubles, they would have traded for furs and skins to send back to Barbados or to markets in Europe. Questions as to whether or not trade between the settlers and Indians developed remain unanswered. Archaeological evidence also indicates that, after the English colonists abandoned Charles Towne, Indians moved in, making it difficult to draw any solid conclusions.[12]

Dr. Thomas Loftfield's excavations at the Charles Towne site were not exhaustive. A significant portion of the site is still unexplored as of this writing, and may yet reveal additional information about the first West Indian settlement on the North American mainland, planted by Barbadians and New England Puritans on the Cape Fear River in 1664.

Endnotes

1. James B. Legg and W. Bryan Watson, "The Exploration, Settlement, and Abandonment of the Lower Cape Fear, 1662-1667: The Historical Record and the Archaeological Evidence at the Supposed Site of Charlestown" (unpublished paper, 1979), 13 (hereafter cited as Legg and Bryan, "Charlestown"); Thomas C. Loftfield, "Lost Charles Towne: Local Manifestation of World Events," *North Carolina Archaeology*, Vol. 54, 2005, 34-48 (hereafter cited as Loftfield, "Lost Charles Towne"). The late Dr. Gerald Shinn (d. 2013) was a philosophy and religion professor, and an enthusiastic amateur archaeologist. His digs initially explored the ruins of James Moore's Old Town Plantation from the later colonial period, adjacent to what turned out to be the Charles Towne site. UNCW's Dr. Chris E. Fonvielle, Jr. participated in the Shinn digs as a high school student. Loftfield's excavations took place over the course of several years, from 1987-1992. In all, the Loftfield excavations uncovered 15,500 square feet of the site. Loftfield notes the exact location of the Charles Towne site as being on a knoll rising ten feet above sea level, one-half mile north of Town Creek. As of 2019 the land is owned by the Hugh MacRae family of Wilmington.
2. Loftfield and Butler, "Barbadians," 15; Loftfield, "Lost Charles Towne," 46. Richard Ligon described Barbadian plantation houses as being "built in a manner of Fortifications and have Lines, Bulwarks, and bastions."

3. Loftfield and Butler, "Barbadians," 19, 30-33.
4. Loftfield and Butler, "Barbadians," 33-35. The lack of a fireplace in the smaller structure between the main building and the gun platform lends credence to the supposition that it was a powder magazine.
5. Loftfield and Butler, "Barbadians," 37. Archaeological evidence has not been discovered that supports Loftfield's conjecture concerning the third entrance on the river side of the compound.
6. Loftfield and Butler, "Barbadians," 39.
7. Loftfield and Butler, "Barbadians," 46; Loftfield, "Lost Charles Towne," *North Carolina Archaeology*, 43.
8. Loftfield and Butler, "Barbadians," 58-59, 63-67. Delftware shards recovered at Charles Towne were fragmented too badly to ascertain designs, but the majority of them were determined to be polychrome, with some floral patterns. As to the porcelain, while it certainly could have originated in the seventeenth century, it is also true it could have come from later periods, as well. The oldest known piece of Barbadian pottery was not recovered on Barbados, but at Charles Towne.
9. Loftfield and Butler, "Barbadians," 66.
10. Loftfield and Butler, "Barbadians," 67.
11. Loftfield and Butler, "Barbadians," 68.
12. Loftfield and Butler, "Barbadians," 74. Given that Native Americans occupied the Charles Towne site after the colony broke up, evidence of trade goods cannot be tied definitively to the Barbadian settlers. The beads and copper fragments could just as easily have come from later trade between natives and settlers along the river, or even from sources in the interior.

GREAT SEAL
of the LORDS PROPRIETORS of
the Province of Carolina
AUTOGRAPHS OF THE LORDS PROPRIETORS

Clarendon C   Ashley

Albemarle   G Cartaret

Craven   John Berkeley

Will Berkely   Jas Colleton

Reverse of
THE GREAT SEAL

Appendix I
Declaration and Proposals of the Lords Proprietors of Carolina (1663)

His majesty having been graciously pleased, by his charter bearing date the 24th of March, in the 15th year of his reign, out of a pious and good intention for the propagation of the Christian faith amongst the barbarous and ignorant Indians, the enlargement of his empire and dominions, and enriching of his subjects, to grant and confirm to us, Edward, earl of Clarendon, high chancellor of England, George, duke of Albemarle, master of his majesty's horse and captain-general of all his forces, William, Lord Craven, John, Lord Berkeley, Anthony, Lord Ashley, chancellor of his majesty's exchequer, Sir George Carteret, knight and baronet, vice-chamberlain of his majesty's household, William Berkeley, knight, and Sir John Colleton, knight and baronet, and all that territory or tract of ground with the islands and islets situate, lying, and being in his dominions in America, extending from the north end of the island called Lucke Island, which lieth in the Southern Virginia sea, and within 36 degrees of the northern latitude, and to the west as far as the South seas, and so southwardly as far as the river St. Matthias, which bordereth upon the coast of Florida, and within — degrees of the northern latitude; in pursuance of which grant, and with a clear and good intention to make those parts useful and advantageous to his majesty and his people; we do hereby declare and propose to all his majesty's loving subjects wheresoever abiding or residing, and do hereby engage inviolably to perform and make good those ensuing proposals in such manner as the first undertakers of the first settlement shall reasonable desire.

1. If the first colony will settle on Charles River near Cape Fear, which seems to be desired, it shall be free for them to do so on the larboard side entering [south side]. If in any other of the territory, then to choose either side, if by a river; we reserving to ourselves twenty thousand acres of land, to be bounded and laid out by our agents in each settlement, in such places as they shall see fit, and in such manner that the colony shall not be thereby incommoded or weakened; which we intend by our agents or assignees in due time to settle and plant they submitting to the government of that colony.

2. That the first colony may have power, when desired, at their own charge to fortify the entrance of the river, as also the sea-coast and island; they engaging to be true and faithful to his majesty, his heirs and successors, by some oath or engagement of their own framing.

3. That the undertakers of that settlement do, before they or any of them repair thither to settle, present to us thirteen persons of those that intend to go, of which number we shall commissionate one to be Governor, for three years from the date of his commission, and six more of the thirteen to be of his council, the major part of which number, the Governor or his deputy to be one, to govern for the time aforesaid; and will also nominate successors to the Governor, who shall be of the six councillors aforesaid, to succeed in the government, in case of death or removal; and likewise councillors out of the remaining six of the thirteen to succeed in case of death or removal of any of the councillors, and after the expiration of the first three years, and so successively for every three years. Upon or before the 25th day of March, before the expiration of the time of the Governor in, being a new presentment by the freeholders of the colony, or by such persons as they shall constitute, to be made of the thirteen persons, four of which shall consist of those that shall be in the government at the time of the election of the thirteen, out of which we will upon or before the 10th day of April following declare and commissionate a Governor and six councillors with their respective successors in case and manner as aforesaid.

4. We shall, as far as our charter permits us, empower the major part of the freeholders, or their deputies or assembly-men, to be by them chosen out of themselves, viz: two out of every tribe, division, or parish, in such manner as shall be agreed on, to make their own laws, by and with the advise and consent of the Governor and council, so as they be not repugnant to the laws of England, but, as near as may be, agreeing with them in all civil affairs, with submission to a superintendency of a general council, to be chosen out of every government of the province, in manner as shall be agreed on for the common defence of the whole; which laws shall, within one year after publication, be presented to us to receive our ratification, and to be in force until said ratification be desired and by us certified; but if once ratified, to continue until repealed by the same power, or by time expired.

5. We will grant, in as ample manner as the undertakers shall desire, freedom and liberty of conscience in all religious or spiritual things, and to be kept inviolably with them, we having power in our charter so to do.

6. We will grant the full benefit of these immunities to the undertakers and settlers which, by the charter, is granted to us (for our services to his majesty) in relation to freedom of customs, of tools of all sorts useful there, to be exported from England for the planters' use; and of certain growths of the plantations, as wine, oil, raisins of all sorts, olivers, capers, wax, currants, almonds, and silks, to be imported into any of his majesty's dominions for seven years for each commodity, after four tons of every respective species is imported as aforesaid in one bottom.

7. We will grant to every present undertaker for his own head, one hundred acres of land, to him and his heires forever, to be held in free and common soccage; and for every man-servant that he shall bring or sent thither, that is fit to bear arms, armed with a good firelock musket, performed bore, twelve bullets to the pound, and with twenty pounds of powder and twenty pounds of bullets, fifty acres of land; and for every woman-servant thirty acres; and to every man-servant that shall come within that time, ten acres after the expiration of his time; and to every woman-servant six acres after the expiration of her time.
Note that we intend not hereby to be obliged to give the proportions of lands above mentioned to masters and servants, longer than in the first five

years, to commence at the beginning of the first settlement.

8. We will enjoin the Governor and council to take care that there lie always one man armed and provided as aforesaid in the colony for every fifty acres which we shall grant, and that there be a supply to make up the number in case of death or quitting the colony by the owners of said lands within twelve months after giving notice of the defect.

In consideration of the premises, we do expect by way of acknowledgment, and towards the charge we have been and shall be at, one half-penny for every acre that shall be granted as aforesaid, within the time before limited and expressed; and that the court-houses and houses for public meetings be erected by the public moneys of the colony on the lands taken up by us; but to be and continue to the country's use forever, they paying some small acknowledgement.

Given under our hands this twenty-fifth day of August, Anno Domini, 1663.

Appendix II
Concessions and Agreement between the
Lords Proprietors of Carolina and William Yeamans et al. (1665)

Articles of Agreement had and made betweene Edward Earle of Clarendon Lord High Chancellor of England George Duke of Albemarle Master of his Majties Horse and Captain Gen: of all his Forces, William Lord Craven John Lord Berkeley Anthony Lord Ashley Chancellor of his Majties Exchequor Sr George Carteret Kt and Barronet Vice Chamberline of his Majties Household Sr John Colleton Kt and Barro and Sr Wm Berkeley Kt the Lords Proprietrs of the Province of Carolina of the one part And Majr Wm Yeamans of Barbados for and on the behalfe of Sr John Yeamans Barro his Father Collonell Edmund Reade Symon Lambert Niccolas Edwards Robert Gibbs Samuell Tidcombe Henry Milles Thomas Lake Tho: Maycoke John Somerhayes Bartholomew Roes John Gibbs Basill Gibbs John Dickenson Thomas Gibbs Benjamin Rees Miles Scottow Nathanyell Meazericke Bartholomew Rees Junor John Arthur Samuell Smith Thomas Partrige John Walice John Brent John Godfrey George Thompson Robt Williams Lawrence Halske Wm Burges John Tothill James Thorpe Robt Tothill Wm Forster Thomas Merricke John Merricke George Phillips Edward Jacobs Robt Hackett Benjamin Waddon Robt Johnston Thomas Dickes Tho: Clutterhooke John Forster Will: Sharpe John Ham John Start Mathew Grey John Kerie Richard Baily Edward Thorneburgh Thomas Liston Anthony Long Thomas Norvill Giles Hall James Norvill Willm

Woodhouse Jacob Scantlebury Samuell Lambart John Forster William Byrdall Richard Barrett Edward Yeamans John Killicott Isaac Lovell Thomas Clarke John Woode John Bellomy John Greenesmith Robt Breoitir Thomas Dowden Niccolas Browne John Wilson Robt Sinckter Thomas Perkins James Thorpe Robt Richards Benjamine Hadlut Christopher Goupher James Walter James Haydensen Wm Birdall Mordecai Bowden Juinor George Nore Humphrey Waterman and himselfe Adventurors to and Setlers of some part of the Province aforesaid and of all others that shall adventure settle and plant in the said Province of the other part as followeth;

Whereas the said Major William Yeamans is Imployed to the said Lords Propriators by the persons above mentioned and by them declared under theire hands to be their Agent and Representative and that they have given him full power to treate propose and conclude with the said Lords about all matters relating to that which they have allready done as alsoe to what shalbe necessary and convenient to be done obligeing themselves and their posterityes to accept of, stand to, and abide by whatsoever the said Major William Yeamans shall conclude of and agree upon in relation to the Setlement of Carolina or any parte thereof, Now in pursuance of the power &c given to the said Major Wm Yeamans by the parties above mencōned. These present Articles doe witnes And it is covenanted graunted and agreed by and between the said partyes as followeth,
Impris The said Lords for their parts their heires Executrs and Administratrs doe covenant and promise to performe fulfill and keepe all the Concessions and particulers that are to bee by them performed and kept mencōned in the Concession and agreemts hereunto annext contayning the manr of Government wth severall Imūnities and priviledges granted to all such persons as shall goe or send to plant or as are already planted in the respective Countyes or Collonys in these Province of Carolina.

Item. The Lords doe further covenant and promis that they will cause to be shipt before the first day of February next twelve peeces of Ordinance with Carrages Saddles Spunges and shott convenient and necessary and twenty barrels of powder one hundred fierlocks and one hundred Matchlocks wth Leade and Bullets fitting as alsoe two hundred pare of Bandalyers for ye Armeing and Providing of a Foart to be erected and built neare Port Royall or neare some other harbour River or Creeke whose mouth or Entrance is Southward or Westward of Cape Romania in the Province aforesaid by the Respective Adventurers before mentioned or by any others under their Authority.

Item The Lords doe further covenant that every one of the Adventurers of the Island of Barbados and their associates of England New England the Leward Islands and Barmothos that hath subscribed and paid or shall subscribe and pay within forty days after notice of this in the Barbados, and the other places unto the Treasurer or Treasurers appointed or to be appointed by the Comittee choosen or to be choosen by the adventurers that are or shalbe to receave the same for the defraying the charge of carrying people that cannot pay for the transportation of themselves to port Royall or some Harbour River or Creeke whose mouth or Entrance is to the Southward or westward of Cape Romania and for ye making of some Fortification therefor and towards a setlement of those and other people in that place, and for other Nessessary Charges concerning the setlement aforesaid And shall send such proporcons of men Armed and provided as their owne Comittee shall agree upon in the first ship or shipes that shalbe sett forth to begin a setlement there, shall have Graunted to them and their heirs for ever for every thousand pound of sugar subscribed and paid five hundred acres of land and soe in proportion for a greater or lessor some subscribed and paid as aforesaid to be taken up within five years after the date hereof and settled as other Lands are to be setled vizt with an able man Armed with a good Firelocke boare twelve Bullets to the pound Tenn pounds of powder and twenty pounds of Bullets with six Monthes provision within one yeare after ye takeing up of the said Land which Land shalbe taken up to the South or Westward of Cape Romania and by Lotts as is proposed and prescribed in the Generall Concessions and Agreements concerning the setlement of the respective Countyes in the said Province And shall pay one halfe penny sterg for every acre English measure yearely in manor as in the Concessions hereunto annexed.

Item. The Lords doe further covenant and promis that whoever shall goe or send in the first Fleete wth Coll: John Yeamans he fayling with the first Governr or Deputy Governr shall have for his own head one hundred and fifty acres of land to him and his heires for ever English measure And for every able man servant he or shee shall carry or send armed and provided as aforesaid one hundred and fifty acres of land like measure, and to every such servant after the expiration of his or their time seaventy five acres of Land to be taken up by Lots as aforesaid in the place before menc̄oned And to every other Sarvt that shall there goe after the first fleete such quantyties as in the Generall Declaration is exprest, upon which hundred and fifty acres of land he shalbe obliged to keepe one able man and noe more and in fayler thereof to forfeite the same as in the Generall Concessions and agreement is exprest for which land there shalbe reserved yearlie to the Lords their heires and assignes one halfe penny per acre English measure to be paid in manner, as for other Lands in the Concessions menc̄oned. In consideration whereof The said Majr Will: Yeamans doth covenant as well on the behalfe of his Father Sr John Yeamans Baro and of Coll: Edmund Reade and of all the adventurers settlers and planters before exprest and of all others that shall adventure setle and plant as of himselfe that they shall for their pte perform fulfill and keepe all ye the particulers that are to bee by them performed menc̄oned in the Concessions and Agreement hereunto annexed And that there shall be provided before the last day of September next two shippes of one hundred and twenty tonns each of them at least with Ordinance convenient in each shipp and with powder shott and provisions necessary for the transportation of such persons as cannot pay for the passage of themselves to the Southward of Cape Romania there to setle and plant and to erect a foart and in it to plant the Artilliry sent by the Lords aforesd for the retreate and preservac̄on of the first settlers and of those that shall follow In witness of truth the said Majr Wm. Yeamans hath hereunto set his hand and Seale this seventh day of January In the sixteenth yeare of his Majties rayne Anno. Dom: 1664.

The Concessions and Agreement of the Lords Propryators of the Province of Carolina to and with the adventurers of the Island of Barbados and their associates of England New England the Carribbia Islands and Barmothos to the Province of Carolina and all that shall plant there In order to the setling and planting of the Countye of Clarendine the County of Albemarle and the County   which latter is to bee to the southward or westward of Cape Romania all within the Province aforesaid.

1. Impris Wee doe consent and agree that the Governor of each County hath power by the advice of his Councill to depute one in his place and Authority in case of death or removall to continue untill our further order unless wee have commissionated one before.

2. Item That he hath likewayes power to make choyce of and to take to him six Councillors at least or twelve at moast or any even Number between six and twelve with whose advice and consent or with at least three of the six or fower of a greater Number all being sumoned he is to govern according to the Lymitacōns and Instructions following during our pleasure;

3. Item That the chiefe Registers or Secretarys which wee have chosen or shall chuse wee fayling that hee shall chuse shall keepe exact enteryes in faire bookes of all publicke affares of the said Countyes and to avoyde deceiptes and lawsuits shall record and enter all Graunts of Land from the Lords to the planter and all conveyances of Land howse or howses from man to man, As alsoe all leases for Land howse or howses made or to be made by the Landlord to any tennant for more than one yeare which conveyance or Lease shalbe first acknowledged by the Grantr or Leasor or proved by the oath of two witnesses to the conveyance or Lease before the Governor or some Chiefe Judge of a Court for the time being whoe shall under our hand us grant upon the backside of the said deede or Lease attest the acknowledgement or proofe as aforesaid which shalbe our grant for the Registers to record the same which Conveyance or Lease soe recorded shalbe good and effectuall in Law notwithstanding any other conveyance deede or Lease for the said Land howse or howses or for any part there although dated before the Conveyance deede or Lease soe recorded as aforesaid And the said Registers shall doe all other thing or things that wee by our Instructions shall direct and ye Governors Councell and Assembly shall ordaine for the good and wellfaire of the said Countyes;

4. Item That the Surveyor Genll that wee have chosen or shall chuse wee fayling that the Governor shall chuse, shall have power by himself or Deputy to survey ley out and bound all such Lands as shalbe granted from the Lords to the Planters (and all other Lands within the said Countyes &c which may concerne particular men as he shalbe desired to doe) And a particuler thereof certifie to the Registers to be recorded as aforesaid Provided that if the said Registers aud Surveyors or either of them shall soe misbehave themselves as that the Governor and Councill or Deputy Governor and Councill or the majr pte of them shall finde it reasonable to suspend their Actings in their respective Imployments it shalbe lawfull for them soe to doe untill further order from us;

5. Item That all choise of officers made by the Governor shalbe for noe longer time then during our pleasure;

6. Item That the Governors Councillors Assemblymen Secretarys Surveyors and all other officers of trust shall sware or subscribe (in a booke to be provided for that purpose) that they will bare trew alleagance to the King of England his heires and successors and that they wilbe faithfull to the Interest of the Lords Propryatrs of the said Province and their heires executors and assignes and endeavor the peace and wellfaire of the said Province and that they will trewly and faithfully discharge their respective trusts in their respective offices and doe equall justice to all men according to their best skill and judgmt without corruption favor or affection, and the names of all that have sworne or subscribed to be entred in a booke; And whosoever shall subscribe and not sware, and shall vyolate his promis in that Subscription shalbe lyable to the same punishmt that the persons are or may be that have sworne and broken their oathes;

7. Item That all persons that are or shalbecome subjects to the King of England and sware or subscribe allegiance to the King and faithfulness to the Lords as above shalbe admitted to plant and become freemen of the Province and enjoy the freedomes & Imunityes hereafter exprest untill some stop or Contradiccōn be made by us the Lords or else by the Governor Councill and Assembly wch shalbe in force untill the Lords see Cause to the Contrary provided yt such stop shall not anywayes prejudice ye right or Continewance of any person that hath beene recd before such stop or order come from the Lords or Genll Assembly.

8. Item That noe person or persons quallifyed as aforesaid within the Province or all or any of the Countyes before exprest at any time shalbe anywayes molested punished disquieted or called in question for any differences in opinion or practice in matters of religious concernment whoe doe not actually disturbe the civill peace of the said Province or Countyes but that all and every such person and persons may from time to time and at all times, freely and fully have and enjoye his and their judgments and contiences in mattrs of religion throughout all the sd Province they behaving themselves peaceably and quietly and not using this liberty to Lycentiousness nor to the Civill Injury or outward disturbance of others, any Law statute or clause conteyned or to be conteyned usage or custom of this

realme of England to the contrary hereof in anywise notwthstanding.
9. Item That noe pretence may be taken by us our heires or assignes for or by reason of or right of patronage and powr of advowson graunted unto us by his Majties Letters pattents aforesaid to infringe thereby ye Genll clause of Liberty of Contience aforemenc̄oned We doe hereby graunt unto the Genll assemblyes of ye sevll Countyes power by act to constitute and appoint such and soe many Ministers or preachrs as they shall thinke fitt, and to establish their maintenance Giving Liberty besides to any person or persons to keepe and mainteyne wt preachers or Ministers they please.

10. Item That the inhabitants being freemen or chiefe agents to others of ye Countyes aforesd doe as soone as this our Com̄ssion shall arrive by virtue of a writt in our names by the Governor to be for ye present (untill our seale comes) sealed and syned make choice of twelve Deputyes or representatives from amongst themselves whoe being chosen are to joyne with him the sd Governor and Councill for the makeing of such Lawes Ordinances and Constitutions as shalbe necessary for the present good and welfare of the severall Countyes aforesd but as soone as Parishes Divisions tribes or districc̄ons of ye said Countyes are made that then ye Inhabitants or Freeholders of the sevll and respective Parishes Tribes Devisions or Districc̄ons of the Countyes aforesd doe (by our writts under our Seale wch wee Ingage shalbe in due time issued) annually meete on ye first day of January and chuse freeholders for each respective denizon Tribe or parish to be ye Deputyes or representatives of ye same, which body of Representatives or ye Majr parte of them shall wth the Governor and Councill aforesd by ye Genll Assembly of the County for which they shalbe chosen, the Governor or his Deputy being present unless they shall wilfully refuse in wch case they may appoint themselves a president during the absence of the Governor or his Deputy Governor.
Which Assemblyes are to have power.

1. Item To appoint their own times of meeting and to adjorne their sessions from time to time to such times and places as they shall thinke Convenient as alsoe to ascertaine ye Number of their Quorum Provided that such numbers be not less than ye third pte of the whole in whome or more shalbe ye full power of the Generall Assembly (vizt)

2. Item To enact and make all such Lawes Acts and Constitutions as shalbe

necessary for the well Goverment of ye County for wch they shalbe chosen and them to repeale provided that the same be consonant to reason and as near as may be conveniently agreable to the Lawes and Customes of his Majties Kingdom of England provided alsoe that they be not against ye Interest of us the Lords Propryators our heires or assignes nor any of these our present concessions Espetially that they be not against the Article for Liberty of Contience abovemenc̄oned, which Lawes &c soe made shall receave publication from the Governor and Councill (but as the Lawes of us and our Genll Assembly) and be in force for the space of one yeare and a halfe and noe more; Unless contradicted by the Lords Propryators within which time they are to be presented to us our heires &c, for our ratification and being confirmed by us they shalbe in continuall force till expired by their owne Limitac̄on or by Act of Repeale in like manner as aforesd to be passed and confirmed;

3. Item by act as aforesd to constitute all Courts for there respective Countyes, togeather wth ye Lymitts powers and jurisdicc̄ons of ye said Courts as alsoe ye severall offices & Number of Officers belonging to each of the sd respective Courts togeather with there severall and respective salleryes fees and perquisites Theire appellations and dignities with the penalltyes that shalbe due to them for breach of their severall and respective dutyes and Trusts.

4. Item by act as aforesd to ley equall taxes and assessments equally to rayse moneyes or goods upon all Lands (excepting the lands of us the Lords Propryators before setling) or persons within the severall precincts Hundreds Parishes Manōrs or whatsoever other denizions shall hereafter be made and established in ye said Countyes as oft as necessity shall require and in such manner as to them shall seeme most equall and easye for ye sd Inhabitants in order to the better supporting of the publicke Charge of the said Government, and for the mutuall safety defence and security of ye Countyes.

5. Item by act as aforesd to erect within ye said Countyes such and soe many Barronyes and Manōrs with their necessary Courts, jurisdicc̄ons freedomes and priviledges as to them shall seeme convenient, as alsoe to devide ye sd Countyes into Hundreds Parishes Tribes or such other denizions and districc̄ons as they shall thinke fitt and the said Divisions to

distinguish by what names we shall order or direct, and in default thereof by such Names as they please As alsoe within any part of ye said Countyes to create and appoint such and soe many ports harbours Creekes and other places for ye convenient ladeing and unlading of goods and merchandize out of shipps, boates and other vessells as they shall see expedient with such jurisdiccōns priviledges and francheses to such ports &c belonging as they shall judge most convenient to the gen1 good of ye said plantacōn or Countyes.

6. Item by these enacting to be confirmed as aforesd to erect rayse and build within the sd Countyes or any part thereof such and soe many Forts Fortresses Castles Cittyes Corporacōns Borroughs Townes Villages and other places of strenkt and defence and them or any of them to incorporate with such Charters and priviledges as to them shall seeme good and our Charter will permit and the same or any of them to fortifie and furnish with such Proportions of ordinance powder shott Armor and all other weapons Ammunition and Habillaments of warr both offensive and defensive as shalbe thought necessary and convenient for the safety and welfare of ye sd Countyes. but they may not at any time demolish dismantle or disfurnish the same without the consent of the Governor and the Major parte of the Councill of the County where such Forts Fortresses &c. shalbe erected and built;

7. Item by act as aforesd to constitute trayne bands and Companys with the number of souldiers for the safety strength and defence of the said Countyes and Province and of the Forts Castles Cittyes &c to suppress all meutinyes and Rebellions. To make warr offensive and defensive with all Indians Strangers and Foraigners as they shall see cause and to persue an Enemy by sea as well as by land if need be out of ye Lymitts and Jurisdiccōns of ye sd County with the perticculer consent of the Governor and under the Conduct of our Leut: Gen: or Comānder in Chiefe or whome he shall appoint.

8. Item by act as aforesd to give unto all strangers as to them shall seeme meete a Naturalizion and all such freedomes and priviledges within the sd Countyes as to his Majties subjects doe of right belong they swearing or subscribing as aforesd wch said strangers soe naturallized and priviledged shall alsoe have the same Imūnityes from Customes as is granted by the

Kinge to us and by us to ye said Countyes and shall not be lyable to any other Customes then the rest of his Majties subjects in the sd Counties are but be in all respects accompted in the Province and Countyes aforesaid as the King's naturall subjects.

9. Item by act as aforesd to prescribe ye quantityes of land which shalbe from time to time alotted to eavery head free or Sarvt male or female and to make and ordaine Rules for the casting of Lotts for Land and leying out of ye same provided yt these doe not their said prescriptions exceed ye severall proportions which are hereby graunted by us to all persons arriveing in ye sd Countyes or adventuring theither;

10. Item the Genll Assembly by act as aforesd shall make provision for the maintenance and Support of the Governor and for the defraying of all necessary Charges of the Goverment as alsoe that the Cunstables of the respective Countyes shall collect the halfe penny per acre payable to ye Lords in theire Countyes and pay ye same to ye receavor yt ye Lords shall appoint to receave the same unless ye sd Generall Assembly shall prescribe some other way whereby the Lords may have their rents duely collected wthout charge or trouble to them.

11. Lastly to enact constitute and ordaine all such other Lawes actes and constitutions as shall or may be necessary for the good prosperity and setlement of ye said Countyes excepting wt by these presents are excepted and conformeing to Limitacōns herein exprest.

The Governors are with theire Councill before exprest:
1. Item to see that all Courts established by the Lawes of ye Genll Assembly and all Ministers and officers Civill or Military doe and execute their severall dutyes and offices respectively according to the Lawes in force and to punish them from swerveing from the Lawes or acting contrary to their trust as the nature of their offence shall require.

2. Item according to the constitutions of the Genll Assembly to nominate and comīssionate the severall Judges, Members and Officers of Courts wheither Majistraticall or Ministeriall and all other civill officers as Justices Coroners &c the Comīssions and powers and Priviledges to revoake at pleasure provided that they appoint none but such as are freeholders in

the Countyes aforesd unless the Generall Assembly consent;

3. Item according to the Constitutions of the Genll Assembly to appoint Courts and officers in Cases Cryminall and to impower them to inflict penaltyes upon offenders against any of the Lawes in force in ye said Countyes as ye said Lawes shall ordaine wheither by fine Imprisonment Banishmt corporall punishmt or to ye taking away of member or of Life itselfe if there be cause for it.

4. Item to place officers and soldiers for the safety strenkt and defence of the Forts Castles Cittyes &c according to ye number appointed by the Genll Assembly to nominiate place and comissionate all military officers under ye dignity of ye Leut: Genll whoe is comissionated by us, over the sevll trayned bands and Companys constituted by ye Genll Assembly as Collonels Capts: &c and theire comissions to revoake at pleasure, ye Leut: Gen: with the advice of his Councill unless some present danger will soe permitt him to advize to muster and trayne all ye soldiers wthin the said County or Countyes to prosecute warr persue an Enemy suppress rebellions and mewtinies as well by sea as Land and to exercise the whole Millitia as fully as by our Letters pattents from the kinge wee can impower him or them to doe Provided yt they appoint noe Military officers but wt are freeholders in the sd Countyes unless ye Genll Assembly shall consent;

5. Item where they see cause after condemnacon to reprieve untill the Case may be presented with a Coppy of ye whole tryall proceedings and proofes to ye Lords who will accordingly eather pardon or comand execution of ye sentence on ye offender who is in ye meane time to be kept in safe custody till the pleasure of ye Lords be knowne

6. Item in case of death or other removall of any of the representatives within the yeare to issue summons by writt to ye respective division or divisions for which he or they were chosen comanding the freeholders of ye same to chuse others in their steade;

7. Item to make warrants and to seale Grants of Land according to theis our Concessions and the prescriptions by ye advice of ye Genll Assembly in such forme as shalbe at large set down in our Instrucons to ye Governor in his Comission and which are hereafter expressed.

8. Item to act and doe all other thing or things yt may conduce to ye safety peace and well Government of ye said Countyes as they shall see fitt soe as they be not contrary to ye Lawes of ye Countyes aforesaid;
For the better security of the proprietyes of all the Inhabitants

1. Item They are not to impose nor suffer to be imposed any tax Custome Subsidy Tallage Assesment or any other duty wtsoever upon any Culler or pretence upon ye sd County or Countyes and the Inhabitants thereof other then what shalbe imposed by ye Authority and consent of ye Generall Assembly and then only in manner as aforesaid;

2. Item they are to take care ye land quietly held planted and possessed seaven yeares after its being first duely surveyed by the Surveyor Generall or his order shall not be subject to any review resurvey or alteration of bounds on wt pretence soever or by any of us or any officrs or Ministers under us.

3. Item they are to take care yt noe man if his Catle straye range or graze on any ground wthin the sd Countyes not actually appropryated or sett out to particuler persons shalbe lyable to pay any trespass for ye same to us our heires &c Provided yt Custome of Comons be not thereby pretended to; nor any person hindred from taking up and appropriating any Lands soe grazed upon and yt noe person purposely doe suffer his Catle to graze on such land.

4. Item it is our will and desire that ye Inhabitants of ye said Countyes and adventurers theither shall enjoye all the same Imunityes from Customes for exporting certine goods from these Realmes of England &c theither as ye Kinge hath been graciously pleased to graunt to us as alsoe for ye Incorragement of ye Manufactrs of wine silke oyle ollives fruite almonds &c. menconed in the pattent have priviledge for bringing them Custome free into any of his Majties dominions for ye same time and upon ye same tearmes as we ourselves may by our Pattent.

And that the planting of the Countyes aforesd may bee the more speedily promoted:

1. Item The Governors are to take notice that wee doe hereby graunt unto all persons whoe have already adventured to Carolina or shall transport themselves or Sarvts before ye first day of January which shalbe in ye yeare of our Lord one thousand six hundred sixty five theis following proporc̄ons of land vizt if to ye County of Clarendon one hundred acres English measure to every freeman and as much to his wife if hee have one And to every freewoman yt already is or shall arrive into ye sd County with a Sarvt or Sarvts to plant within ye Province aforesd one hundred acres like measure To a Mastr or Mistres for every able man Sarvt he or shee hath brought or sent or shall bring or send as aforesd being each of them armed with a good firelocke or Matchlocke boare twelve bullets to the pound ten pounds of powder and twenty pounds of bullets wth Match proportionable and victualled for six monthes fifty acres of like measure for every weaker Sarvt hee or shee hath brought or sent or shall bringe or send as aforesd as woemen children and slaves above ye age of fowerteene yeares, And fifty acres like measure for every Christian Sarvt yt is brought or sent within ye sd time to his or her proper use and behoofe when their time of servitude is expired;

2. Item to every freeman and freewoman yt shall arrive in ye sd County armed and provided as aforesd within the second yeare from ye first daie of January one thousand six hundred sixty five to ye first of January one thousand six hundred sixty six with an intenc̄on to planting seaventy five acres of Land and seaventy acres for every able man Sarvt that he or they shall carry or send armed and provided as aforesaid:

3. Item for every weaker sarvant or slave adged as aforesd yt shalbe carryed or sent theither within ye second yeare as aforesd forty acres of Land To every christian sarvant yt shall arrive ye second yeare forty acres of Land of like measure after ye expiration of his servitude.

4. Item to every freeman or freewoman armed and provided as aforesd yt shall goe and arrive with an intention to plant within ye third yeare from January one thousand six hundred sixty six to January one thousand six hundred sixty seaven fifty acres of Land like measure and for every able man sarvt yt he or they shall carry or send within ye sd time armed and provided as aforesd the like quantity of Land and for every weaker sarvt or slave adged as aforesd yt he or they shall carry or send within the third

yeare twenty five acres of Land and to every Christian sarvant soe carryed or sent in the third yeare twenty five acres of Land of like measure after the expiraĉon of his or their time of Sarvice;

5. Item we do hereby graunt unto all persons whoe have already adventured to Carolina or shall transport themselves or sarvants before ye first daie of January which shalbe in ye yeare of our Lord one thousand six hundred sixty five theis following proporĉons of Land If to ye County of Albemarle eighty acres English measure to every freeman and as much to his wife if he have one And to every freewoman yt already is or shall arrive into ye sd County with a Sarvt to plant within ye time aforesd eighty acres like measure To a Master or Mistres for every able man Sarvt he or shee hath brought or sent or shall bringe or send as aforesd being each of them armed with a good firelock or matchlock boare twelve bullets to ye pound tenn pounds of powder and twenty pounds of bullets wth match proportionable and victualed for six monthes eighty acres of like measure and for every weaker Sarvt he or she hath brought or sent or shall bringe or send as aforesd as woemen children and slaves above the age of fowerteene yeares, forty acres like measure And for every Christian Sarvt yt is brought or sent within ye said time to his or her proper use and behoofe when their time of Sarvitude is expired forty acres of like measure;

6. Item to every freeman and freewoman yt shall arrive in ye sd County armed and provided as aforesd within ye second yeare from ye first day of January one thousand six hundred sixtie five to ye first day of January one thousand six hundred sixty six wth an intenĉon to plant sixtie acres and sixty acres for every able man Sarvt yt he or they shall carry or send Armed and provided as aforesaid;

7. Item for every weaker Sarvt or slave adged as aforesd yt shall be carryed or sent theither wthin ye second yeare as aforesd Thirty acres like measure To every Christian sarvt yt shall arrive ye second yeare Thirty acres of Land of like measure after ye expiraĉon of his or there time of servitude.

8. Item to every freeman and freewoman armed and provided as aforesd yt shall goe and arrive wth an intenĉon to plant wthin ye Third yeare from January one thousand six hundred sixty six to January one thousand six

hundred sixty seaven Forty acres of Land like measure, and for every able man sarvt that he or they shall carry or send wthin ye sd time armed and provided as aforesd ye like quantity of land, And for every weaker sarvt or slave adged as aforesd yt he or they shall carry or send within ye Third yeare Twenty acres of Land like measure, And to every Christian Sarvt so carryed or sent wthin ye Third yeare Twenty acres of land of like measure after ye expiracōn of his or there time of servitude;

9. Item we doe hereby graunt unto all persons who have already adventured to Carolina or shall transport themselves or Sarvts before ye first day of January which shalbe in ye yeare of our Lord one thousand six hundrd sixty five these following proporcōns vizt to every freeman yt shall goe wth ye first Governr from ye port where hee imbarkes (or shall meete him at ye Randeyvous he appoints) and from thence goe with him to ye southward or westward of Cape Romania wthin the province aforesd for ye settlemt of a Plantacōn there which we name to be ye County of Armed wth a good muskett boare twelve bullets to ye pound wth Tenn pounds of powder & Twenty pounds Bullets wth Bandalears and match convenient and wth six monthes provision, for his owne person arriveing there, one hundred and fifty acres of Land English measure And for every able man Sarvt yt hee shall carry wth him Armed and provided as aforesd and arriveing there ye like quantity of one hundred and fifty acres and whoever shall send Sarvts at yt time shall have for every able man Sarvt hee or they shall send armed and provided as aforesd and ariving there ye like quantity of one hundred and fifty acres and for every weaker Sarvt or slave male or female exceeding ye age of fowerteene yeares which any one shall send or carry arriving there seaventy five acres of land and to every Christian Sarvt exceeding ye age aforesd after ye expiracōn of their time of service, seaventy five acres of land for there owne use.

10. Item to every Mastr or Mistress yt shall goe before ye first day of January wch shalbe in ye yeare of our Lord one thousand six hundrd sixty five one hundrd and Twenty acres of land and for every able man Sarvt yt hee or shee shall carry or send armed and provided as aforesd and arriveing wthin ye time aforesd ye like quantity of one hundrd & Twenty acres of Land and for every weaker Sarvt or slave male or female exceeding ye age of fowerteen yeares ariving there sixty acres of land and to every Christian Sarvt to there owne use and behoofe sixty acres

11. Item to every freeman and freewoman yt shall arrive in ye sd County armed and provided as aforesd wthin ye second yeare from ye first of January one thousand six hundred sixty five to ye first of January one thousand six hundrd sixty six wth and Intencon to plant ninety acres of Land English measure and for every able man Sarvt yt hee or shee shall carry or send Armed and provided as aforesd Ninty acres of Land of like measure.

12. Item and for every weaker Sarvt or slave adged as aforesd yt shalbe soe carryed or sent theither wthin ye second yeare as aforesd forty five acres of Land of like measure, and to every Christian Sarvt yt shall arrive ye second yeare forty five acres of land of like measure after ye expiration of his or there time of servitude, for there owne use and behoofe, all wch Lands soe granted in ye 9: 10: 11: and 12: articles preceeding and ye 13th following are ment and intended to be taken up and given in ye County of and not elsewhere,

13. Item to every freeman and freewoman armed and provided as aforesd yt shall goe and arrive wth intencon to plant wthin ye Third yeare from January one thousand six hundred sixty six to January one thousand six hundred sixty seaven armed and provided as aforesd sixty acres of land like measure and for every able man Sarvt yt hee or they shall carry or send wthin ye sd time armed and provided as aforesd ye like quantity of sixty acres of land and for every weaker Sarvt or slave adged as aforesd yt he or they shall carry or send wthin ye Third yeare thirty acres of land, and to every Christian Sarvt soe carryed or sent in ye third yeare thirty acres of Land of like measure, after ye expiracon of his or there time of service, All which land and all other yt shalbe possessed in sd Countyes are to be held on ye same tearmes and Condicons as is before mentoned and as hereafter in the following Pharagraphes is more at large exprest Provided yt all ye before mentoned Land and all other wtsoever yt shalbe taken up and soe setled in ye sd Province shall afterwards from time to time for ye space of thirteene yeares from ye date hereof be held upon ye Condicon aforesd of continewing one able man Sarvt or two such weaker Sarvts as aforesd on every hundred acres Master or Mistres shall possess besides wt was graunted for his or her owne person, In failer of wch upon Notificacon to ye present Occupant or his assignes, there shalbe three yeares given to such for there compleating the said Number of persons or for there sayle

or other disposure of such part of there Lands as are not soe peopled wthin ye time of three yeares if any person holding any Lands shall faile by himselfe his agents executors or assignes or some other way to provide such number of persons, Unless the Genll Assembly shall without respect to poverty judge yt it was impossible for ye party soe fayleing to keepe or procure his or her Number of Sarvts to be provided as aforesd In such case wee ye Lords to have power of disposeing of soe much of such Land as shall not be planted wth its dew Number of persons as aforesd to some other yt will plant ye same; Provided alwayse yt any person who hath a stocke of Catle sheepe or such like on his hands shall for every greater soart of Cattle wch hee hath at ye time of such forfeiture as horses Kine &c, retain two acres, and for every lessor sorte as sheepe hoggs &c one acre Provided alsoe yt noe persons arriveing into ye sd Countyes wth purpose to setle (they being subjects or Naturallized as aforesd) be denyed a graunt of such proporc̄ons of Land as at ye time of there arrivall are due to themselves or Sarvts by Concession from us as aforesd but have full Lycence to take up and setle ye same in such order and manner as is granted or prescribed all Lands notwthstanding (ye powers in ye Assembly aforesd) shalbe taken up by warrant from ye Governor and confirmed by ye Governor and Councill under a Seale to be provided for yt purpose in such order and meth-hood as shalbe set downe in this declaration and more att Large in ye Instrucc̄ons to ye Governor and Councill.

And that the lands may be the more regulerly layd out and all persons the better ascertayned of there titles and possessions.

1. Item in the bounding of ye County of Clarendon the Governor and Councill (and Assembly if any bee) are to make choyce of (and confine themselves and planters to) one side of ye mayne river neare Cape Faire, on which some of ye adventurers are already setled or intend to setle and ye Islands in or neare ye said River next ye side they setle on, Unless they have already setled some Island neare ye other side which if they have they may continew thereon;

2. Item the Governor of ye County of   with ye advice of his Councill is to bound ye said County as he shall see fitt not exceeding Forty myles square or sixteene hundred Square myles.

3. Item they are to take care and direct yt all Lands bee devided by Genll Lotts none less then two thousand two hundred acres nor more then two and twenty thousand acres in each Lott excepting Cittyes Townes &c and ye neare Lotts of towneshipps and yt ye same be undecimally devided one eleventh part by lott to us our heires and Assignes ye Remayndr to persons as they come to plant ye same in such proporcons as is allowed;

4. Item that ye Governor of each County or whome he shall depute in Case of death or absence if some one be not before Comissionated by us as aforesd doe give to every person to whome land is due a warrant syned & sealed by himselfe and ye Major pte of his Councill and directed to ye Surveyor Genll or his Deputy comanding him to ley out Lymitt and bound acres of Land (as his due proporcon is) for such a person in such allotmt according to wch warrant ye Register having first recorded ye same and attested the record upon ye warrant ye Surveyr Genll or his Deputy shall proceed and certifie to ye Chiefe Secretary or Register ye Name of ye person for whome he hath layde out land, by virtue of wt authority ye date of ye authority or warrant ye Number of acres ye bounds and on wt poynt of ye Compass ye Severall Lymitts thereof lye which Certificate the Register is likewayse to enter in a booke to be prepared for yt purpose with an Alphabeticall table referring to ye booke soe ye Certificate may be ye easier found and then to file ye Certificates and ye same to Keepe safely The Certificate being entered a warrant comprehending all ye particculers of Land mencioned in ye Certificate aforesd is to be syned and sealed by him and his Councill or ye Major pte of them as aforesd (they haveing seen ye entry) and directed to ye Register or Chiefe Secretary for his preparing a Graunt of ye land to ye party for whome it is layd out wch Graunt shalbe in the forme following vizt The Lords Proprietors of the Province of Carolina doe hereby graunt unto A. B. of ye county of Clarendon (or in wt County ye same shalbe) in ye province aforesd a plantacon in ye said County Conteyning   Acres English measure Bounding as in ye said Certificates to hold to him (or her) his (or her) heires and Assignes for ever Yielding and paying yearly to ye said Lords Proprietors their heires or Assignes every twenty fifth day of March according to ye English Acco one halfe penny of Lawfull English mony for every of ye said Acres To be holden of ye manner of   in free and Comon Soccage, ye first paymt of wch rent to beginn ye twenty fifth day of March which shalbe in ye yeare of our Lord one thousand six hundrd and seaventy according

to ye English Account, Given under ye seale of ye County of Clarenden ye   day of   in ye yeare of our Lord   To which Instrument ye Governor or his Deputy hath hereby full Authority to put yee seale of ye said County and to subscribe his Name as alsoe ye Councell or Majr pte of them are to subscribe there Names and then ye Instrument or Graunt is to be by ye Register recorded in a Booke of Records for yt purpose all wch being done according to these instrucc̄ons we hereby declare yt the same shalbe effectuall in Law for ye Injoymt of ye said plantac̄on and all ye benefitts and profitts of and in ye same, except ye halfe part of Mynes of Gold and Silver paying ye rent as aforesd Provided yt if any plantac̄on so granted shall by ye space of three yeares be neglected to be planted with a sufficient Number of Sarvts as is before menc̄oned yt then it shalbe lawfull for us otherwayse to dispose thereof in whole or in part This graunt notwthstanding.

5. Item We doe alsoe graunt convenient proporc̄ons of land for highways and for streetes not exceeding one hundred foote in bredth in Cittyes Townes Villages for churches Forts wharfs Keys Harbours and for publicke houses and to each parish for ye use of there Ministers one hundred Acres in such places as ye Genll Assembly shall appoynt;

6. Item ye Governors are to take notice yt all such lands leyd out for ye uses and purposes in ye next preceeding Article shall be free and exempt from all rents Taxes and other Customes or dutyes wtsoever payable to us our heires or Assignes.

7. Item that in leying out Lands for Cittyes Townes Villages Burroughes or other Hamlets ye said lands be undecimally devided one eleaventh part to be by lott layd out for us and ye rest devided to such as shalbe willing to build thereon they paying after ye rate of one halfe penny per Acre yearely to us, as for there other lands as aforesd wch said Lands in Cittyes Townes &c is to be assured to each possessor by ye same way and Instrewment as is before menc̄oned.

8. Item That all Rules relating to building of each streete or quantity of ground to be alotted to each house within ye said respective Cittyes Burroughs and Townes be wholy left by act as aforesd to ye wisdome and discrecc̄on of ye Generall Assembly;

9. Item That ye Inhabitants of ye said County have free passage through or by any Seas bounds Creekes Rivers &c. in ye said Province of Carolina through or by which they must necessarily pass to come from ye Mayne Ocean to ye Countyes aforesd or any part of ye Province aforesd;

10. Lastly it shalbe Lawful for ye Representatives of ye freeholders to make any address to ye Lords touching ye Governor and Councill or any of them or concerning any Greivances whatsoever or for anything they shall desire without the Consent of the Governor and Councell or any of them,

(Endorsed)

Sealed and Delivered in ye presence of us
JO: PERYN.
THO: WALKER

January 7th 1664-5
It is this day agreed by the Lords Propryators of Carolina that although the County of Clarendon neare Cape Faire, and all the tract of ground as farr as to the southward of the river St Mathias and west as far as the South Seas, be for the present, under the Government of Sir John Yeamans, yet notwithstanding it is ment and intended, that that parte of it which is about to be setled to the southward and westward of Cape Romania be a distinckt Government from the County of Clarendon, and that there be a distinckt deputy Governor for the present and that it be called the County of Craven and as soone as it shalbe conveniently setled by the said Sir John Yeamans or any other that there be a distinckt Governor comissionated to governe there.

Appendix III

**Persons Known to have Explored Cape Fear with William Hilton, Jr.,
or who
Settled at Charles Towne with John Vassall or Sir John Yeamans.**

No extant list of the people who actually settled at Cape Fear in 1664 has ever been found, but some of the expedition's leadership is known. All of the following were part of the first expedition to the Charles River with John Vassall:

John Nevinson, George Cary, Samuel Hardy, Joseph Woory, Richard Abravall, Thomas Giles, Richard Whittney, Robert Sandford, Robert Gobbs, John Knight, Humphrey Davenport, Thomas Clifton, Henry Brayne, John Brent, Will Grig, Thomas Gibbes, Sam Hames, John Vassall. Edward Hassell (or his son, also named Edward) were likely members of the group too. Hassell had a close relationship with both John Vassall and Humphrey Davenport on Barbados.

Via legal papers involving Henry Douglas of "Doggles R[iver]," who was a part of Hilton's 1662 exploratory voyage, and from other documents, we know of probable explorers and certain migrants. The migratory voyages were less family affairs than the exploratory voyage had been:

• **Henry Douglas** paid Capt. **John Long**, of the ship *Consent*, passage for himself, his son **Thomas** of Boston, their sow, and their goods suitably packed in one hogshead, three barrels, and two chests. Henry, to be safe, wrote his will the next day, leaving his Cape Fear lands to his infant grandson, **Samuel Hett**. When the expedition aborted the Cape Fear settlement, Douglas' sow may have been among the livestock set loose on Bald Head Island. Henry Douglas wanted to stay at Cape Fear, or sail up to Albemarle and settle, but he was overruled by the rest of the colonists. Miffed, he refused to pay his return passage to Boston, so Capt. Long sued him upon their return to Massachusetts. Douglas lost his case, and the documents from the affair are a prime source for information about the early New Englanders who attempted to settle at Cape Fear.

• **John Greene** and **Enoch Greenleefe** (spelled as they signed their names) made both journeys to Cape Fear with Hilton. **Thomas Burges** likely did, too.

• **Richard Price** was the master of a second ship that went to Cape Fear, in addition to Long's. Price was captain of the bark *Plyer*. Price, also a merchant of Boston, was back in Massachusetts by May 1663.

• **Joseph Winslow** (younger brother of **Edward**) may have captained a third ship to Cape Fear, the *Content*. After the Puritans abandoned the Cape Fear, just enough time elapsed for Joseph to sail his ship to the Chesapeake's Patuxent River, where authorities seized his ship for loading tobacco without giving bond first. Winslow claimed he intended to do so on departure.

• **William** Courser was a cordwainer and later an innholder, who also served a year as town crier in Boston. Courser was part of both New England voyages to the Cape Fear River, the exploratory and migratory. He is said to have been a closet member of an underground Church of England congregation in Massachusetts (which was not public in Boston until after his death in 1687), and the Scots Charitable Society.

• **Simon Mellens**, son of **Richard Mellens**, had a bit of a wandering streak that helped him make contacts in a number of Massachusetts towns. He was on the migratory voyage.

• **Captain Elias Rowe/Row, Jr.** of Charlestown and Malden, Massachusetts, married John Long's sister, Rebecca. After Cape Fear he was involved in shipping around Port Royal, Jamaica.

• **Captain William Walley**, of Newbury Massachusetts, married another Long sister, Ruth.

• **John Pike, Jr.,** of Newbury Massachusetts, was a very young member of the company that sailed for Cape Fear in 1663.

• **Daniel Pierce/Pearse, Sr.,** of Watertown and Newbury, was a blacksmith who gave his son the legal power to act for him "when he went to Cape Faire."

• **Abraham Shepard**, of Malden Massachusetts, may have ended up on the Cape Fear expedition to dodge the consequences of a teenage prank, as his father answered for him at court saying son had "Gone to Cape faire." As his father was a tailor, it is likely young Abraham had some skill in that regard, too.

New Englanders Involved with Later Voyages:

• **Pyam Blowers**, of Boston, was with William Hilton in the Barbadian voyage to the Cape Fear River in 1663.

• **Matthew Barnes** was a miller who was likely part of the Vassall settlement in 1664-65. He may or may not have died there sometime around June 8, 1667.

• **George Davis**, weaver, did die at Cape Fear on July 14, 1667. His will left all he had to his son, **Joseph**, who also went to Charles Towne with him. The will said: "I giue all that I haue now in the ship, and that we cary with vs to Cape feare with the weauers-loome."

• **Joseph Davis**, his son, made the Cape Fear trip too. After the Vassall colony failed, he returned to Reading, Massachusetts.

• **Col. John Phillips**, captain of the ship *Ann and Katherine*, sailed for Cape Fear on December 8, 1664, no doubt with a load of New Englanders for the colony.

Known members of the Yeamans colony at Charles Towne (Not all of these may have been settlers. Some may have been Barbadian investors who never went to Carolina):

Sir John Yeamans (Governor), Major William Yeamans (John's son), Col. Edmund Reade, Symon Lambert, Niccolas Edwards, Robert Gibbs, Samuell Tidcombe, Henry Milles, Thomas Lake, Thomas Maycoke, John Somerhayes, Bertholomew Roes, John Gibbs, Basill Gibbs, John Dickenson, Thomas Gibbs, Benjamin Rees, Nathanyell Meazericke, Bartholomew Rees, Jr., John Arthur, Samuell Smith, Thomas Partridge, John Walice, John Brent, John Godfrey, George Thompson, Robert Williams, Lawrene Halske, William Burges, John Tothill, James Thorpe, Robert Tothill, William Forster, Thomas Merricke, George Phillips, Edward Jacobs, Robert Hackett, Benjamin Waddon, Robert Johnston, Thomas Dickes, Thomas Clutterhooke, John Forster, William Sharpe, John Ham, John Start, Mathew Grey, John Kerie, Ricahrd Baily, Richard Thorneburgh, John Liston, Anthony Long, Thomas Norvill, William Woodhouse, Jacob Scantlebury, Samuell Lambart, John Forster, William Byrdall, Richard Barrett, Edward Yeamans, John Killicott, Isaac Lovell, Thomas Clarke, John Woode, John Bellomy, John Greenesmith, Robert Breoitir, Thomas Dowden, Nicholas Browne, John Wilson, Robert Sinckter, Thomas Perkins, James Thorpe, Robert Richards, Benjamine Hadlut, Christopher Goupher, James Walter, James Haydensen, William Byrdall, Mordecai Bowden, Jr., George Nore, Humphrey Waterman.

Appendix IV
William Hilton, Jr.'s Description of Cape Fear (1663)

From Tuesday the 29th of September, to Friday the 2d of October, we rang'd along the Shoar from Lat. 32 deg. 20 min. to Lat. 33 deg. 11 min. but could discern no Entrance for our Ship, after we had pass'd to the Northward of 32 deg. 40 min. On Saturday, Octob. 3. a violent Storm overtook us, the Wind between North and East; which Easterly Winds and Foul Weather continu'd till Monday the 12th; by reason of which Storms and Foul Weather, we were forced to get off to Sea, to secure Ourselves and Ship, and were driven by the Rapidity of a strong Current to Cape Hatteras in Lat. 35 deg. 30 min. On Monday the 12th aforesaid we came to an Anchor in seven Fathom at Cape-Fair Road, and took the Meridian Altitude of the Sun, and were in Latitude 33 deg. 43 min. the Wind continuing still easterly, and foul Weather, till Thursday the 15th; and on Friday the 16th, the Wind being at N. W. we weigh'd and sail'd up Cape-Fair-River, some 4 or 5 Leagues, and came to an Anchor in 6 or 7 Fathom, at which time several Indians came on board, and brought us great Store of fresh Fish, large Mullets, young Bass, Shads, and several other Sorts of very good well-tasted Fish. On Saturday the 17th, we went down to the Cape, to see the English Cattle, but could not find 'em, tho' we rounded the Cape: And having an Indian Guide with us, here we rode till Oct. 24. The Wind being against us, we could not go up the River with our Ship; but went on shoar, and view'd the Land of those Quarters.

On Saturday, we weigh'd, and sail'd up the River some 4 Leagues, or thereabouts. Sunday the 25th, we weigh'd again, and row'd up the River, it being calm, and got up some 14 Leagues from the Harbour's Mouth, where we mor'd our Ship. On Monday Oct. the 26th, we went down with the Yawl, to Necoes, an Indian Plantation, and view'd the Land there. On Tuesday the 27th, we row'd up the main River, with our Long-Boat, and 12 Men, some 10 Leagues, or thereabouts. On Wednesday the 28th, we row'd up about 8 or 10 Leagues more. Thursday the 29th, was foul Weather, with much Rain and Wind, which forc'd us to make Huts, and lie still. Friday the 30th, we proceeded up the main River, 7 or 8 Leagues. Saturday the 31 st, we got up 3 or 4 Leagues more, and came to a Tree that lay cross the River; but because our Provisions were almost spent, we proceeded no farther, but return'd downward before Night, and on Monday the 2d of November, we came aboard our Ship. Tuesday the 3d, we lay still, to refresh ourselves. On Wednesday the 4th, we went 5 or 6 Leagues up the River, to search a Branch that run out of the main River towards the N. W. In which Branch we went up 5 or 6 Leagues; but not liking the Land, return'd on board that Night about Midnight, and call'd that Place Swampy-Branch. Thursday, November the 5th; we stay'd aboard. On Friday the 6th, we went up Greens-River, the Mouth of it being against the Place at which rode our Ship.

On Saturday the 7th, we proceeded up the said River some 14 or 15 Leagues in all, and found it ended in several small Branches; The Land, for the most part, being marshy and Swamps, we return'd towards our Ship, and got aboard it in the Night. Sunday November the 8th, we lay still, and on Monday the 9th, went again up the main River, being well stock'd with Provisions, and all things necessary, and proceeded upwards till Thursday noon, the 12th, at which time we came to a Place, where were two Islands in the Middle of the River; and by reason of the Crookedness of the River at that Place, several Trees lay cross both Branches, which stop'd the Passage of each Branch, so that we could proceed no farther with our Boat; but went up the River side by Land, some 3 or 4 Miles, and found the River wider and wider. So we return'd, leaving it, as far as we could see up a long Reach, running N. E. we judging ourselves near fifty Leagues North from the River's Mouth. In our Return, we view'd the Land on both Sides the River, and found as good Tracts of dry, well-wooded, pleasant, and delightful Ground, as we have seen any where in the World, with abundance of long thick Grass on it, the Land being very level, with steep Banks on both Sides the River, and in some Places very high, the Woods stor'd every where, with great Numbers of Deer and Turkies, we never going on Shoar, but we saw of each Sort; as also great Store of Partridges, Cranes, and Conies, in several Places; we like-wise heard several Wolves howling in the Woods, and saw where they had torn a Deer in Pieces. Also in the River we saw great Store of Ducks, Teal, Widgeon; and in the Woods, great Flocks of Parrakeeto's.

The Timber that the Woods afford, for the most part, consists of Oaks of four or five Sorts, all differing in Leaves, but each bearing very good Acorns. We measur'd many of The Oaks in Several Places, which we found to be, in Bigness, some Two, some Three, and others almost Four Fathom in Height, before you come to Boughs or Limbs; forty, fifty, sixty Foot, and some more; and those Oaks very common in the upper Parts of both Rivers; also a very tall large Tree of great Bigness, which some call Cyprus, the right Name we know not, growing in Swamps. Likewise Walnut, Birch, Beech, Maple, Ash, Bay, Willow, Alder, and Holly; and in the lowermost Parts innumerable Pines, tall and good for Boards of Masts, growing, for the most part, in barren and sandy, but in some Places up the River, in good Ground, being mixt amongst Oaks and other Timbers. We saw Mulberry-Trees, Multitudes of Grape-Vines, and some Grapes which we eat of. We found a very large and good Tract of Land, on the N. W. Side of the River, thin of Timber, except here and there a very great Oak, and full of Grass, commonly as high as a Man's Middle, and in many Places to his Shoulders, where we saw many Deer, and Turkies; one Deer having very large Horns, and great Body, therefore call'd it Stag-Park. It being a very pleasant and delightful Place, we travell'd in it several Miles, but saw no End thereof. So we return'd to our Boat, and proceeded down the River, and came to another Place, some twenty five Leagues from the River's Mouth on the same Side, where we found a Place, no less delightful than the former; and as far as we could judge, both Tracts came into one. This lower Place we call'd Rocky Point, because we found many Rocks and Stones, of several Sizes, upon the Land, which is not common.

We sent our Boat down the River before us; ourselves travelling by Land, many Miles. Indeed we were so much taken with the Pleasantness of the Country, that we travell'd into the Woods too far to recover our Boat and Company that Night. The next day being Sunday, we got to our Boat; and on Monday the 16th of November, proceeded down to a Place on the East-Side of the River, some 23 Leagues from the Harbour's Mouth, which we call'd Turky-Quarters, because we kill'd several Turkies thereabouts; we view'd the Land there, and found some Tracts of good Ground, and high, facing upon the River about one Mile inward, but backwards some two Miles, all Pine Land, but good Pasture Ground: We return'd to our Boat, and proceeded down some 2 or 3 Leagues, where we had formerly view'd, and found it a Tract of as good Land, as any we have seen, and had as good Timber on it. The Banks on the River being high, therefore we call'd it High-Land-Point. Having view'd that, we proceeded down the River, going on Shoar in several Places on both Sides, it being generally large Marshes, and many of them dry, that they may more fitly be calld Meadows. The Wood-Land against them is, for the most part, Pine, and in some Places as barren, as ever we saw Land, but in other Places good Pasture-Ground.

On Tuesday, November the 17th, we got aboard our Ship, riding against the Mouth of Green's River, where our Men were providing Wood, and fitting the Ship for the Sea: In the interim, we took a View of the Country on both sides of the River there, finding some good Land, but more bad, and the best not comparable to that above. Friday the 20th was foul Weather; yet in the Afternoon we weigh'd, went down the River about two Leagues, and came to an Anchor against the Mouth of Hilton's River, and took a View of the Land there on both sides, which appear'd to us much like that at Green's River. Monday the 23d, we went, with our Long-Boat well victuall'd and mann'd, up Hilton's River; and when we came three Leagues, or thereabouts, up the same, we found this and Green's River to come into one, and so continu'd for four or five Leagues, which makes a great Island betwixt them. We proceeded still up the River, till they parted again, keeping up Hilton's River on the Larboard side, and follow'd the said River five or six Leagues farther, where we found another large Branch of Green's River to come into Hilton's, which makes another great Island.

On the Starboard side going up, we proceeded still up the River some four Leagues, and return'd, taking a View of the Land on both sides, and then judg'd ourselves to be from our Ship some 18 Leagues W. and by N. One League below this Place, came four Indians in a Canoe to us, and sold us several Baskets of Acorns, which we satisfy'd them for, and so left them; but one of them follow'd us on the Shoar some two or three Miles, till he came on the Top of a high Bank, facing on the River; and as we row'd underneath it, the Fellow shot an Arrow at us, which very narrowly miss'd one of our Men, and stuck in the upper edge of the Boat; but broke in pieces, leaving the Head behind. Hereupon, we presently made to the Shoar, and went all up the Bank (except Four to guide the Boat) to look for the Indian, but could not find him: At last, we heard some sing, farther in the Woods, which we look'd upon as a Challenge to us, to come and fight them. We went towards them with all Speed; but before we came in Sight of them, heard two Guns go off from our Boat; whereupon we retreated, as fast as we could, to secure our Boat and Men. When we came to them, we found all well, and demanded the Reason of their firing the Guns: They told us, that an Indian came creeping along the Bank, as they suppos'd, to shoot at them; and therefore they shot at him at a great distance, with small Shot, but thought they did him no Hurt; for they saw him run away. Presently after our Return to the Boat, and while we were thus talking, came two Indians to us, with their Bows and Arrows, crying Bonny, Bonny. We took their Bows and Arrows from them, and gave them Beads, to their Content; then we led them, by the Hand, to the Boat, and shew'd them the Arrow-head sticking in her Side, and related to them the whole Passage; which when they understood, both of them shew'd a great Concern, and signify'd to us, by Signs, that they knew nothing of it; so we let them go, and mark'd a Tree on the Top of the Bank, calling the Place Mount-Skerry.

We look'd up the River, as far as we could discern, and saw that it widen'd, and came running directly down the Country: So we return'd, viewing the Land on both sides the River, and finding the Banks steep in some places, but very high in others. The Bank-sides are generally Clay, and as some of our Company did affirm, some Marl. The Land and Timber up this River is no way inferiour to the best in the other, which we call the main River. So far as we could discern, this seem'd as fair, if not fairer, than the former, and we think runs farther into the Country, because a strong Current comes down, and a great deal more Drift-Wood. But, to return to the Business of the Land and Timber: We saw several Plots of Ground clear'd by the Indians, after their weak manner, compass'd round with great Timber Trees, which they are no-wise able to fell, and so keep the Sun from Corn-Fields very much; yet nevertheless, we saw as large Corn-stalks, or larger, than we have seen any where else: So we proceeded down the River, till we found the Canoe the Indian was in, who shot at us.

In the Morning, we went on Shoar, and cut the same in pieces. The Indians perceiving us coming towards them, ran away. Going to his Hutt, we pull'd it down, broke his Pots, Platters, and Spoons, tore the Deer-Skins and Matts in pieces, and took away a Basket of Acorns; and afterwards proceeded down the River 2 Leagues, or thereabouts, and came to another Place of Indians, bought Acorns and some Corn of them, and went downwards 2 Leagues more.

At last, espying an Indian peeping over a high Bank, we held up a Gun at him; and calling to him, Skerry, presently several Indians came in Sight of us, and made great Signs of Friendship, saying Bonny, Bonny. Then running before us, they endeavour'd to persuade us to come on shoar; but we answer'd them with stern Countenances, and call'd out, Skerry, taking up our Guns, and threatning to shoot at them, but they still cry'd Bonny, Bonny: And when they saw they could not prevail, nor persuade us to come on shoar, two of them came off to us in a Canoe, one paddling with a great Cane, the other with his Hand. As soon as they overtook us, they laid hold of our Boat, sweating and blowing, and told us, it was Bonny on shoar, and at last persuaded us to go on shoar with them.

As soon as we landed, several Indians, to the Number of near 40 lusty Men, came to us, all in a great Sweat, and told us Bonny: We shew'd 'em the Arrow-Head in the Boat-Side, and a Piece of the Canoe we had cut in Pieces: Whereupon, the chief Man amongst them made a long Speech, threw Beads into our Boat, which is a Sign of great Love and Friendship, and gave us to understand, that when he heard of the Affront which we had receiv'd, it caus'd him to cry; and that he and his Men were come to make Peace with us, assuring us, by Signs, that they would tye the Arms, and cut off the Head, of the Fellow who had done us that Wrong; And for a farther Testimony of their Love and Good-Will towards us, they presented us with two very handsome, proper, young Indian Women, the tallest that ever we saw in this Country; which we suppos'd to be the King's Daughters, or Persons of Distinction amongst them.

Those young Women were so ready to come into our Boat; that one of them crowded in, and would hardly be persuaded to go out again. We presented the King with a Hatchet and several Beads, and made Presents of Beads also to the young Women, the chief Men, and the rest of the Indians, as far as our Beads would go. They promis'd us, in four Days, to come on board our Ship, and so departed from us. When we left the Place, which was soon after, we call'd it Mount-Bonny, because we had there concluded a firm Peace. Proceeding down the River 2 or 3 Leagues farther, we came to a Place where were 9 or 10 Canoes all together. We went ashoar there, and found several Indians; but most of them were the same which had made Peace with us before. We staid very little at that Place, but went directly down the River, and came to our Ship, before day. Thursday the 26th of November, the Wind being at South, we could not go down to the River's Mouth; but on Friday the 27th, we weigh'd at the Mouth of Hilton's River, and got down a League towards the Harbour's Mouth. On Sunday the 29th, we got down to Crane-Island, which is 4 Leagues or thereabouts, above the Entrance of the Harbour's Mouth.

On Tuesday the 1st of December, we made a Purchase of the River and Land of Cape-Fair, of Wat-Coosa, and such other Indians, as appear'd to us to be the chief of those Parts. They brought us Store of fresh Fish aboard, as Mullets, Shads, and other sorts very good. This River is all fresh Water, fit to drink. Some 8 Leagues within the Mouth, the Tide runs up about 35 Leagues, but stops and rises a great deal farther up. It flows at the Harbour's Mouth, S. E. and N. W. 6 Foot at Neap-Tides, and 8 Foot at Spring-Tides. The

Channel on the East side, by the Cape-Shoar, is the best, and lies close aboard the Cape-Land, being 3 Fathoms at high Water, in the shallowest Place in the Channel, just at the Entrance; But as soon as you are past that Place, half a Cables Length inward, you have 6 or 7 Fathoms, a fair turning Channel into the River, and so continuing 5 or 6 Leagues upwards. Afterwards the Channel is more difficult, in some Places 6 or 7 Fathoms, in others 4 or 5, and in others but 9 or 10 Foot, especially where the River is broad. When the River comes to part, and grows narrow, there it is all Channel from side to side, in most Places; tho' in some you shall have 5, 6, or 7 Fathoms, but generally 2 or 3, Sand and Oaze.

We view'd the Cape-Land, and judg'd it to be little worth, the Woods of it being shrubby and low, and the Land sandy and barren; in some Places Grass and Rushes, in others nothing but clear Sand: A Place fitter to starve Cattle, in our Judgment, than to keep'em alive; yet the Indians, as we understand, keep the English Cattle down there, and suffer them not to go off of the said Cape, (as we suppose) because the Country Indians shall have no Part with them; and therefore 'tis likely, they have fallen out about them, which shall have the greatest Share. They brought on board our Ship very good and fat Beef several times, which they sold us at a very reasonable Price; also fat and very large Swine, good and cheap; but they may thank their Friends of New-England, who brought their Hogs to so fair a Market. Some of the Indians brought very good Salt aboard us, and made Signs, pointing to both sides of the River's Mouth, that there was great Store thereabouts. We saw up the River, several good Places for the setting up of Corn of Saw-Mills. In that time, as our Business call'd us up and down the River and Branches, we kill'd of wild Fowl, 4 Swans, 10 Geese, 29 Cranes, 10 Turkies, 40 Ducks and Mallards, 3 dozen of Parrakeeto's, and 6 dozen of other small Fowls, as Curlues and Plover, &c.

Whereas there was a Writing left in a Post, at the Point of Cape-Fair River, by those New-England-Men, that left Cattle with the Indians there, the Contents whereof tended not only to the Disparagement of the Land about the said River, but also to the great Discouragement of all such as should hereafter come into those Parts to settle: In answer to that scandalous Writing, We, whose Names are underwritten, do affirm, That we have seen, facing both sides the River and Branches of Cape-Fair aforesaid, as good Land, and as well timber'd, as any we have seen in any other Part of the World, sufficient to accommodate Thousands of our English Nation, and lying commodiously by the said River's Side. On Friday the 4th of December, the Wind being fair, we put out to Sea, bound for Barbados; and, on the 6th of February, 1663/4, came to an Anchor in Carlisle-Bay; it having pleas'd God, after several ap-

parent Dangers both by Sea and Land, to bring us all in Safety to our long-wish'd for and much desir'd Port, to render an Account of our Discovery; the Verity of which we do assert.
Anthony Long.
William Hilton.
Peter Fabian.

Appendix V
Signatures of the Lords Proprietors of Carolina
and a
Facsimile of the Lone Surviving Record Book of the
Lords Proprietors of Carolina

Carolina Lords Proprietors Account of Disbursements & Receipts

1663 – 1666

The Lords Proprietors of Carolina are Debtor

1663		£	s	d
June y̆ 6	To Cash paid for this booke	00	04	03
	To mōn. Laprerey for 1 monthes Sallery	04	00	00
July 12	To ditto for another monthes Sallery	04	00	=
25	For y̆ sight of S.ʳ Robᵗ Heathes Instrucc͠ions in y̆ Signet Office in relation to his Pattent for Carolina	00	02	=
Sept.ᵇʳ 5	For parchm.ᵗ & wax for y̆ Ingroseing & Sealeing of S.ʳ Wᵐ Berkeleye's Commission & powʳ for y̆ commissionateing of a Gov.ⁿ.ʳ &c upon Albemarle river	00	00	10
9	For an order of y̆ King & his Councell abrogateing S.ʳ Robᵗ Heathe's Pattent, wᶜᴴ was pᵈ S.ʳ Richᵈ Browne's Clarke	00	10	=
January 5.ᵗʰ	for y̆ Charge of y̆ Pattent of his Ma.ᵗⁱᵉˢ Grannt for Carolina, pᵈ by S.ʳ Geo. Carteret wᵗʰ an Exemplification Thereof as by S.ʳ Carteret's note	106	11	6
19	To S.ʳ Wᵐ Morris Clarke for 2 Lettʳˢ from y̆ Kinge & To Serient Towntayne for his advice in y̆ Lord's Pattent	02	00	=
		03	06	=
29	For a box to put sᵈ Pattent in	00	03	=
1664 July 19	To Cash given S.ʳ Anthony Morgan for drawing Sev.ᵉʳˡ Commissions	05	00	=
August 22	To ditto pᵈ for a diner, at a meeting w.ᵗʰ M.ʳ Sampson & M.ʳ Vassall about a treaty wᵗʰ Them Concerneing Carolina	01	04	00

		£ s d
1664		
November 22	To ditto for 2 Skins of Partchm.t & Ingroceing Mr Vassalls Comission for Deputy Govern.r	00 09 0
December 15	To ditto p.d Mr Symonds for Ingraveing a Greate Seale	40 00 =
January 10	To ditto for 4 Skins of Partchm.t for y.e Concessions for Mai: Yeamans to Signe to y.e Lords	00 06 =
14	To ditto for 4 tynn boxes to put Seales in & 2 lether ones for y.e Concessions & Comissions sent to S.r John Yeamans	00 05 02
1665		
March 31	To ditto p.d Mr Carrington a Scrivenr for Ingroseing y.e Concessions &.t y.e Lords signed to S.r Jn:o Yeamans; and Comissions, done by Mr Westlake & my man	06 00 =
	To Sev.ll Disbursem.ts as Armes, Amunicon, Shot, & other necessaryes w.ch y.e Lords undertooke to furnish towards y.e Settlem.t of Port Royall as p Pticulars	284 12 03
	To 100 firelockes, Custome, fraught & Charges w.ch was sent upon y.e Lords accompt to be sold at Barbados	52 19 08

		£	s	d
1665				
uch 31	To 3ˢ pᵈ more in shiping, Cocket, & Custome	00	03	=
	To Cash pᵈ for pˡ of Letters about this bussiness	00	08	0
	To ditto pᵈ for ye Dockets of 2 pattents to send Govnor Drumond	00	05	00
	To ditto pᵈ Mr Symonds for a little Seale for ye County of Albemarle — for a screw for ye Greate Seale	08	00	=
	For fees pᵈ Mr Westlake for ye last pattent as by his Note appeares	71	02	09
	To Mr Symonds for a little Seale wᵗʰ an Ivery handle for ye County of Clarendon	06	00	=
		600	08	03

⅌ Contra is Creditor

1663		£	s	d
ult 2d	By his Grace ye Duke of Albemarle recd of him	25	00	00
	By Wm Lord Craven recd of him	25	00	=
ⁿ⁹ 6	By John Lord Berksley recd of him	25	00	=
	By Anthony Lord Ashley recd of him	25	00	=
	By Sr Geo. Carteret recd of him	25	00	=
	By Sr John Colleton I place to this acct	25	00	=
'664				
ny 3d	By Wm Earle of Craven recd of him	50	00	=
	By John Lord Berksley recd of him	50	00	=
	By Sr John Colleton I place to this acct	50	00	=
ny 9	By ye Duke of Albemarle recd of him	50	00	=
'666				
ill 13	By Wm Earle of Craven recd of him	25	00	=
14	By ye Duke of Albemarle recd of him	25	00	=
	By Sr Geo. Carteret recd of him	75	00	=
	By Anthony Lord Ashley recd of him	75	00	=
	By John Lord Berksley recd of him	25	00	=
	By Sr John Colleton I place to this acct	25	00	=
		600	00	00

Particular of things sent for setling Port Royal

1664

A Perticuler of Ordinance Armes powdr Shott & other things sent to ye Barbados ₱ ye ship John & Thomas in ordr to ye planting & Setling of Port Royall December 28th 1664

		£	s	d
	For ye Kings warrant for ye 12 Great Guns	06	00	00
	For shipping wharfage, Leighterage, & fees at ye Tower for ye sd Guns	03	13	00
4	minion Carriages at 18s ₱ Carriage is	03	12	00
6	great Seacar Carriages at 24s ₱ Carriage is	07	04	00
2	field minion Carriages at	04	00	00
2	paire of Wheeles & Iron worke	04	10	00
5c	of Iron worke to build 10 Carriages at 32s ₱ Ct is	08	00	00
44	Lince pins at 2d a peece is	00	07	04
24	Strait fore Lockses at	00	02	00
	1c 0qr 9li of Iron worke for ye two field Carriages at 32s ₱ Ct	01	14	07
	for carrying ye Carriages to ye Smythes house	00	02	06
10c	of Musket shott at 19s ₱ Ct is	09	10	00
3c	of Swan Shott at 20s ₱ Ct is	03	00	00
	for 13 barrells at 8d ₱ barrell is	00	08	08
	for porterage to ye water side	00	01	00
6c	of Match at 28s ₱ Ct is	08	08	00
200	Collers of Bandaleares at 16d ₱ coller is	13	06	08

	£	s	d
of fire Locke Muskets at 10ˢ ℔ musket is	50	00	00
of Match Locke Muskets at 8ˢ ℔ musket is	40	00	00
of halfe picke heads at 3ᵈ ℔ peece is	02	10	00
of broaken flints at 12ᵈ ℔ cᵗ is	01	00	00
fn 20 matts & 20ᴸᵇ Spun yarne fn yᵉ 200 Muskets	00	18	04
fn a Chest for yᵉ picke heads & flints	00	03	06
fn whole flint stones	00	02	06
pᵈ carrying aboard	00	03	04
pᵈ yᵉ Searcher when they were shipt of	00	05	00
pᵈ porterage to yᵉ waterside	00	01	00
barrels of powdr at 3ˡⁱ 10ˢ ℔ barrell is	70	00	00
of round minion & Saber shott weying 12.1.6 at 13ˢ ℔ Cᵗ is	08	00	00
of burr shott at 13ˢ ℔ Cᵗ is	01	06	00
horner at 12ᵈ is	00	06	00
primeing Irons	00	03	00
bitts at 6ᵈ ℔ peece is	00	01	06
fn charges in sending them aboard	00	12	06
doz. of ramers at 2ˢ ℔ peece is	00	04	00
doz. of spunges at	00	07	06
powdr Ladles at	01	02	06
dimy Collvering Ladle at	00	06	06
feild Tomkins	00	14	00
doz. of burshott cases at	01	01	00

		£	s	d
18	Cartrages for pound: at	01	05	06
12	sheepe skins at	01	10	00
2	doz. of Spunge staves	01	10	00
6	Lanthornes	00	13	00
2	bond barrells	00	07	00
1	Reame of Cartrage paper	00	18	00
6	Wadhookes	00	06	00
1	great packe basket 2/ and Carrying aboard 2/	00	04	00
	for Custome, Searcher' fees Cocketts, shiping & carrying aboard most of yt goods. above	02	10	06
	fraught & primage	22	10	01
		285	12	00
	To deduct for rebate on yt Sevʳᵃˡˡ Bills paid above	000	19	09
		284	12	03

Invoyce of 100 fire Lockes sent to yͤ Barbados by yͤ John & Thomas for yͤ accͦ of yͤ Lord Proprietͬˢ of Carolina to be soald to such psons as shall desire to goe to Carolina but wante armes

		£	s	d
100	fire Locke muskets at 10ˢ ₱ peec is	50	00	00
	for 10 Matts & 10ᴸᴮ of spunn yarne for ye Muskets	00	09	02
	Custome & other Charges in shiping them	00	09	08
	fraught & Primage	02	00	10
		52	19	09
	The some ₱ contra is	284	12	03
	To Mͬ Symonds for a Little Seale & a screw for yͤ great one	00	00	00
		284	12	03

Fees in Passing y:e Charter & Duplicate of Carolina

	£	s	d
Fees in passing ye Charter & Duplicate of Carolina			
For ye Kings warrant ye Secrytary takeing noe fee	01	02	06
For Mr Anthony Denn^{ll} & his Clarkes fee for drawing & Ingroseing ye bill	17	17	06
For ye Kings signeing ye bill (ye Secrytary takeing noe fee	01	02	06
For ye fees of ye Signet & privy Seale 8 each	16	00	00
For fees to ye Mr of ye pattent Office & for Velom, ruleing, painting & Ingroseing ye pattent for ye broad Seale & to ye Clarke	25	05	00
For Lord Chancellors purseberar & his Clerke	01	09	00
For Lord Chancellors Servants	02	00	00
For fees of ye Hannop Office	24	00	00
For fees of ye Duplicate of ye Pattent office, & for ye velom & ingroseing it & to ye clerkes	15	00	00
For fee at ye Hannape Office	02	15	00
	106	11	06

Fees p^d in passing ye last pattent for Carolina

	£	s	d
For ye Kings warrant & Signeing ye bill, ye Secrytary takeing noe fee	04	00	00

	£	s	d
for Mr Attorney Genll & his Clarkes fee for drawing & Ingrossing ye bill &c	11	05	00
for fees pd at ye Signet Office & ye Privy Seale	17	06	08
for my Lord Chancellors purse bearer & Clarkes	01	04	00
for ye Master of ye pattent office for velome ruling &c, & Ingrossing ye pattent & to ye Clarkes	16	15	06
for fees at ye Hanop Office &c	20	07	08
for Expences there in attending ye Great Seale	00	03	06
	71	02	04

Bibliography

Primary Sources

Cabeza de Vaca, Alvar Nunez. Rolena Adorno and Patrick Charles Pautz, editors. *The Narrative of Cabeza de Vaca*. Lincoln, NE: University of Nebraska Press, 2003.

"Concessions and Agreement of the Lords Proprietors of the Province of Carolina, 1665." Harvard University Law School. *The Avalon Project: Documents in Law, History & Diplomacy*. http://avalon.law.yale.edu/17th_century/nc03.asp. (accessed 11/27/10)

Cooper, Anthony Ashley. *The Shaftesbury Papers*. Charleston, S.C.: Tempus Publishing, 2000. (reprint)

Grant, William Lawson and Munro, James. *Acts of the Privy Council of England: Colonial Series, Vol. I*. London: HM Stationery Office, 1908.

Hilton, William, Jr. "William Hilton Explores the Cape Fear River (1663)." Learn NC, published 2008. http://learnnc.org/lp/editions/nchist-colonial/1899. (accessed   12/6/09).

Horne, Robert. "A Brief Description of the Province of Carolina." London, 1666. Reprinted in Alexander S. Salley, Jr., ed. *Narratives of Early Carolina, 1650-1708* (New York, 1911), pp 66-73. Accessed from Learn NC website. http://http:www.learnnc.org/lp/pdf/a-brief-description-of-the-p2043.pdf. (accessed 7/17/2010).

Lawson, John. *A New Voyage to Carolina*. Edited by Hugh Lefler. Chapel Hill: University of North Carolina Press, 1984; originally published 1709.

Ligon, Richard; Karen Ordahl Kupperman, editor. *A True and Exact History of the Island of Barbados*. Indianapolis, IN: Hackett Publishing Company, 2011. (reprint of 1657 original)

Lords Proprietors' Accounts, 1663-1664. C.O. 5/286/-)

Lords Proprietors of Carolina. "A Declaration and Proposals of the Lords Proprietors of Carolina (1663)." *LearnNC.org* website. http://www.learnnc.org/lp/editions/nchist-hist/1666. (accessed 8/14/13).

Colonial and State Records of North Carolina. http://docsouth.unc.edu/csr/ (accessed 9/1/12-9/30/12)

North Carolina Under the Lords Proprietors: A Series of Original Documents (many signed by the Lords Proprietors) to Governor Stephens and Governor Carteret between the years 1664 and 1674, including The Form of Government of 1667, the original document signed by the Lords Proprietors. London: Maggs Brothers, 1933.

Parker, Mattie Erma Edwards, et. al., editors. *Colonial Records of North Carolina: Colonial Records Project*. Raleigh: North Carolina Colonial Records Project, and North Carolina State Dept. of Archives and History, 1964.

Quinn, David B. and Alison M., editors. *The First Colonists: Documents on the Planting of The First English Settlements in North America, 1584-1590*. Raleigh: N.C. Department of Cultural Resources, Division of Archives & History, 1982.

Sainsbury, William Noel, editor. *Calendar of State Papers, Colonial Series, America and West Indies, 1661-1668: preserved in Her Majesty's Public Record Office.* London: Longman & Co., 1880.

------------- *Calendar of State Papers, Colonial Series, America and West Indies, 1669-1674.* London: Her Majesty's Stationery Office, 1889.

Salley, Alexander S., editor. *Narratives of Early Carolina, 1650-1708, Vol. 11,* New York: Charles Scribner's & Sons, 1911.

Vassall, John. "Letter From John Vassall to John Colleton (1667)." From Documenting the South: Colonial and State Records of North Carolina, http://docsouth.unc.edu/csr/index.html/document/csr01-0061(accessed 9/1/12-9/30/12)

Verrazano, Giovanni de. "Letter to King Francis I of France, 8 July 1524: reporting on his voyage to the New World." National Humanities Center, http://nationalhumanitiescenter.org/pds/amerbegin/contact/text4/verrazzano.pdf (accessed 1/17/12).

Withington, Lothrop. "Virginia Gleanings in England." *The Virginia Magazine of History and Biography*, Vol. 12, No. 3 (January 1905): 297-310.

Unpublished Manuscripts, Theses, and Dissertations
Beckles, Hilary M. *"White Labor in Black Slave Plantation Society and Economy: A Case Study of Indentured Labour in Seventeenth Century Barbados,"* unpublished Ph.D dissertation, University of Hull, 1980.

Buchanan, J.E. "The Colleton Family and the Early History of South Carolina and Barbados, 1646-1775." Ph.D dissertation, University of Edinburgh, 1989.

Butler, Lindley S. "The Historical Significance of Charles Towne on the Cape Fear." Manuscript. From the collection of the N.C. Maritime Museum at Southport.

Colson, Tammy L. "A Family Feud: The Origins of Settlement of the Cape Fear River and Wilmington, North Carolina." Unpublished paper, June 18, 1999. http://www.fortunecity.com/millenium/hollyoaks/410/colonial.htm. (accessed 5/22/2010).

Fagg, Daniel W., Jr. "Carolina, 1663-1683: The Founding of a Proprietary." Ph.D dissertation, Emory University, 1970.

Grady, Timothy Paul. "On the Path to Slavery: Indentured Servitude in Barbados and Virginia during the Seventeenth Century." Master's thesis, Virginia Polytechnic Institute and State University, 2000.

Harrington, Matthew Craig, ""The Worke Wee May Doe in the World": The Western Design and the Anglo-Spanish Struggle for the Caribbean, 1654-1655." Masters Thesis, Florida State University, 2004. Electronic Theses, Treatises and Dissertations. Paper 4248. http://diginole.lib.fsu.edu/etd

Howell, Andrew J. "Promoting Real Estate In 1666." Andrew J. Howell Papers, October 1931. N.C. Room, New Hanover County Public Library.

Legg, James B. and Watson, W. Bryan Jr. "The Exploration, Settlement, and Abandonment of the Lower Cape Fear, 1662-67: The Historical Record and the Archaeological Evidence at the Supposed Site of Charles Towne." Unpublished manuscript, May 1979. Author's collection.

Loftfield, Thomas C. "Historical Archaeology at the Site of Charles Towne On the Cape Fear River (1663-1667)." Unpublished paper presented to the Southeastern Archaeology Conference, 1989.

Loftfield, Thomas C. and Butler, Lindley S. "Barbadians on the Cape Fear: The Sugar Business and Seventeenth Century Carolina." Unpublished paper, author's collection, n.d.

Lowry, Charles Bryan. "Class, Politics, Rebellion and Regional Development in Proprietary North Carolina, 1697-1720," unpublished Ph.D dissertation, University of Florida, 1979.

Paschal, Herbert Richard, Jr. "Proprietary North Carolina: A Study in Colonial Government." Ph.D dissertation, University of North Carolina, 1961.

Rugemer, Ed. "Making Slavery English: Comprehensive Slave Codes in the Greater Caribbean during the Seventeenth Century." Presentation, Yale University, British Studies Colloquium, 2011.

Seaman, Rebecca M. "Native American Enslavement in Proprietary North Carolina: A Causality Study." Ph.D dissertation, Auburn University, 2001.

South, Stanley. "The Unabridged Version of Tribes of the Carolina Lowland: Pedee- Sewee-Winyaw-Waccamaw-Cape Fear-Congaree-Wateree-Santee." (1972). Research Manuscript Series. Book 16. http://scholarcommons.sc.edu/archanth_books/16

South, Stanley and Hartley, Michael. "Deep Water and High Ground: Seventeenth Century Low Country Settlement" (1980). *Research Manuscript Series*, Book 159. http://scholarcommons.sc.edu/archanth_books/159.

Suttlemeyre, Charles Greer, Jr. "Proprietary Policy and the Development of North Carolina, 1663-1729." Ph.D dissertation, St. Benet's Hall, Oxford University, 1991.

Waddell, Alfred M. "Early Explorers of the Cape Fear." Delivered before the North Carolina Society of Colonial Dames at Brunswick Town site. William R. Reaves Collection, New Hanover County Public Library.

Compilations/Anthologies/Collections/References

Bailyn, Bernard and Morgan, Philip D., editors. *Strangers within the Realm: Cultural Margins of the First British Empire*. Chapel Hill: University of North Carolina Press, 1991.

Billings, Warren M. *The Old Dominion in the Seventeenth Century: A Documentary History of Virginia, 1606-1689*. Chapel Hill: University of North Carolina Press, 1975.

Coclanis, Peter, editor. *The Atlantic Economy during the Seventeenth and Eighteenth Centuries: Organization, Operation, Practice, and Personnel*. Columbia: University of South Carolina Press, 2005.

Garraty, John A. and Carnes, Mark C., editors. *American National Biography, Volume 10*. New York: Oxford University Press, 1999.

Greene, Jack P., editor. *Settlements to Society, 1607-1763*. New York: W.W. Norton & Company, 1975.

Jackson, Claude V. III; Fryar, Jack E. Jr. (ed.). *The Big Book of the Cape Fear River*. Wilmington: Dram Tree Books, 2008.

N.C. Museum of History Timeline http://ncmuseumofhistory.org/nchh/seventeenth.html (accessed 9/29/12)

Powell, William S. *Dictionary of North Carolina Biography, Vol. 6*. Chapel Hill, N.C.: University of North Carolina Press, 1996.

Shilstone, E.M. "Nicholas Plantation and Some of Its Associations" in *Chapters in Barbados History*, Peter F. Campbell, ed. Bridgeport: Barbados Museum and Historical Society, 1986.

Withington, Lothrop. *Virginia Gleanings in England: Abstracts of 17th and 18th-century English Wills and Administrations Relating to Virginia and Virginians: a Consolidation of Articles from The Virginia Magazine of History and Biography*. Genealogical Publishing Co., 1980.

Monographs

Ackroyd, Peter. *Rebellion: The History of England from James I to the Glorious Revolution*. New York: Thomas Dunne, 2014.

Andrews, Charles M. *Our Earliest Colonial Settlements: Their Diversity of Origin and Later Characteristics*. New York: New York University Press, 1933.

Armitage, David and Braddick, Michael J., editors. *The British Atlantic World, 1500-1800*. New York: Palgrave Macmillan, 2009.

Bailyn, Bernard. *The Barbarous Years: The Peopling of British North America: The Conflict of Civilizations, 1600-1675*. New York: Vintage Books, 2012.

Beckles, Hilary. *A History of Barbados: From Amerindian settlement to nation-state*. Cambridge: Cambridge University Press, 1990.

Beer, George Louis. *The Origins of the British Colonial System, 1578-1660*. Gloucester, MA: Peter Smith, 1959.

------------- *The Old Colonial System, 1660-1754, Pt. I*. New York: Peter Smith, 1933.

Bell, Walter George. *The Great Plague in London in 1665*. London: John Lane, The Bodley Head, 1924.

Billings, Warren M. *Sir William Berkeley and the Forging of Colonial Virginia*, Baton Rouge: Louisiana State University Press, 2004.

Boles, John B. *Black Southerners, 1619-1869*. Lexington: University of Kentucky Press, 1984.

Bridenbaugh, Carl. *No Peace Beyond The Line: The English in the Caribbean, 1624-1690*. New York: Oxford University Press, 1972.

------------- *Vexed and Troubled Englishmen, 1590-1642*. New York: Oxford University Press, 1967.

Burk, Kathleen. *Old World, New World: Great Britain and America from the Beginning*. New York: Grove Press, 2009.

Burns, Sir Alan. *History of the British West Indies*. London: George Allen and Unwin. Ltd., 1965.

Calder, Charles Maclear. *John Vassall and his Descendants*. First published 1921.

Canny, Nicholas. *The Origins of Empire*. Oxford: Oxford University Press, 1998.

Carlton, Charles. *Going to the wars: the experience of the British Civil Wars, 1638-1651*. London and New York: Routledge, 1992.

------------- *Archbishop William Laud*. London: Routledge, 1987.

Carpenter, Stanley D. M. *Military leadership in the British civil wars, 1642–1651: The Genius Of This Age*. Abingdon, UK: Frank Cass, 2005.

Carse, Robert. *The Seafarers: A History of Maritime America, 1620-1820*. New York: Harper & Row, 1964.

Craven, Wesley Frank. *The Southern Colonies in the Seventeenth Century: 1607-1689*. Baton Rouge: Louisiana State University Press, 1949.

Culver, Henry B. *The Book of Old Ships and Something of their Evolution and Romance*. New York: Bonanza Books, 1924.

Davis, Ralph. *English Merchant Shipping and Anglo-Dutch Rivalry in the Seventeenth Century*. London: Her Majesty's Printing Office, National Maritime Museum, 1975.

Dunn, Richard S. *Sugar and slaves: The rise of the planter class in the English West Indies, 1624-1713*. New York: Norton, 1973.

Fenn, Elizabeth A. and Wood, Peter H. *Natives & Newcomers: The Way We Lived in North Carolina before 1770*. Chapel Hill: University of North Carolina Press, 1983.

Ferguson, James. *A Traveller's History of the Caribbean*. Northampton, MA: Interlink Books, 2008.

Fraser, Antonia. *King Charles II. London*. London: Weidenfeld and Nicolson, 1979.

Fuller, J.F.C. *A Military History of the Western World: From the Defeat of the Spanish Armada to the Battle of Waterloo*. New York: Da Capo Press, 1955.

Galenson, David W. *Traders, Planters, and Slaves: Market Behavior in Early English America*. London: Cambridge University Press, 1986.

Gallay, Alan. *The Indian Slave Trade: The Rise of the English Empire in the American South, 1670-1717*. Yale University Press, 2002.

Gardiner, Samuel Rawson. *History of the Commonwealth and Protectorate, 1649-1656: 1655-1656*. Vol. 4. London: Longmans, Green, and Co., 1903.

Gragg, Larry. *Englishmen Transplanted: The English Colonization of Barbados, 1627-1660*. Oxford: Oxford University Press, 2003.

Gregg, Pauline. *King Charles I*. Berkeley: University of California Press, 1984.

Handler, Jerome S. and Lange, Frederick W. *Plantation Slavery in Barbados: An Archaeological and Historical Investigation*. Cambridge: Harvard University Press, 1978.

Hanson, Neil. *The Great Fire of London: In That Apocalyptic Year, 1666.* Hoboken, New Jersey: John Wiley and Sons, 2002.

Hatfield, April Lee. *Atlantic Virginia: Intercolonial Relations in the Seventeenth Century,* Philadelphia: University of Pennsylvania Press, 2007.

Hawks, Francis L. *History of North Carolina with Maps and Illustrations, Vols. I & II* Fayetteville, N.C.: E.J. Hale & Son, 1857.

Horn, James. *Adapting to a New World: English Society in the Seventeenth-Century Chesapeake.* Chapel Hill: University of North Carolina Press, 1994.

-------------- *A Land As God Made It: Jamestowne and the Birth of America.* New York: Basic Books, 2005.

Hudgins, James P. *Tropical Cyclones Affecting North Carolina since 1566: An Historical Perspective.* Blacksburg, VA: National Weather Service, 2003.

Hudson, Charles. *The Juan Pardo Expeditions: Exploration of the Carolinas and Tennessee, 1566-1568.* Washington, D.C.: Smithsonian Institution Press, 1990.

Johnston, William Dawson. *The History of England from the Accession of James the Second.* New York: Houghton Mifflin & Co., 1901.

Klein, Herbert S. and Vinson, Ben. *African Slavery and the Caribbean.* Oxford: Oxford University Press, 2007.

Koot, Christian J. *Empire at the Periphery: British Colonists, Anglo-Dutch Trade, and the Development of the British Atlantic, 1621-1713.* New York: New York University Press, 2011.

Kupperman, Karen Ordahl. *Indians & English: Facing Off in Early America.* Ithaca: Cornell University Press, 2000.

La Vere, David. *The Lost Rocks: The Dare Stones and the Unsolved Mystery of Sir Walter Raleigh's Lost Colony*. Wilmington, N.C.: Dram Tree Books, 2010.

Lee, E. Lawrence. *The History of Brunswick County, North Carolina*. N.p., n.d.

-------------- *The Lower Cape Fear in Colonial Days*. Chapel Hill, N.C.: University of North Carolina Press, 1965.

Lefler, Hugh T. and Powell, William S. *Colonial North Carolina*. New York: Charles Scribner's Sons, 1973.

LeMaster, Michelle and Wood, Bradford J. *Creating and Contesting Carolina: Proprietary Era Histories*. Columbia: University of South Carolina Press, 2013.

Lockridge, Kenneth A. *Settlement and Unsettlement in Early America*. Cambridge: Cambridge University Press, 1981.

McClelland, J.S. *A History of Western Political Thought*. London: Routledge, 1996.

McIlvenna, Noellen. *A Very Mutinous People: The Struggle for North Carolina, 1660-1713*. Chapel Hill: University of North Carolina Press, 2009.

McCusker, John J. and Menard, Russell R. *The Economy of British America, 1607-1789*. Chapel Hill: University of North Carolina, 1985.

Marley, David F. *Wars of the Americas*. Santa Barbara: ABC-CLIO, 1998.

Martin, Colin and Parker, Geoffrey. *The Spanish Armada*. New York: Penguin   Books, 1999.

Menard, Russell R. *Sweet Negotiations: Sugar, Slavery, and Plantation Agriculture in Early Barbados*. Charlottesville: University of Virginia Press, 2006.

Miller, John. *Restoration England: The Reign of Charles II*. New York: Longman, Inc., 1985.

Moote, A. Lloyd and Dorothy C. Moote. *The Great Plague: The Story of London's Most Deadly Year*. Baltimore: Johns Hopkins University Press, 2004.

Morison, Samuel Eliot. *The European Discovery of America: The Northern Voyages*. New York: Oxford University Press, 1971.

Nash, Gary B. *Red, White, and Black: The Peoples of Early America*. Engelwood Cliffs, N.J.: Prentice-Hall Publishers, 1982.

National Maritime Museum. *The Second Dutch War: Described in pictures & manuscripts of the time*, London: Her Majesty's Printing Office, 1967.

Osgood, Herbert L. *The American Colonies in the Seventeenth Century*. New York: The Macmillan Company, 1904.

Parry, J.H., Sherlock, Philip and Maingot, Anthony. *A Short History of the West Indies*, New York: St. Martin's Press, 1987.

Pestana, Carla Gardina. *The English Atlantic in an Age of Revolution, 1640-1661*. Cambridge, MA: Harvard University Press, 2004.

Pipes, Richard. *Property and Freedom*. New York: Alfred A. Knopf, 1999.

Powell, William S. *North Carolina Through Four Centuries*. Chapel Hill: University of North Carolina Press, 1989.

-------------- *The Proprietors of Carolina*. Raleigh, N.C.: The Carolina Tercentenary Commission, 1963.

-------------- *The Carolina Charter of 1663: How It Came to North Carolina and It's Place in History*. Raleigh: N.C. State Department of Archives & History, 1954.

Puckrein, Gary A. *Little England: Plantation Society and Anglo-Barbadian Politics, 1627-1700*. New York: New York University Press, 1984.

Quattlebaum, Paul. *Land Called Chicora: The Carolinas Under Spanish Rule With French Intrusion, 1520-1670*. Spartanburg, S.C.: The Reprint Company, 1973.

Quinn, Arthur. *A New World: An Epic of Colonial America from the Founding of Jamestown to the Fall of Quebec*. Boston: Faber & Faber, 1994.

Quinn, David Beers. *North America from Earliest Discovery to First Settlements: The Norse Voyages to 1612*. New York: Harper & Row, 1977.

Quinn, David B. and Alison M., editors. *The First Colonists: Documents on the Planting of The First English Settlements in North America, 1584-1590*. Raleigh, N.C.: Division of Archives & History, Dept. of Cultural Resources, 1982.

Raper, Charles Lee. *North Carolina: A Study in English Colonial Government*. New York: The Macmillan Company, 1904.

Rawley, James A. *The Transatlantic Slave Trade: A History*. Lincoln, NE: University of Nebraska Press, 2005 (revised edition).

Rodger, N.A.M. *The Command of the Ocean: A Naval History of Britain 1649 —1815*. London: Penguin Group, 2004.

Roper, L.H. *Conceiving Carolina: Proprietors, Planters, and Plots, 1662-1729*. New York: Palgrave Macmillan, 2004.

Schama, Simon. *A History of Britain, Vol. II: The Wars of the British, 1603-1776*. New York: Hyperion Books, 2001.

Silver, Timothy. *A New Face On The Countryside: Indians, colonists, and slaves in South Atlantic forests, 1500-1800*. Cambridge: Cambridge University Press, 1990.

Smith, Merril D. *Women's Roles in Seventeenth-Century America*. Connecticut: Greenwood Press, 2008.

Sprunt, James. *Chronicles of the Cape Fear River: 1660-1916*. 2nd ed. Wilmington, N.C.: Dram Tree Books, 2005.

Steele, Ian K. *The English Atlantic, 1675-1740: An Exploration of Communication and Community*. Oxford: Oxford University Press, 1986.

Tinniswood, Adrian, *By Permission of Heaven: The True Story of the Great Fire of London*. New York: Riverhead Books, 2003.

Tree, Ronald. *A History of Barbados*. London: Hart-Davis, MacGibbon, 1972.

Walsh, Lorena S. *Motives of Honor, Pleasure, & Profit: Plantation Management in the Colonial Chesapeake, 1607-1763*. Chapel Hill: University of North Carolina Press, 2010.

Wedgewood, C.V. *The King's War: 1641-1647*. London: Fontana Press, 1970.

Wright, Louis B. *The Colonial Search for a Southern Eden*. Tuscaloosa, AL: University of Alabama Press, 1953.

-------------- *The Colonial Civilisation of North America, 1607-1763*. London: Eyre & Spottiswoode, 1949.

-------------- *The Dream of Prosperity in Colonial America*. New York: New York University Press, 1965.

Articles and Essays

Armitage, David. "John Locke, Carolina, and the Two Treatises of Government." *Political Theory*, Vol. 32, No. 5 (October 2004): 602-627.

Beckles, Hilary McD. "The Hub of Empire: The Caribbean and Britain in the Seventeenth Century" in *The Origins of Empire: British Overseas Enterprise to the Close of the Seventeenth Century*. New York: Oxford University Press, 1998.

Billings, Warren M. "Sir William Berkeley and the Carolina Proprietary." *North Carolina Historical Review*, Vol. 72, No. 3 (July 1995): 329-342.

Butler, Lindley S. "The Early Settlement of Carolina: Virginia's Southern Frontier." *The Virginia Magazine of History and Biography*, Vol. 79, No. 1, Part One (Jan., 1971): 20-28.

Butler, Lindley S. and Paschal, Herbert R. "Yeamans, Sir John." *NCpedia* website. http://ncpedia.org. (accessed 1/15/13).

Carney, Richard. "Roanoke Island." *N.C. History Project* http://northcarolinahistory.org/encyclopedia/25/entry (accessed 9/12/12)

Chisolm, Hugh, ed. Entry for "Gonzalo Oviedo Y Valdes." *Encyclopedia Brittanica* (1911). http://www.studylight.org/encyclopedias/bri/view.cgi?number=13504. (accessed 2/2/2015).

Cumming, William P. "Naming Carolina." http://www.ah.dcr.state.nc.us/sections/hp/colonial/Nchr/Subjects/cumming.htm. (accessed 11/17/10)

Dunn, Richard S. "The English Sugar Islands and the Founding of South Carolina." *The South Carolina Historical Magazine*, Vol. 101, No. 2 (April 2000): 142-154.

-------------- "The Barbados Census of 1680: Profile of the Richest Colony in English America." *The William & Mary Quarterly*, Vol. 26, No. 1 (January 1969): 3-30.

Earle, Carville V. "The First English Towns in North America." *Geographical Review*, Vol. 67, No. 1 (January 1977): 34-50.

Edelson, S. Max. "Clearing Swamps, Harvesting Forests: Trees and the Making of a Plantation Landscape in the Colonial South Carolina Lowcountry." *Agricultural History*, Vol. 81, No. 3 (Summer 2007): 381-406.

-------------- "Defining Carolina: Cartography and Colonization in the North American Southeast, 1657-1733," in Michelle LeMaster and Bradford J. Wood, *Creating and Contesting Carolina: Proprietary Era Histories*. Columbia: University of South Carolina Press, 2013.

Eltis, David. "The Volume of the Transatlantic Slave Trade: A Reassessment." *The William & Mary Quarterly* (2001): 17-46.

-------------- "A Brief Overview of the Trans-Atlantic Slave Trade." Emory University, 2009. http://slavevoyages.org/tast/assessment/essays-intro-01.faces. (accessed 1/17/2013)

Fagg, Daniel W., Jr. "Sleeping Not with the King's Grant: A Rereading of Some Proprietary Documents, 1663-1667." *North Carolina Historical Review*, Vol. XLVIII, No. 2 (April 1971): 171-185.

Farnie, D.A. "The Commercial Empire of the Atlantic, 1607-1783." *The Economic History Review*, New Series, Vol. 15, No. 2 (1962): 205-218.

Gaston, George H. "The Boundaries of Virginia." *Tyler's Quarterly Historical and Genealogical Magazine*, Vol. X, No. 4 (1929): 217-237.

Grady, Timothy P. "'Vomit His Fury and Malice': English Fears and Spanish Influences on the Exploration and Establishment of Carolina through 1670." *The Proceedings of the South Carolina Historical Association*, 2010: 31-42. http://www.palmettohistory.org/scha/proceedings 2010.pdf.

Green, William A. "Caribbean Historiography, 1600-1900: The Recent Tide." *The Journal of Interdisciplinary History*, Vol. 7, No. 3 (Winter 1977): 509-530.

Greene, Jack P. "Colonial South Carolina and the Caribbean Connection." *The South Carolina Historical Magazine*, Vol. 88, No. 4 (October 1987):192-210.

Hall, Louise. "New England at Sea: Cape Fear Before the Royal Charter of 24 March 1662/3." *The New England Historical and Genealogical Register*, Vol. 124, No. 2 (April 1970): 88-108.

Handler, Jerome S. and Pohlmann, John T. "Slave Manumissions and Freedmen in Seventeenth-Century Barbados." *The William & Mary Quarterly*, Third Series, Vol. 41, No. 3 (July 1984): 390-408.

Harvard University Library Open Collections Program. "The Great Plague of London, 1665." http://ocp.hul.harvard.edu/contagion/plague.html. (accessed 11/6/2010).

"Capt. William Hilton of Newbury and Charlestown, MA." *Hilton*. Accessed 06/15/2014. http://freepages.geneaology.rootsweb.ancestry.com/~maingenie/HILTON.htm.

Hutton, Ronald. "Monck, George, first duke of Albemarle (1608-1670)." *Oxford Dictionary of National Biography*. Oxford University Press. http://www.oxforddnb.com/index/18/101018939. (accessed 6/11/11).

"Isle of Wight County Records." *The William & Mary Quarterly*, Vol. VII, No. 4 (April 1899): 205-216.

Kelsey, Sean. "The Trial of Charles I." *English Historical Review*, Vol. 118 , No. 477: 583–616

Kidwell, Clara Sue. "Indian Women as Cultural Mediators." *Ethnohistory*, Vol. 39, No. 2 (Spring 1992): 97-107.

Kinloch, Bull. "Barbadian Settlers in Early Carolina: Historiographical Notes." *The South Carolina Historical Magazine*, Vol. 96, No. 4 (October 1995): 329-339.

Kniffen, Fred and Glassie, Henry. "Building in Wood in the Eastern United States: A Time-Place Perspective." *Geographical Review*, Vol. 56, No. 1 (January 1966): 40-66..

Kopperman, Paul E. "Profile of Failure: The Carolana Project, 1629-1640." *North Carolina Historical Review* 59 (1982): 1-23.

Kupperman, Karen Ordahl. "Fear of Hot Climates in the Anglo-American Colonial Experience." *The William & Mary Quarterly*, Third Series, Vol. 41, No. 2 (April 1984): 213-240.

Leech, Roger H. "Impermanent Architecture in the English Colonies of the Eastern Caribbean: New Contexts for Innovation in the Early Modern Atlantic World." *Perspectives in Vernacular Architecture*, Vol. 10, Building Environments (2005):153-167.

Lewis, J.D. "A History of Clarendon County – One of the Three Original Counties of Carolana." http://www.carolana.com/Carolina/Settlement/clarendon_county_original.html (accessed 6/17/2009).

Loftfield, Thomas C. "Lost Charles Towne: Local Manifestation of World Events." *North Carolina Archaeology*, Vol. 54 (2005): 34-48.

McBride, Ransom. "Early Settlements Along The Carolina Coast." *N.C. Genealogical Society Journal*, Vol. 11, No. 2 (May 1985): 74-88.

Martin, Jonathan. "Bertie County (1722)". North Carolina History Project. http://www.northcarolinahistory.org/encyclopedia/613/entry (accessed 9/29/12).

Merrill, Gordon. "The Role of Sephardic Jews in the British Caribbean Area during the Seventeenth Century." *Caribbean Studies*, Vol. 4, No. 3 (October 1964): 32-49.

Nash, R.C. "South Carolina and the Atlantic Economy in the Late Seventeenth and Eighteenth Centuries." *The Economic History Review*, New Series. Vol. 45, No. 4 (Nov. 1992): 667-702.

N.C. Museum of History Timeline http://ncmuseumofhistory.org/nchh/seventeenth.html (accessed 9/29/12)

Nickson, Chris. "Tracing Huguenot History in England." http://www.exploregenealogy.co.uk/tracing-huguenot-history-england.html (accessed 11/17/10)

Osgood, Herbert L. "The Proprietary Province as a Form of Government." *The American Historical Review*, Vol. 2, No. 4 (July 1897): 644-664.

"Owner's History." *St. Nicholas Abbey* website. http://www.stnicholasabbey.com/Learn/Owners-History. (accessed 1/15/13)

Parramore, Thomas C. "The Lost Colony Found: A Documentary Perspective." *North Carolina Historical Review*, Vol. 78, No. 1 (January 2001): 67-83.

Paschal, Herbert R. "The Tragedy of the North Carolina Indians." In *The North Carolina Experience: An Interpretive and Documentary History*, edited by Lindley S. Butler and Alan D. Watson, 3-12. Chapel Hill: University of North Carolina Press, 1984.

Plant, David. "The Western Design, 1655." *BCWProject: British Civil Wars, Commonwealth & Protectorate, 1638-1660*. http://bcw-project.org/military/anglo-spanish-war/western-design

Rickard, J. "The Second Anglo-Dutch War (1665-1667)." http://www.historyofwar.org/articles/wars_anglodutch2.html, 12 December 2000 (accessed 11/6/2010).

Rutman, Darrett B. and Ruttman, Anita H. "Of Agues and Fevers: Malaria in the Early Chesapeake." *The William & Mary Quarterly*, Vol. 33, No. 1 (January 1976): 31-60.

"Seventeenth-Century North Carolina History Timeline." http://thomaslegion.net/seventeenthcenturynorthcarolinahistorytimeline.html. (accessed 5/8/2010).

Shoemaker, Nancy. "How Indians Got to be Red." *The American Historical Review*, Vol. 102, No. 3 (June 1997): 625-644.

Sluyter, Andrew. "The role of Black Barbudans in the establishment of open-range cattle herding in the colonial Caribbean and South Carolina." *Journal of Historical Geography*, Vol. 35 (2009): 330-349.

Smith, Frederick H. and Watson, Karl. "Urbanity, Sociability, and Commercial Exchange in the Barbados Sugar Trade: A Comparative Colonial Archaeological Perspective on Bridgetown, Barbados in the Seventeenth Century." *International Journal of Historical Archaeology*, Vol. 13 (2009): 63-79.

Spindel, Donna J. and Thomas, Stuart W., Jr. "Crime and Society in North Carolina, 1663-1740." *The Journal of Southern History*, Vol. 49, No. 2 (May 1983): 223-244.

Sweeney, William Montgomery. "Higginbotham Family of Virginia." *The William & Mary Quarterly*, Vol. 26, No. 3 (January 1918): 205-213.

Thomas, Jno. P., Jr. "The Barbadians in Early South Carolina." *The South Carolina Historical and Genealogical Magazine*, Vol. 31, No. 2 (April 1930): 75-92.

Tomlins, Christopher. "The Legal Cartography of Colonization, the Legal Polyphony of Settlement: English Intrusions on the American Mainland in the Seventeenth Century." *Law & Social Inquiry*, Vol. 26, No. 2 (April 2001): 315-372.

"Virginia in 1667." *The Virginia Magazine of History and Biography*, Vol. 21, No. 2 (April 1913):122-135.

Waterhouse, Richard. "England, the Caribbean, and the Settlement of Carolina." *Journal of American Studies*, Vol. 9, No. 3 (December 1975): 259-281.

"William Hilton Explores the Cape Fear River." Learn NC website. http:www.learnnc.org/lp/pdf/William-hilton-explores-the-p1899.pdf. (accessed 7/17/2010).

Wright, J. Leitch Jr. "William Hilton's Voyage to Carolina in 1662." *Essex Institute Historical Collections* (April 1969): 96-103.

Index

Italics indicates reference is in a footnote

Andrews, Peter - 85, 86, *96-97*
Anglo-Spanish War - 18
Asheville (NC) - 13
Ashley River - 148
Ayscue, Sir George - 44
Bald Head Island - 93, 108, 190
Barbados - 1, 2, 4, 6, 28, 30, 35-58
Battle, John - 21
Batts, Nathaniel - 18, 20, 21, *24, 25*
Bennett, Richard - 19
Berkeley Hundred Plantation - 84
Berkeley, John - 66, 68, 70, 71, 148
Berkeley, William - *24*, 66, 68, 70, 72, 73, *75, 76*, 93, 148, 165
Berringer, Benjamin - 103-104
Berringer, Margaret Foster - 104
Bland, Edward - 89, *97*
Blower, Pyam - 91, 191
Boswell, William - 83, 84, *96*
Brazil - 44-47, *56*
Brower, Pieter - 47
Brunswick Town/Fort Anderson State Historic Site - 156, 161,
Calvert, George - 80
Cape Fear River - 1, 2 10 *22*, 53, *98*, 107, *110*, 115, 120, 121, 123, 124, 127, 128, 138, 140, 141, 143, 146, 147, 157, 162, 190, 191
Cape San Romano - 88, 90, *129*

Carolana - *24*, 61, 66, 79-86, *95*
Carolina Charter - 18, *23, 69, 72, 77*, 87, 93, *95, 97 99*, 145
Carteret, George - 67-68, 69, 71, 72, *75*, 165 169
Charles River (Cape Fear River) - 94, 108 120, 140 166, 189
Charles Stuart (King Charles II) - 32, 33, 50, *56*, 60, 61, 62, 63, 64, 65, 67, 68, 70, *74, 76*, 93, 101, 140
Chicora - 12, *22*
Chief Watcoosa - 108, 109
Chowan River - 19, 20, *24*, 79
Church of England - 63, 70, 77, 84, 89, 93, *96*, 190
Cock Pit, the - 72, *76*, 94
Colleton, John - 43, 44, *54, 56*, 58, 68, 70, 71, 72, 73, *76, 77*, 93, *95, 97, 99*, 102, 103, 104, *110*, 120, *130*, 138, 140, 146, 147, 148, *152*, 165, 169
Colleton, Peter - 99, 102, *110*, 114, 125, 126, 136, 137
Columbus, Christopher - 10, 144
Comberford, Nicholas - 21
Committee for Cape ffaire at Boston - 90, 94
Concessions and Agreement - 117, 118, 119, 120, *130*, 136, 137, 145, 146, 147, 148, 169
Cooper, Anthony Ashley (1st Earl of Shaftesbury) - 3, 43, 70, 146, 148, *152*
Cooper River - 139

Corporation of Barbados Adventurers - 102, *109*, 136
Council of Foreign Plantations - 71, *74*
Courteen, Sir William - 35
Craven, William - 65, 68, 71, *76*, 142, 148, *150*, 165, 169
Cromwell, Oliver - 27, 28, 29, 30, 31, 32, 33, 44, 57, 63, 64, 67, 71, *75*, 87, 106
Cromwell, Richard - 31
Dare, Ananias - 16
Dare, Virginia - 16
de Narvaez, Panfilio - 12, *22*
de Aviles, Gen. Pedro Menendez - 12, 13
de Ayllon, Lucas (Luis) Vazquez - 10-12, *22*
de Morales, Hernando Moyano - 13
de Ridouet, Antoine (Baron de Sance) - 81, 82, 83, *96*
de Licques, Peter - 84
Declarations and Proposals - *76*
Dew Thomas - 19
Drake, Sir Francis - 15, 86
Dunkin, Orpheus - 85, 86
Durant, George - 22, *24*
Dutch West India Company - 46, 47, *56*
English Civil War - 2, *25*, 27, 38, 44, 50, 53, 63, 66, 86
Fort San Juan - 10
Frying Pan Shoals - 12
Fundamental Constitutions of Carolina - 67, 119, 146, 148
Gent, E.W. - 87

Gerard, John - 47
Gibbes, John - 126
Great Fire of London (1666) - 142, *150*
Great Plague of London (1665) - 142, 143, *150*
Grenville, Sir John - 32
Grenville, Sir Richard - 15, 63
Guinea Company - 106
Hacket, Robert - 126, 169
Hakluyt, Richard - 14
Harvey, Sir John - 21, 86
Heath, Sir Robert/Heath Patent - *23,* 72, *77,* 80-89, *95, 96, 97,* 106
Henry, William R. - 155
Hilton, William Jr. - 4, 8, 9, 54, 88, 89-92, 94, *97, 98,* 102, 107-109, *110, 111*
Hispaniola - *22,* 29, 30, *33,* 44
Holland/the Dutch - 4, 41, 44, 45, 46, 47, 52, 53, *56, 57,* 62, 63, 70, *76,* 82, 114, 139, 140, 141, 149, *150*
Howard, Henry Frederick (Lord Maltravers) - 84, 86
Hyde, Anne - 62
Hyde, Edward - 62-63, 66, 67, 69, 71, 73, *74,* 140
Huguenots - 82, 84, 106
indentured servitude - 30, 38, 39, 41, 42, 48-50, 51, 53, 54, *55,* 117, 118
Indian River - 91, *98,* 127
Interregnum, the - 32, 33, 62, 71, *76,* 106
Jamestown (VA) - 12, 14, 18, 21, 52, *58,* 87, 89, 113, 141, *150*
Jarvis, Thomas - 22
Jenkins, John - 22
Jews - 44-47, *56, 57*
Kendal, Thomas - 43, 65, *77*

King Charles I - 27, 28, 62, 65, 80, 82, 83, 86
King Kiscutanaweh - 21
King Philip II of Spain - 12, 17, *23, 24*, 105
Kingswell, Edward - 85, 86, *96, 97,* 106
Known Charles Towne Settlers - 189-192
Lake, Thomas - 126, 170, 192
L'Amy, Hugh - 84
Lambert, John - 31
Lambert, Simon - 126
Leslie, David - 28
Ligon, Richard - 38, 39, 42, 43, 48, *162*
Linville (NC) - 13
Locke, John - 67, 84, 119, 146, 148
Loftfield, Dr. Thomas C. - *59, 132,* 155, 157, 158, 160, 161, 162, *163*
Long, Anthony - 91, 170, 192, 200
Lords Proprietors of Carolina - 2, 3, 4, 18, *24,* 26, 33, 43, 62-74, *74-77,* 79, 87, 88, 89, 93, 94, *95-97, 99,* 102, *109, 110,* 113, 114, 116-117, 118, 119, 120, 122, *129-130, 131,* 135, 136, 138, 139, 140, 141, 142, 143, 144, 145, 146, 147, 148, *149-152*
Lost Colony - 10, 18, *23, 24*
Mace, Samuel - 18
Massachusetts Bay Colony - *89, 99*
Modyford, Sir Thomas - 43, 44, 48, 65, 68, 102, *110,* 114, *129, 130,* 136, 137
Monck, George - 28, 31-32, 62, 63-65, 68, 69, 70, 71, 72, *75, 76, 77,* 140, 141,

142
Morganton (NC) - 10, 13
Mount Skerry - 108, 128. 197
Nansemond (VA) - 19, 53, 140, 147
naval stores - 41, 120, 122
Necoes - 91, 108, 127, 194
Nevis - 30, *58,* 141
Nicholas, Edward - 81
Nicholas Plantation - 103, *109, 110*
Pardo, Juan - 10, 12, 13, *22*
Penn, William - 30
Pepys, Samuel - 31
Plumpton, Henry - 19, *24*
Port Royal - 2, 5, 88, *97,* 107, 115, 116, 119, 120, 128, 130, 135, 138, 139, 140, 146, 147, 148, *149,151,152,* 170, 171, 191
Pory, John - 18
Powell, Henry - 35
Providence Plantations - 85, 106
Puritans - 1, 2, 4, 9, 30, 66, 89, 91, 93, 94, *99,* 102, 113, 114, 122, 124, 129, 144, 162, 190
Queen Elizabeth I - 10, 14, 15, 105
Raid on the Medway - 62, 141
Raleigh, Sir Walter - 10, 14, 15, 16, 17, 18, *23,* 80, 86
Reade, Edward - 125, 169, 172, 192
Relfe, Thomas - 21
Rich, Robert (Earl of Warwick) - 85
Roanoke Island (NC) - 10, 14-18, *24,* 63, 80
Rocky Point - 91, 196
Royal African Company - 53, 79

Rump Parliament - 31
Russell, Anna - 105
St. Augustine (FL) - 12, 18, 86, 87, 88, *97,* 113, 116, 120
St. Kitts - 30
Salmon (Fletts) Creek - 21
Sandford, Robert (a.k.a., Sampson or Sanford) - 114, 115, 117, 129, 135, 138, 139, *149, 151,* 189
Santa Elena (GA) - 12, 13, *23*
Scituate (MA) - 105, 106, *110*
Searle, Daniel - 30, 71
"seasoning" - 42, 43
Second Anglo-Dutch War - 63, *75,* 140, 141
Shapley, Nicholas - 90, 91, 92, *98*
Sharpe, William - 126, 169, 192
Shinn, Dr. Gerald - 154-157, *162*
Ships:
Adventure - 9, 88, 89, 90, 107, 109, 128, 129
Blessing - 107
Brave - 17
George of London - 85
Henry - 85, 86
Hopewell - 17
La Dauphine - 10, 11
La Normande - 10, 11
Little Toby - 105
Mayflower - 85, *97*
Moonlight - 17
Prince - 33
Roe - 17
St. Claude - 81
Samuel - 105
Sir John - 115, 130, 138, *158*
Thomas of London - 85
slaves/slavery - 1, 2, 6, 13, 16, 38, 39, 40, 41, 45, 46, 48, 51-54, *55, 56, 57, 58*
South, Dr. Stanley - *98, 133,* 155
Spanish Armada - 17, 105
Stag Park - 91, *195*
Stanyon, Edward - 138, 139
Stone, Garry W. - 155
Stuart, James (Duke of York) - 67, 71, 72
Sugar - 4, 6, 35, 38, 40, 41, 42, 43, 44-50, 51, 52, 54, *55, 56, 57, 58, 59,* 72, 73, 74, *76,* 100, 101, 102, 104, *109,* 126, 127, 144, 171
Taverner, Henry - 85, 86, *96*
Took (Tuke), Thomas - 19, *24*
Town Creek - 1, 91, *98,* 107, 108, 114, 121, 128, 154, 155, 157, 159, 161, *162*
Turkey Quarter - 91
Tybee Island (GA) - 11, 12
Vassall, Henry - *110,* 114, 116, *129, 130, 131,* 136, 138, 139, 150
Vassall, John - 2, 4, 5, 27, 53, 54, 84, 89, *98,* 102, 104, 106, 107, *110,* 113, 114, 115, 117, 120, *130, 132,* 134, 135, 136, 138, 139, 140, 143, 147, 148, *149, 150, 151,* 189
Vassall, Samuel - *77,* 83, 84, 85, 86, 89, *97, 98, 99,* 105, 106
Venables, Robert - 30, 44, 71
Verney, Thomas - 38
Verrazzano, Giovanni de - 9
Vespucci, Amerigo - 10
Virginia - 2, 9, 15, 17, 18, 19, 21, *24, 25,* 28, 33, 41, 43, 44, 46, 51, 52, 53, 54, *56, 57, 58,* 66, 68, 70, 73, *76, 77,* 79, 80, 82, 84, 85, 86, 93, *95, 96, 97,* 106, 115, 139, 140, 141, 146, 147, 149, 159, 165
Ware, Nicholas - 53, 55, 58, 106
"Western Design" - 29
White, John - 15, 16, 17
Williams, Roger - 22, *99,* 106
Wingina - 16, 18
Woodward, Dr. Henry - 139
Yeamans, Sir John - 2, 102, 103-104, *110,* 112, 113, 115, 116, 119, 120, 125, 126, *130, 131,* 135, 136, 138, 139, 140, 141, 144, 145, 147, 148, 149, 151, 169, 171, 172, 188, 189, 192
Yeamans, William - 117, 169, 170, 172, 192
Yeardley, Francis - 19, 21, *25*

Also by Jack E. Fryar, Jr.

- *The Coastal Chronicles Volume I* - 0972324003
- *The Coastal Chronicles Volume II* - 097232402X
- *A History Lover's Guide to Wilmington & The Lower Cape Fear* - 097234011
- *The Story of Brunswick Town & Fort Anderson* with Franda D. Predlow - 0972324062

The Young Reader's Series of North Carolina History

- *The Battles for Fort Fisher* - 0978624807
- *Pirates of the North Carolina Coast* - 9780978624897
- *Under Three Flags: The Fort Johnston Story* - 9780978624828
- *The Yellow Death: Wilmington & The Epidemic of 1862* - 9780978624873
- *"King George and Broadswords!" The Story of the Battle at Widow Moores Creek* - 9780978624811

Edited Works

- *The Big Book of the Cape Fear River* - 9780981460314
- *Revolutionary Incidents: Sketches of Character Chiefly in the Old North State Vol. I* - 9780981460390
- *Revolutionary Incidents: Sketches of Character Chiefly in the Old North State Vol. II* - 9780984490004
- *A Sketch of the LIfe of Brig. Gen. Francis Marion* - 9780981460307
- *Buccaneers & Pirates of Our Coasts* - 097862484X
- *A James Sprunt Reader* - 9780981460369
- *Derelicts* - 0972324097
- *Lossing's Pictorial Field-Book of the Revolution in the Carolinas & Georgia* - 0972324046
- *Lossing's Pictorial Field-Book of the Revolution in Virginia & Maryland* - 9780978624859
- *Blue Tide Rising: A Memoir of the Union Army in North Carolina* - 9780978624835
- *One Good Man: Rev. John Lamb Prichard'sLife of Faith, Service, and Sacrifice* - 0978624882

These books and more available from Dram Tree Books through your favorite bookstore!

dramtreebooks@gmail.com

About the Author...

Jack E. Fryar, Jr. is a life-long resident of southeastern North Carolina. He has been a professional writer and publisher since 1994. In 2000, Jack founded Dram Tree Books, a small publishing house whose titles tell the story of North and South Carolina and the Carolina coast. He has authored or edited twenty-four volumes of North Carolina and Cape Fear history, and is a frequent lecturer for historic groups in the region. Jack is also the editor and publisher of the digital magazine, *Carolina Chronicles*, covering the history of North and South Carolina. His historical specialty is colonial North Carolina, particularly during the seventeenth century. Jack has served as a United States Marine, worked as a broadcaster, freelance magazine writer, sports announcer, and book designer. He holds a Masters in History and a Masters in Teaching from the University of North Carolina Wilmington, and currently teaches history at E.A. Laney High School in Wilmington.

www.ingramcontent.com/pod-product-compliance
Lightning Source LLC
Chambersburg PA
CBHW061252110426
42742CB00012BA/1892